Filled with the Spirit

Filled with the Spirit

Sexuality, Gender, and Radical Inclusivity in a Black Pentecostal Church Coalition

ELLEN LEWIN

University of Chicago Press   Chicago and London

The University of Chicago Press, Chicago 60637
The University of Chicago Press, Ltd., London
© 2018 by The University of Chicago
All rights reserved. No part of this book may be used or reproduced in any manner whatsoever without written permission, except in the case of brief quotations in critical articles and reviews. For more information, contact the University of Chicago Press, 1427 East 60th Street, Chicago, IL 60637.
Published 2018

27 26 25 24 23 22 21 20 19 18   1 2 3 4 5

ISBN-13: 978-0-226-53717-7 (cloth)
ISBN-13: 978-0-226-53720-7 (paper)
ISBN-13: 978-0-226-53734-4 (e-book)
DOI: https://doi.org/10.7208/chicago/9780226537344.001.0001

Library of Congress Cataloging-in-Publication Data
Names: Lewin, Ellen, author.
Title: Filled with the spirit: sexuality, gender, and radical inclusivity in a Black Pentecostal church coalition / Ellen Lewin.
Description: Chicago; London : University of Chicago Press, 2018. | Includes bibliographical references and index.
Identifiers: LCCN 2017030693 | ISBN 9780226537177 (cloth: alk. paper) | ISBN 9780226537207 (pbk: alk. paper) | ISBN 9780226537344 (e-book)
Subjects: LCSH: Homosexuality—Religious aspects—Christianity. | African American sexual minorities—Religious life. | Pentecostalism.
Classification: LCC BR115.H6 L48 2018 | DDC 289.9/408660973—dc23
LC record available at https://lccn.loc.gov/2017030693

Contents

Acknowledgments vii

Invocation: The Anthropology Ministry 1

1 "I've Been 'Buked": The Double Consciousness of Being LGBT and Black 27

2 "Lead Me, Guide Me": The Charisma of Bishop Flunder 53

3 "Just as I Am": Revealing Authentic Selves 89

4 "Old-Time Religion": Invoking Memory 115

5 "What a Fellowship": Radically Inclusive Futures 145

Benediction: Continuities and Departures 174

Notes 185   *References Cited 197*   *Index 217*

Acknowledgments

Like most people who have completed books after years of research, writing, and consulting, I owe enormous debts to many different people, including those who so generously invited me into the Fellowship, colleagues from my own institution and elsewhere, and friends and family. Part of what happened in the course of writing this book is that the boundaries between these categories became hazy, particularly as colleagues and interlocutors became friends and family.

The Fellowship connected me with so many loving and supportive people that it is difficult for me to be able to thank all of those whose encouragement and enthusiasm sustained me while I worked on this project. I not only had the privilege of working with people whose willingness to share their spiritual lives gave my research meaning, but I gained deep and nurturing friendships that will continue to be important to me in the years to come. Unlike other research I have done, I had no sense at the "end" of this project that I could say good-bye to those with whom I have worked or, indeed, that my connection with TFAM had come to an end. One Fellowship friend asked me in the summer of 2016 what would "happen" after I finished the book. "What do you mean?" I asked. "Will you still come to our events?" she continued. When I told her that I most certainly would, she said, "Good. Because otherwise we would miss you." And I would miss them.

With the caution that I am certainly going to miss mentioning some TFAM people who were constant sources of support, I want to particularly thank Bishop Yvette Flunder,

ACKNOWLEDGMENTS

who, along with her partner, Mother Shirley Miller, opened the coalition to me, making every aspect of its operation accessible to me and showing enormous confidence in the ability of an outsider to document TFAM's story. Their warm embrace has framed every interaction I've had with the Fellowship. Pastor Kevin Tindell invited me to the first service I attended and made the declaration that started my connection to TFAM. Bishop Phyllis Pennese and Vickie Sides were constant friends as I pursued the research and as I watched their son, Brandon Sides, turn into a fabulous adult.

Veronica Jordan, who is the official photographer for TFAM and a member of City of Refuge, provided the pictures that appear in this book; my only regret is that I couldn't include much more of her beautiful work. I apologize for any omissions in this list: the folks who helped me find my footing in TFAM are really too numerous to list here, and include some people whose names I still don't know.

I also owe gratitude to Bishop Wyatt Greenlee and Bishop Joseph Tolton, and a host of others (titles mostly omitted): Glenn Alexander, Dr. Lucki Allen, Dr. P. J. Anderson, Vanessa Brown, Bishop Alex Byrd, Yunus Coldman, James Darby, Pei des Rosiers, Toni Dunbar, Nubian Flunder, Darlene Garner, Twanna Gause, Phil Gray, Candy Holmes, Ann Jefferson, Lesley Jones and Noni Gordon-Jones, Taunya Kinney, Charla Kouadio and Theresa Coley-Kouadio, Paul Lucas, Carl Madgett, Katrina Marsh, Tanya Maryoung, James Pearman, Darren Phelps, Joi Rhone, Marvin Roberts, Deneen Robinson, Troy Sanders, Anthony Sullivan, Sherry Thomas, Andrea Vassell, Alvis Ward, and Alex Williams, and many members of City of Refuge UCC, Pillar of Love UCC, and Rivers@Rehoboth, the congregations where I spent the most time. Veronica Jordan, who is the official photographer for TFAM and a member of City of Refuge, provided the pictures that appear in this book; my only regret is that I couldn't include much more of her beautiful work. I apologize for any omissions in this list: the folks who helped me find my footing in TFAM are really too numerous to list here and include some people whose names I still don't know.

One of the special friends I made at TFAM convocations is Tim Wolfe, divinity student extraordinaire, who spent enormous amounts of time unraveling the theological mysteries of Christianity and especially Pentecostalism and who also served as my guide to black churches and gospel music in Chicago. Tim provided vital clarifications that helped me improve the manuscript, which he read while he juggled a nearly impossible schedule of academic and professional obligations. I'm also grateful for having met a new colleague, Terry Todd, at TFAM, and for his insightful comments on the manuscript.

ACKNOWLEDGMENTS

I was very fortunate while working on this project to receive funding from the Arts and Humanities Initiative at the University of Iowa (2010–11), a Martin Duberman Fellowship from the Center for Lesbian and Gay Studies (CLAGS) at the City University of New York (2010–11), and research fellowships from the Louisville Institute and the National Endowment for the Humanities (2015–16). I also benefited enormously from the opportunity to enjoy the tranquility of the Obermann Center for Advanced Studies at the University of Iowa during my sabbatical semester in spring of 2012, along with the collegial support of the other scholars who worked there that semester. I never would have known about the resources of the Louisville Institute without the advice of Kristy Nabhan-Warren, so I am grateful for her suggestion that I apply there for funding.

I received meticulous and challenging comments from the two University of Chicago Press readers, who graciously allowed their identities to be revealed to me: E. Patrick Johnson and Dawne Moon. These two scholars are perfectly positioned to make astute critiques of my work, so I am grateful that they supported my efforts even as they caught just about every error I could have made. They very appropriately held my feet to the fire, and I cannot thank them enough for taking the work so seriously.

A number of friends and colleagues read the manuscript at various stages of its preparation and offered comments that helped me clarify my argument and do away with confusing language. First, my friend and partner in crime, Leni Silverstein, used the proverbial fine-tooth comb to examine the text, and imposed logic and intelligibility on what were often confusing first drafts. Others who read the work and who deserve my thanks are Susan Birrell, Tom Boellstorff, Ann Merrill, Carol Shepherd, Susan Stanfield, and Miriam Thaggert.

As always, the support and encouragement of my partner in life, Liz Goodman, made everything possible. She (usually) showed patience and fortitude, even when I was being cranky, and went on to help me make the book as good as it could be, given my limitations. She provided glasses of wine when they were most urgently needed. And she reminded me that I always fall into a state of despair about a book right before I figure out how to finish it. Our four-footed family—Dinah, Benny, Vanya, and Pasha—helped as best they could, sometimes by barking their enthusiasm for particularly felicitous phrases, and at other times just going to sleep on the manuscript.

Doug Mitchell has been a wonderfully supportive and critical editor, as he was on an earlier project. He was both enthusiastic about my moving forward on this work and then amazingly patient as it took me much longer to finish than I had at first optimistically predicted. I know that

ACKNOWLEDGMENTS

editors like Doug are not easily found in the world of academic publishing, so I am deeply appreciative of having had the good fortune to work with him, and to have known him now for over fifty years! His assistant, Kyle Wagner, shepherded the manuscript through the later stages of completion, and I am grateful to him for being so responsive and smart about everything that needed to be done.

Invocation: The Anthropology Ministry

I never expected to study religion. Even after decades as an anthropologist, my firmly secular upbringing had left me with a skepticism about faith that made it hard to take it seriously, even as an academic pursuit. Certainly my anthropological training, especially its deeply relativistic stance on pretty much everything, meant that I understood in some remote intellectual way that religious sentiments and beliefs are important parts of people's lives as well as the cultural wholes that are the foundation of our work (and our world), and that they are not to be taken lightly. But I never felt entirely comfortable participating in religious rituals. Though I went to many such events during my study of lesbian and gay commitment ceremonies, I focused on what else they meant besides worship of the divinity, and in the case of weddings and commitment ceremonies, that was usually a lot. I understood that belief and faith were real, but I didn't internalize this understanding enough to find my footing when I played a role in a ritual setting.

These qualms are nowhere more intense for me than at the Jewish services I unfailingly attend at the High Holy Days of Rosh Hashanah and Yom Kippur. I have been going to these events since 1974 because (I think) I want to situate myself within a history and set of ethics that I find compelling, and because my first desire to do that coincided with the founding of Congregation Sha'ar Zahav, a progressive and predominantly lesbian and gay synagogue in San Francisco, where I then lived. But still, I remain a bit mystified

INVOCATION

about the allure of these rituals. I don't know Hebrew and so almost all of the liturgy slides by as if it were music. I also attend for sentimental reasons: my father died on Yom Kippur more than forty years ago, and I feel a strong obligation to mark the anniversary of his death in the traditional Jewish manner of lighting a candle and attending a *yizkor* (memorial) service. The irony that underlies this observance doesn't escape me. My father was an uncompromising nonbeliever, though he had a strong Jewish identity, intensified by his flight from Nazi Germany in the 1930s. He viewed religious beliefs with something between humor and condescension, and the idea that I have been lighting a *yahrzeit* (anniversary) candle for him every year since his death in 1973 might have struck him as a foolish, but perhaps endearing, waste of time. These days, I also set work aside to observe the High Holidays, in part because I now live in Iowa City, a place with few Jews and occasional episodes of (relatively low-key) anti-Semitism. Being Jewish now also seems a matter of ethnic pride that demands expression, even if my notion of what this means differs substantially from the understandings of other Jews and my non-Jewish Iowa neighbors.

So my connection to the Fellowship of Affirming Ministries (TFAM), now of more than ten years' standing, has come as a bit of a surprise to me, if not to the members of Fellowship congregations who have become my dear friends and interlocutors and who have provided me with the material that forms the substance of this book. It all started, like many anthropological inspirations, with a serendipitous connection. In the fall of 2002, I was doing fieldwork in Chicago for a study of gay fathers (Lewin 2009). I quickly learned that a good place to meet fathers (or other parents) was in churches and synagogues, as many Americans are inspired to begin or return to some sort of religious observance when they become parents. As I focused on meeting more gay dads, I contacted clergy in open and affirming congregations or gay/lesbian–oriented congregations, using referrals each offered me to find other such churches and specific members who were gay dads. One of these contacts, a woman I met soon after I arrived to work in Chicago, told me about a service in celebration of National Coming Out Day, held annually on October 11 (the anniversary of the 1987 National March on Washington for Lesbian and Gay Rights), at the Chicago Theological Seminary (CTS). This seemed like an event that might offer me access to lots of gay men with children, so I went.

During part of the service, various people in attendance stood to testify about recent events that they wanted to share with fellow worshippers. In the midst of these testimonies, a tall black man stood to announce that he and his partner had just finalized the adoption of their son. When the service came to an end, I rushed to intercept the man at the door. I told him about my research, and he invited me to his home to interview him and his partner.

The interview, held in the two men's large Hyde Park flat, offered me important insights into the way that African American men typically anchor their decisions to be parents within a larger awareness of social justice and knowledge of the predicament of black children, especially boys, in foster care. As we conversed, Kevin Tindell,[1] the man I'd met at CTS, suddenly told me, "You know, I am pastoring a church, the Praise Center. You should really come." He mentioned the church again later in the interview, told me where and when it met on Sundays, and again urged me to attend.

This wasn't something I had envisioned as part of my research on gay dads. I didn't think it was related to my project, and since I had never been to a black church before, I was somewhat apprehensive about making an appearance. But Kevin's invitation was so warm and sincere, I felt a bit like I'd been offered something unfamiliar to eat by an informant, a situation that in the past had always compelled me to consume whatever it was with at least apparent gusto and appreciation. It didn't hurt that the location of the service was in the vicinity of the University of Chicago, an area I knew well from my undergraduate years. So I said I would come.

A couple of weeks after my meeting with Kevin and his partner, I made my way to the chapel where the service would be held. In classic anthropological fashion, I tried to make myself inconspicuous by sitting in a rear corner of the chapel, but two women came barreling over to me as soon as I sat down, took me by the elbows, and said, "Don't sit there by yourself. Come sit here with us." I joined them in their pew.

By the time the service started, about a dozen worshippers had arrived, gay men and lesbians, and a transgender woman, all African American. Kevin, who was a divinity student at the time, began the service with hymns, the words of which were projected on a screen in the front by another man in the congregation. The gathering being small, we soon moved into a circle, all holding hands, as Kevin invoked gratitude to God for the many gifts He had endowed on his people. "Thank you, Lord," he intoned, "for waking me up this morning." "Thank you for keeping my family members safe." "Thank you for curing my mother of the illness she recently suffered." "Thank you for leading us to this place." These invocations went on for some time, some delivered in tongues (glossolalia).[2] Worshippers responded to Kevin's prayers, saying, "Yes, yes," "Thank you, Lord," and other amplifications of Kevin's expressions of thanks. One woman began to weep and slid to the floor, with the worshippers on each side supporting her. These prayers went on for quite a while, and I began to lose track of how much time had elapsed. Then, without warning, Kevin said, "And thank you, Lord, for bringing us Sister Ellen, who is going to tell our stories."

It is difficult to describe how I felt when I heard these words. On one level, I had been congratulating myself for having landed in a place where people were speaking in tongues and experiencing trance. This felt like an anthropologist's dream. But on another level, I feared that things were getting out of control, that there were meanings attached to my participation in the Sunday service that were beyond my comprehension.

The service, which I had expected to be an interesting curiosity, moved me deeply, though clearly not in the same way as for the other participants. And the warmth of the reception I received made me want to come back. So I started attending on a regular basis. I met some men in the congregation who were hoping to become fathers and connected through them to another predominantly black, lesbian, gay, bisexual, and transgender (hereafter LGBT) church (Church of the Open Door) that met later in the day in another part of the city. I started going to that one, too, and soon became acquainted with its two pastors and some congregants.

The connection at the Praise Center became more intense after I met Phyllis Pennese there in late 2002. A divinity student at CTS at the time, she went on to become the pastor of a Fellowship congregation in Chicago and later a bishop in TFAM. Phyllis preached some Sundays, always offering eloquent and emotionally grounded sermons that drew on innovative interpretations of Scripture. And she was there the day I arrived in great distress, after learning that my next-door neighbor in Iowa City, a black woman originally from the South Side of Chicago, had succumbed to lung cancer. My partner and I had been friends with her, chatting over the fence between our gardens and sometimes sharing a beer on one of our front porches. I had visited her during her last weeks at her mother's home in the Woodlawn neighborhood of Chicago, only blocks away from CTS. I sat down and cried when I arrived at church that day, perhaps moved by my proximity to my neighbor's roots, my feeling that I was honoring her memory by being in a black church. I really can't remember now what Phyllis said to me that was so comforting. But we formed a bond, as I did with her partner, Vickie, and their son, Brandon, that continued after the Praise Center ceased operation, and after I ended my work in Chicago and returned to Iowa City. We stayed in touch over the years that followed. Not long after my time in Chicago, the now-ordained Pastor Phyllis started her own ministry in Chicago, Pillar of Love, and on the occasional weekend when I visited the city, I tried to attend. She told me about her involvement in the Fellowship, a coalition of like-minded churches—mainly African American, LGBT, and Pentecostal in worship style—and explained that the name of her new church was one that the Holy Spirit conveyed to her during intense prayer at a Fellowship meeting.

A few years after I first discovered the Praise Center and Church of the Open Door (which has since closed) in 2002 and 2003, I began to imagine that I could turn this new set of connections into a research venture and talked with Pastor Phyllis in general terms about this idea. In 2009 she told me that she thought I should attend the national convocation of the Fellowship, scheduled for Atlanta that summer. I hesitated, but Pastor Phyllis urged me to register for the convocation and to make my hotel reservation without further ado if I wanted to get a room in the main hotel. A few weeks later, she called me. "The Holy Spirit spoke to me yesterday," she began. ("Oh my," I thought, "she wants me to do something.") "So I called Bishop [Flunder] and we agreed that you should lead a workshop at the convocation."

I was amazed, particularly since I had yet to meet Yvette Flunder, the presiding bishop of the Fellowship. "Really, you want me to do that? What sort of workshop?"

"We thought you could lead a session on lesbian and gay relationship issues over the life course."

"Yes, I think I can do that," I responded. "But I'm overwhelmed that you would ask me. You know I'm not black, not Christian, and have never been to a Fellowship event before. I'm so honored that you would invite me to do this."

"Well," said Pastor Phyllis, "we want you to know that you're part of the family."

This conversation launched my research on the Fellowship, renamed the Fellowship of Affirming Ministries (TFAM) in 2011 (both names will be used interchangeably in this book as they are in the usage of members). Initially, I really didn't know exactly what I was trying to find out, so my early visits to TFAM events and interviews with members and leaders allowed me to survey the scene and see what jumped out at me. There's no question that at the outset my work was inspired by how much I liked attending Fellowship events. After the first exploratory trip to the 2009 convocation, I attended three regional meetings in 2010 (Eastern, Southern, and Midwestern), an international conference of the Metropolitan Community Church (MCC) in 2010 that the Fellowship co-sponsored, and the next series of convocations, held in Las Vegas in 2011 and 2013, in Oakland in 2015, and, as I complete this book, the Leadership Gathering held in Palm Springs in the summer of 2016. I also went to various regional meetings in 2012 and 2014, and attended services at the Chicago church and at congregations in New York City; Washington, DC; Springfield, Massachusetts; and Dallas, Texas, in addition to going several times to the "mother church," Bishop Flunder's City of Refuge in San Francisco (since relocated to Oakland). With her permission, I made audio recordings of worship services, music, testimonies, and sermons; I interviewed pastors and other leaders (deacons, ministers, prophets) as well as ordinary members. Out of approximately forty interviews I completed, most were conducted face-to-face, but for others I relied on Skype. I also benefited from the audio recordings TFAM makes of its national events, so I was able to use the CDs of four convocations to listen to sermons delivered and many of the other events that took place at these meetings, though I also made my own recordings of many ceremonial events and workshops.

In this book, I examine the seemingly paradoxical relationship between TFAM and traditional black churches, particularly focusing on how congregations and individual members of the coalition both reclaim the worship practices of these churches and simultaneously challenge their authority. The set of ideas that guides TFAM, enunciated by Bishop Flunder as "radical inclusivity" (Flunder 2005), directs the coalition to promote the embrace of all those who have been rejected by or alienated from the black church, but also calls for the inclusion of people of every religious, racial, and ethnic background. The aim of this expansive philosophy, also sometimes described as "extravagant hospitality," is to nurture a new ethic of love and acceptance, and to thereby fuel the kind of social justice activism that TFAM espouses. As I shall show, TFAM both reenacts forms of Christian worship that have deep histories among African Americans and reframes them with the assistance of intellectual and interpretive perspectives combined with a recognition of the connectedness of all human beings.

Pentecostalism and Black Christianity

Pentecostalism is widely understood to have originated in the United States with the Azusa Street Revival that took place in Los Angeles between 1906 and 1909, led by William J. Seymour, a black pastor originally from Louisiana.[3] It was noteworthy for its egalitarian ethos of worship, with race and gender not determining leadership roles, but later collapsed and fragmented, possibly because such racial and gender equality presented too radical a departure from prevailing social norms. It then splintered into (eventually) racially segregated denominations, primarily the black Church of God in Christ (COGIC) and the white Assemblies of God, along with too many other sects to enumerate here (Cox 2001; Synan 1971), though this was a process that proceeded unevenly and sometimes included churches that were racially mixed, at least for a period of time (Alexander 2011). Although the black church in the United States is not solely Pentecostal in tradition, many of the spiritual practices familiar to African Americans have been influenced by Pentecostal worship, with its emphasis on the experience of inhabitation by the Holy Spirit and on extravagant expressions of that inhabitation. Trance and glossolalia figure prominently in churches inspired by Pentecostalism, as does elaboration of the personal experience of spiritual grace through charismatic gifts including dancing, shouting, and "being slain in the Spirit" or "falling out" (Anderson 1979). Many scholars have argued that the expressive style of worship that characterizes Pentecostalism fits comfortably into spiritual practices that have their origins in the African diaspora (Herskovits 1990 [1941]; Mintz and Price 1992 [1976]; Pitts 1993; Raboteau 1999). Such worship was historically associated with the less privileged strata of African American populations because after slavery some upwardly mobile blacks chose a more restrained style of worship that resembled the practices of white Christians as a way to claim refinement and to repudiate stereotypes of blacks as primitive (Best 2005; Jefferson 2015).

Pentecostalism, of course, has been expanding around the globe in recent years (Alexander 2009; Austin-Broos 1997; Espinosa 2014; Robbins 2004), though its origins are American and it maintains a solid presence among Christians in the United States. It has also expanded in the United States, with the spread of the new Pentecostal movements that have appeared among mostly white, often middle-class Christians, including the formation of megachurches (Bielo 2009, 2011; Elisha 2011; Luhrmann 2012).

Pentecostalism takes its name from the New Testament, Acts 2:2–4, which describes the experience of the Apostles on the day of Pentecost:

When the day of Pentecost had come, they were all together in one place. And suddenly from heaven there came a sound like the rush of a violent wind, and it filled the entire house where they were sitting. Divided tongues, as of fire, appeared among them, and a tongue rested on each of them. All of them were filled with the Holy Spirit and began to speak in other languages, as the Spirit gave them ability. (National Council of Churches of Christ in the USA 1989: 123)

This "baptism of fire" provides a direct experience of the Holy Spirit, revealed in various spiritual gifts or charismatic phenomena among worshippers—especially glossolalia. But Fellowship preachers also pointedly invoke Azusa Street as a way to authorize the doctrine of "radical inclusivity." Descriptions of the Revival often speak of what theologian Estrelda Alexander calls the "radically egalitarian nature" of Azusa Street. She explains, "Though most worshippers were from the lower and working classes, there was no stratification either by class, race, gender or age in involvement or leadership of the services. Men and women, adults and children, Black, white, yellow, and red freely worshipped God and admonished each other to holiness of life through speaking in tongues and interpretation, prophecy, song, prayer, miraculous signs and preaching" (Alexander 2011: 121).

The hallmark of Pentecostalism, flowing from this and other biblical texts, is an emphasis on *experience*, more than textual interpretation, as the source of spiritual fulfillment. Pentecostals experience God through being filled with the Holy Spirit, an ecstatic or mystical condition that may lead to speaking in tongues, dancing, divine healing and exorcism, but which also may inspire worshippers to devote themselves to community projects and political involvement. Pentecostal liturgies are "primarily oral, narrative, and participatory" (Anderson 2004: 201). As Harvey Cox explains, a core belief is "that the Spirit of God needs no mediators but is available to anyone in an intense, immediate, indeed interior way" (Cox 2001: 87). What is central in this formulation is a kind of spatial understanding of the spiritual experience. The Holy Spirit can take up residence within a person, allowing her an intense feeling of spiritual fulfillment, but just as easily sin, demons, disease, and other undesirable elements also can establish themselves, extending influence over one's decisions and behaviors. Being filled with the Holy Spirit is thus especially important as it will enable the individual to ward off sinful and demonic influences.

The Fellowship

The Fellowship's origins are anchored in this Pentecostal history. In preaching and other forms of devotion, it makes the powerful assertion that everyone, no matter how seemingly flawed or corrupted, has holiness within—whether the person is LGBT, has HIV/AIDS, has been in prison, abuses drugs and/or alcohol, is homeless or otherwise compromised and marginalized. Mistreatment based on race, gender, sexuality, poverty, or other bases are overturned in this environment, as each person is welcomed according to the tenets of "radical inclusivity." Such welcome makes identity legible; regardless of what else you might be, you are one of God's creations. At one of the first services I attended at the Praise Center, Pastor Kevin told the worshippers, "If you want to see the face of God, look in the mirror." In other words, the Fellowship gives members a number of vital routes to establishing coherence in both spiritual and social locations. The Fellowship brings individuals who have been shunned or isolated in their home churches back into communication with God, telling them that they are made in God's image and that God sees himself in each of them.

The Fellowship also allows African American worshippers who have been distanced from the churches in which they were raised to reclaim blackness by situating them in the racial history that the black church communicates. As we shall see in the chapters that follow, Fellowship churches avoid newfangled forms of Pentecostal worship, the kinds of innovations that scholars have reported in studies of middle-class white Pentecostals who have converted to charismatic spiritual practices (Csordas 1997; Luhrmann 2012; Neitz 1987). Instead, worship is notably "old-time," adhering to what most congregants recognize from the churches where they grew up, churches that recapitulated the spiritual routines that are historically African American. The hymns are those to which everyone (except the anthropologist!) knows the words; the order of service is what anyone with a background in the Church of God in Christ, the Baptist Church, or an Apostolic church would recognize; the exhortation to tithe and the collection of offerings follow established routine, with the familiar addition of the "love offering" when there is a guest preacher or other special need; time is provided for the children to make a presentation or for dancers to perform; the food served at church-sponsored meals is the solidly southern fare of fried chicken, greens, and corn bread. Congregants pray intensely, and at most services, many call out encouragement and appreciation as the preacher delivers the Word, while some speak in tongues, dance, stomp, and fall out—charismatic gifts that confirm that they are filled with the Spirit. True, the service is substantially shorter than the all-day worship typical of many Pentecostal churches, and women can wear makeup, jewelry, and slacks, which are frowned on in the traditional churches. There may be cross-dressing, and same-sex couples may sit together and hold hands, with their anniversaries and other family events marked and celebrated. Congregants are not forbidden to attend movies or to listen to the "devil's music" (rhythm and blues, rock and roll, and all other forms of secular music), nor do all refrain from drinking alcohol.

Much work in LGBT studies has focused on the formation of "queer space," or the strategies that LGBT people devise to locate safe places where they can live their lives not only shielded from homophobic disparagement and violence, but where their identities can receive active support (Beemyn 1997; Kennedy and Davis 1993; Murray 1979; Newton 1993). In many ways, Fellowship churches offer such refuge, with a welcome to LGBT people at the heart of their mission. That is, they provide the foundation for the formation of a community of black LGBT Christians that sustains and nourishes multiple identities, where worshippers can let down their guard and perform all aspects of their identities. In this way, they resemble other LGBT-centered religious spaces that have come into existence since the early 1970s: the Metropolitan Community Church (MCC), affirming congregations in mainstream denominations like the Unitarians and the United Church of Christ (UCC), the support groups available to LGBT members of non-affirming (and often virulently homophobic) denominations such as Dignity for Roman Catholics and Affirmation for Mormons, and synagogues like the one I belonged to in San Francisco (Shallenberger 1998; Shokeid 1995; Thumma 2006; Wilcox 2003).

But I will argue in the pages that follow that these TFAM congregations must be understood as more than sites of community solidification and as more than safe spaces. Members and leaders of Fellowship congregations told me over and over that they don't see themselves as being affiliated with a "gay church" or, for that matter, with a black church, though they conceded that others may so label them. They do offer LGBT people and others who have been marginalized in some way, particularly when they are African American, a safe haven—a place where the stigma they deal with elsewhere in their lives can be left at the door. But, as one congregant in Washington, DC, told me: "I don't want to come to church to hear over and over that it's okay to be gay. I know that. I come to worship God. I want to talk about God." It is the spiritual experience that is transformative in Fellowship worship, rather than just the opportunity to be told that LGBT people deserve respect and support and to find relief from the pressures of a stigmatized, marginalized existence.

The story I will tell about the Fellowship is animated by a desire to move beyond conceptualizations of LGBT life constrained by unidimensional accounts of identity. Paradoxically, perhaps, both lesbian and gay studies and queer studies have tended to make this very misstep. Despite its vociferous disavowal of identity-based theories of LGBT/queer experience, much recent scholarship still tends to proceed as though our interest in such people rests solely on their non-heteronormative sexual/gender identity or presentation. As I have argued elsewhere (Lewin 2009), the politics and scholarship that I have characterized as "queer fundamentalism" assume that LGBT/queer sexualities or genders should naturally engender subversive cultural formations and sensibilities. The preoccupation with "queer culture" that such assumptions spawn have led us into bottomless debates about whether marriage equality is a worthwhile goal or primarily a form of assimilation, and hence an unworthy political objective, just to mention one such discussion (see, for example, Polikoff 2009). In contrast, I would contend that if the study of LGBT topics more thoroughly adheres to empirical realities, it can be more truthful. By moving outside the boundaries of LGBT personal identifications, it can more readily take note of how ephemeral such identities may be and how they are inflected by the other identity positions individuals and groups may adopt, whether intentionally or not. This would also mean giving serious recognition to the spirituality of those with non-heteronormative identities, and the need many have to engage with the divine.

Doing an Anthropology of Faith

I've been an anthropologist for a long time and have completed several ethnographic studies that became books. So any project I undertake has a shape based on ethnographic practice: a commitment to try to get inside how other people think as fully as possible and to translate their understandings into terms that various audiences can comprehend. In the current (postcolonial, feminist-informed) climate in anthropology, I recognize that one such audience must be the interlocutors themselves; while people who act as informants for an anthropological study might not embrace all of my interpretations, they should still be able to see descriptions of themselves as accurate and perhaps as thought-provoking.

I struggled for some time to construct an intellectual foundation for my research, as a succession of ideas on how to conceptualize a study of the Fellowship took shape and then collapsed with further thought or fresh information. I was new to the study of both religion and African American culture, and while I am a long-standing student of LGBT life in the United States, there had been little attention among scholars to the specificities of African American LGBT experience. There were a few tantalizing readings that I identified, with the work of William Hawkeswood in anthropology, E. Patrick Johnson in performance studies, Mignon Moore in sociology, and Kevin Mumford in history being the most germane to situating the experience of the people I met in the Fellowship (Hawkeswood 1996; Johnson 2003, 2008; Moore 2011; Mumford 2016). I spent considerable time, in between my regular faculty duties and during three semesters when I was on leave, reading works in history, religious studies, folklore, anthropology, linguistics, sociology, and autobiography/personal narratives, to try to situate myself in various dimensions of the Fellowship's operation. I learned a lot about how anthropologists study religion in general, and Christianity in particular. I became aware of a huge literature on the spread of Pentecostalism throughout the world, though this work diverged sharply from the issues on which I was focusing.

Some of this reading was inspiring; some reminded me of the kind of work I didn't want to do or that didn't suit my intellectual inclinations. As always, I wanted to write ethnographically driven work, work that depends on what I see and hear, and even more on what people tell me through their personal narratives—which generates questions and answers, and determines what theoretical connections would be most appropriate and illuminating. I quickly learned that I would have to go to some lengths to convince many of my academic colleagues that I hadn't fallen into the hands of right-wing crazies, that I hadn't myself been spiritually hijacked, and that, especially for non-anthropologists, a close study of religion is a worthwhile pursuit for a feminist ethnographer whose previous work had focused on LGBT families. The extent to which scholars in the humanities and social sciences tend to be suspicious of, or even hostile to, religion impressed me in new ways (and mirrored my own earlier misconceptions); people were both curious and skeptical about my new area of research, and not easily convinced that my work was worthwhile.

Studying the Fellowship sparked a set of challenges I had not previously faced in doing research. On the most basic level, there were practical difficulties having to do with time and space. Fellowship congregations are spread across the United States, from Bishop Flunder's church in Oakland (City of Refuge) to congregations, large and small, stable and ephemeral, all around the country (and now in some non-US locations as well). Unfortunately, the small black and LGBT population in Iowa, even in "diverse" Iowa City, is not sufficient to support a Fellowship congregation (or even a Metropolitan Community Church), so I knew from the start that to do this work, I would have to travel. Still, from the outset, I felt that the focus of my work needed to be on the Fellowship as a coalition and not any single church or congregation. While my first sustained exposure to TFAM and radical inclusivity—a concept that will be explored at length in later chapters—was at Pillar of Love in Chicago, my trips to other congregations showed me that specific cultural and economic features of their location, variations in the populations drawn to them, and the particular appeal of the founding pastor made each of them a unique site, worthy of exploration. So my project, inevitably, became what anthropologists called "multi-sited research."

Anthropologist George Marcus has offered a particularly succinct statement in support of conducting multi-sited ethnographic research. He explains, "Multi-sited research is designed around chains, paths, threads, and junctions, or juxtapositions of locations in which the ethnographer establishes some form of literal, physical presence, with an explicit, posited logic of association or connection among sites that in fact defines the argument of the ethnography" (Marcus 1998: 90). In Marcus's terms, my objective is to "follow the thing"—that is, spiritual practices as they are performed in related, but differing, institutional contexts.

But following the thing can be challenging on many levels.[4] Given the problem of not being able to do continuous fieldwork in any one of the settings where Fellowship churches operate, I had to determine what sorts of "things" would be the focus of my work. This meant picking moments in time to observe and hoping that a sufficient number of these observations would constitute a reasonably representative portrayal of what happens at Fellowship ritual and liturgical events. It also meant choosing interlocutors through a combination of careful strategy and serendipity. I knew I wanted to interview Fellowship leadership in addition to Bishop Flunder; after attending multiple events, it became clear who the most significant leaders were. They included regional administrators (bishops), the pastors of various member congregations, other leaders in those congregations (e.g., music ministers, deacons, elders, and prophets), and those who worked in particular kinds of outreach (e.g., drug and alcohol rehabilitation, HIV/AIDS services, services to the homeless). But I also relied on happenstance to recruit others to be interviewed: people who were sitting near me at Fellowship events, people who approached me with expressions of interest in the research, people with whom I struck up pleasant conversations and with whom I simply "hit it off." The latter circumstance meant that a potential interlocutor might be more interested in finding time in a busy schedule for an interview than someone who found the whole venture (or perhaps just me) less compelling.

Another hurdle to be overcome was contained in the dynamics of scheduling. People in the Fellowship, especially the leaders, proved to be uncommonly busy. Most pastors don't earn enough in the pulpit to support themselves and their families, and thus hold various kinds of "day jobs" that are often quite time-consuming. Bishop Flunder maintains a schedule of visiting teaching positions at divinity schools around the country; Bishop Pennese was, for a time, the chaplain at a large senior residential facility; others are in fields including health care, education, corporate administration, and government work. Many of those in leadership roles, as well as some lay members, are enrolled in full- or part-time programs in seminaries and divinity schools. Many are parents, some of whom have complicated arrangements with co-parents and child-care providers; many have obligations in the care of elderly family members. These folks do not have much time, and getting them to sit down for long, open-ended interviews is difficult no matter how eager they are to contribute to the work.

I was challenged, as well, by the need to situate my work within the larger study of religion in general, religion in the United States, and African American religion. A voluminous literature exists on fundamentalism, Bible-believing Christianity, evangelical religion, and Pentecostalism that examines the history and sociology of these movements and their proliferation in the United States and throughout the developing world. Much of this work focuses on the rise of charismatic churches in the United States and in other countries, and particularly on their growth through new members abandoning their former religious affiliations and seeking more spiritual fulfillment in expressive worship. Other scholars have focused on the relationship between these religious trends and the rise of a highly organized, extreme right wing, especially in the United States.

I will discuss some of these intersections later, but for now it is vital to note that this underscores how different the Fellowship is from other kinds of expressions of Bible-believing Christianity in the United States. Fellowship members are engaged in a process of reclamation rather than finding a new kind of religious commitment, as is frequently the case in the Emerging Church movement and other new Pentecostal groups (Bielo 2011). Memory and sentiment are key ingredients of this process, along with efforts to instill pride in members' affirming their "authentic" identities, understood to be God-given. Further, the emphasis on identifying areas beyond church walls where members should focus social action has been on progressive causes and the formation of coalitions with social justice organizations that reflect the inclusive politics espoused not only by the leadership but by the congregants of TFAM. Frequent guests at national convocations are representatives of Lambda Legal, the National Center for Lesbian Rights, the National Association for the Advancement of Colored People (NAACP), and the Human Rights Campaign. Such participation may involve the organization setting up a table with literature, giving out souvenir items like tote bags or T-shirts, sponsoring an event like a lunch, conducting a workshop, or providing a representative who delivers an address at a plenary session.

These practices remind me of the porous nature of LGBT community life that has also been central to my work in other ethnographic settings. The Fellowship is a site where LGBT, black, and Christian identifications all converge upon one another, further enlarged by commitments to progressive political action, community service, and amplified by understandings of Christianity as requiring a deeply interpretive process that often calls for formal religious education. The object of study is never "just" LGBT, any more than it can be limited to Christianity, African American culture, or churches as the engines of political mobilization. Identities shift and ramify depending on circumstances and context, a process that is further encouraged by the doctrine of radical inclusivity, a commitment that assaults boundaries of all sorts.

But besides my long-standing focus on LGBT people, clear areas of continuity emerged between my previous work and my new involvement with the Fellowship. Like other people I had studied—lesbian mothers, gay fathers, and same-sex couples staging commitment ceremonies in the years before any kind of legal marriage equality existed—the LGBT Christians I met in the Fellowship struggled with the issue of incommensurability (Boellstorff 2005; Povinelli 2001). That is, their full performance of identity claims involved resolving problems of legibility: according to conservative religious thinking, LGBT people are inherently sinful and cannot achieve salvation in the ways available to other Christians (Barton 2012; Erzen 2006; Gerber 2011; Moon 2004). Explicit revelation of a non-heteronormative gender or sexual identity would almost always lead to their being distanced from the most important black community institution in the United States—the church—and would often involve rejection from kinship networks, neighborhoods, and other social locations that shape and reinforce black identity. Beyond this, being distanced from the black church might mean being distanced, as well, from the possibility of direct communication with the Holy Spirit, thus losing the chance to achieve salvation and sanctification, and to receive inspiration and gifts of the spirit (charisma). While access to the latter experience is not uniformly desired or experienced by black LGBT people, even those with long histories in Pentecostal and other charismatic denominations, the revelations that can proceed from collective prayer are vitally important to many of those I met in the Fellowship.

My inquiry, then, is grounded in an understanding of how the Fellowship promotes solutions to these diverse difficulties in a manner that sets it apart from other inclusive religious and social institutions. On the one hand, TFAM mediates between African American LGBT people and their heritage, allowing them to return to cultural practices that had seemed to be permanently out of reach. On the other hand, by promoting a concept of radical inclusivity, the Fellowship opens these resources to the rest of humanity, allowing black LGBT people potentially to lead others to a condition of ethical wholeness and spiritual harmony. While the story of radical inclusivity is aspirational rather than consistently realized, as I will argue more fully later, it engages with the most troubling ways in which people are deprived of access to full humanity based on their race, sexual/gender identity, gender, nationality, and class. The story is also consistent with the Christian roots of TFAM; the emphasis on social justice and the embrace of those most despised, while not always honored in other Christian institutions, resonate both with biblical accounts of the mission of Jesus Christ and with many other exemplars of faith-based service and self-sacrifice.[5]

In telling the stories of the Fellowship, I continue the focus on narrative that has characterized all of my earlier ethnographic research (Lewin 1993, 1998, 2009). I understand narrative to be a verbal form that is distinct from actual experience; it is produced in a particular social context and, in the words of literary scholar Greg Sarris, "is not a life but an account or the story of the life" (Sarris 1993: 85). Anthropologist Renato Rosaldo's work on how the Ilongot of the Philippines craft hunting narratives shows that these not only offer accounts of particular events, but reveal fundamental cultural understandings. "Huntsmen in fact seek out experiences that can be told as stories. In other words, stories often shape, rather than simply reflect, human conduct" (Rosaldo 1989: 129). Stories, then, are both about how life was or is, but also about how it should be; it is the latter that allows stories to constitute or represent culture.

Anthropological linguist William Leap calls this process "retrospective narratization," referring to how "narratives reconstruct original action more than they actually reproduce it" (Leap 1996: 138–39; see also Kleinman 1988). Kath Weston makes a similar argument in *Families We Choose*, showing how coming-out stories not only tell how life events unfolded—in this case, the experience narrators had of revealing their homosexuality to family members—but depend on obligatory elements expected in such accounts. Thus, the coming-out story not only tells how a person came to reveal her/his homosexuality to others, but also reveals basic notions of what homosexual identity is all about and what sorts of concerns preoccupy narrators and audiences (Weston 1991; see also Zimmerman 1984 and Lewin 1991).

Narrative analysis has been especially influential in the work of feminist anthropologists and in that of feminists in other disciplines (Abu-Lughod 1991; Ginsburg 1989; Krasniewicz 1992; Personal Narratives Group 1989; Steedman 1987; Wolf 1992). All of these works use different approaches to representing narratives, but all also make the point that narrators construct meaning in the course of explaining action and that narratives ought to be viewed as evidence of how cultural systems shape verbal performances. Audiences (including the ethnographer) are witnesses to narratives, but the storytellers themselves are also a kind of audience, as they explain their own worlds to themselves and thereby conceptualize who they are.

The narratives that animate the pages that follow occurred in particular settings and in relation to ritual occasions, diverse experiences of prayer, and specific personal histories. They also were told to me—a Euro-American, non-Christian who nonetheless was (often) embraced as a family member. Stories also reveal callings to specific ministries or forms of social action and education. Narrative is the mechanism by which I can offer accounts of how Fellowship members experience prayer, how they achieve inhabitation by the Holy Spirit, and how they explain these experiences. How do specific liturgical and ritual elements enhance or inhibit spiritual fulfillment, and how do these relate to what narrators understand to be the most authentic worship practices?

In these pages, I tell the stories of TFAM participants situated at different levels in the life of the coalition and of their individual congregations, navigating between narratives and ritual language to tell the story of the Fellowship. The voices of ordinary congregants—the people who come week after week, but who don't (yet) hold leadership positions—will contribute to the larger account, as will narrative materials gathered from Fellowship members who play leadership roles, including those who are deacons, ministers of music, pastors, elders, prophets, and bishops. These interlocutors shared stories with me about the topics that constitute the individual chapters that follow. Some of their accounts appear in the text; most others inform the analysis even when I do not quote from them.

Along with these stories, I draw on the texts of sermons to illustrate the way particular themes are elaborated and used to construct TFAM's identity as a religious movement. I do not embark on a technical analysis of these texts in the way that scholars of religious expression have done so effectively (Davis 1985; Hinson 2000), as my interest in them lies less in their formal or musical attributes than in the specific cultural and aspirational messages they convey.

The Anthropology Ministry

I have already mentioned that I was surprised by my intense desire to become involved with the Fellowship, but that the members and leaders I met took my arrival in stride. Indeed, as I talked with people, I learned about the ways that they came to understand what sorts of life decisions and work they should undertake, choices they nearly always called "ministries." One woman told me that she had been called to the "administrative ministry," discovering that she had a previously unrecognized talent for managing the financial and organizational dimensions of her church that she found extremely satisfying to enact. That God had led her in this direction was absolutely clear to her; the proof that this was the correct path for her to take was to be found in her uncommon competence as an administrator. The music minister of another church explained how the call to assume responsibility for the diverse musical activities in her congregation came to her. There's a lot of work associated with the music ministry: rehearsing with the gospel choir, planning the Praise and Worship sessions that are held before the start of Sunday services, the choice of hymns and the music that accompanies other parts of the service. Though not herself LGBT—she told me before I even asked that she is heterosexual—she feels spiritually called to this work, building on a lifetime in the music industry as a gospel and R&B recording artist, and inspired by the "authenticity" of worship in TFAM and in the church she attends.

The characteristic of all of these ministries—whether they involve time-consuming duties and major responsibility or are more short-term commitments—is that the individuals feel "called" to do them and experience great satisfaction from performing them. Typically, the Holy Spirit spoke to them during prayer, but sometimes without warning or preparation, as occurred for Pastor Carl, a transgender man who belongs to Pillar of Love in Chicago, who often heard and conversed with the Spirit in the shower. As I will detail later, this communication may sometimes have the attributes of a literal voice, but more often involves a strong feeling of having been entered and changed, told what to do next.

During the convocation in 2011 at a large hotel in Las Vegas, I spent many hours talking with Fellowship members about their ministries and how they were inspired to take these particular directions in their lives and to contribute to their churches in these ways. In the course of these conversations, I realized, rather suddenly, that I have the anthropology ministry, that my drive to do anthropology comes out of some deep place within me, that my commitment to this work is passionate, and that the work could contribute in some way to the mission of the Fellowship. I saw Bishop Flunder shortly after I had this revelation and shared it with her. She nodded as if to say, "I've known that all along."

Bishop's response clarified the wholehearted welcome I received when I first approached leaders of the Fellowship with my plan to conduct research. Perhaps reflecting the lack of confidence I felt as I decided to study a religious organization, I was a bit nervous about whether members and leaders would be enthusiastic about my work. I didn't understand until later that my feelings about the work, and my steady appearance at events around the country over a period of more than seven years (from 2009 through 2016), would convince Fellowship members that I had the "anthropology ministry," and that, beyond this, I was "the Fellowship's anthropologist." When I asked permission to record local, regional, and national events, Bishop Flunder told me to do "anything you want." I suspect that regular attendance coupled with my clear position as an outsider secured my position. It was understood that I would be unlikely to speak in tongues or fall out, but that my participation was sincere. That is, I was in a unique position as a person distant enough to record the Fellowship's stories, but not so distant as to be untrustworthy. It hasn't hurt that the principle of "radical inclusivity" offers an embrace to me as well as to all sorts of people whose involvement might not be predictable. After all, Bishop Flunder reminded me, after I mentioned not being a Christian, "Jesus was one of your people." And my work is clearly understood like all other worldly phenomena, as something that God has intended.

The embraces have been literal as well as figurative. Services at Fellowship churches almost invariably involve a period of greeting one's fellow worshippers that can go on for as long as it takes for every person to embrace almost everyone else present. "Bless you," "So glad you're here," "Happy to see you again" accompany the hugs and kisses one receives at these times. Mere handshakes don't speak to the pleasure congregants take in each other's presence; almost everyone's embrace seems sincere, and perhaps these feelings of closeness are part of what people come to church to experience. People I have met in the Fellowship have "friended" me on Facebook, a connection that has led me to receive dozens of birthday greetings over the past few years, and to have photos of me at Fellowship events "tagged" and circulated.

I was also undeniably drawn to work with TFAM because of the extraordinary empathy and generosity of spirit I have encountered among members and leaders. Bishop Phyllis Pennese's way of being in the world, for example, exemplifies these qualities. As mentioned earlier, for some years, her "day job" was serving as the chaplain at an upscale (and nearly

INVOCATION

all white) retirement residence in the Chicago suburbs operated by the United Church of Christ. Although it must have taken most residents aback to have a very large black lesbian serving in this position, her spirituality and eloquence won them over and they grew to love her. As a result, a group of residents asked her if she would do a presentation for them about her family and her life, and she put a talk and PowerPoint show together for them. This was when they learned that she is biracial, the daughter of an African American mother and an Italian immigrant father. After the talk, one woman in her nineties thanked Phyllis and then remarked that she was so fortunate to have her Italian father, that is, to be biracial, because that was why she was so smart. I was appalled when I heard this and asked Phyllis how she responded. She told me, "I said thank you." She then explained that despite her limitations, the woman meant well, and that there was nothing she could do to make someone so old change their preconceptions about race.

The stories I will tell in the following chapters are embedded in this complex experience of being an outsider who has been granted a kind of insider status and has, in a sense, fallen in love with the people I study. This is, of course, the story of anthropology as a discipline, something that ought not to have caught me unawares. But it's a story that isn't always acknowledged in our research, and that doesn't always affect us with equally deep emotion. I know it was the story that drew me to anthropology when I was an undergraduate, overwhelmed (perhaps naively) with the possibilities of giving all cultures equal respect, with the simple beauty of transmitting people's ideas and utterances as inherently valid and meaningful. I do believe that the romance of anthropology, the risk taking that accompanies leaping into the worlds of others, is still alive and still animates much of the work we do.

Anthropological Perspectives

All of the practices and histories that undergird TFAM worship have been subjected to intensive study by anthropologists and others. Scholars have been concerned with understanding ritual and cultural performance (Bauman 1977; Geertz 1973; Myerhoff 1992; Turner 1969, 1987), the phenomenology of prayer (Csordas 1997, 2002; Luhrmann 2012; Schmidt 2000), the links between religiosity and conservative politics (Harding 2001; Heineman 1998; Hunter 1991; Wilcox and Robinson 2011), the increasing appeal of Pentecostal denominations in the United States and elsewhere (see Anderson et al. 2010; Brusco 1995; Keane 2007; Miller and

Yamamori 2007; Robbins 2004, among many others), and the cultural foundations of such phenomena as trance, glossolalia, and spirit possession (Bourguignon 1973; Goodman et al. 1974; Rouget 1985; Samarin 1972). Scholars who have studied religious movements have been particularly concerned to document the way that the charisma of church leaders shapes the trajectories of such movements (Harding 2001; Lindholm 2013; Willner 1984). Recently, some scholars of sexuality and gender have brought their work into conversation with examinations of religion (Ramberg 2014).

Recent scholarship on US churches has been particularly attentive to the relationship between specific spiritual directions and conservative or neoliberal political agendas, the intersections or collisions between race/ethnicity, class, gender, and sexuality with political commitments and economic accessibility; the rapid pace of change in these domains, however, makes it difficult to summarize the state of the field. The attention of anthropologists and other scholars of religion has been drawn to the massive growth in various kinds of fundamentalist and charismatic movements, both the Emerging Church movement and the rise of megachurches, and the highly visible pastors who lead them, among mostly white and middle-class Americans (Bielo 2009, 2011; Elisha 2011; Luhrmann 2012), where an emphasis on personal communication with God as a route to sanctification recalls some of the flavor of black churches but clearly has a very different genealogy. Some of these movements stress informal organizing through the "planting" of churches in worshippers' homes; others are grandiose and ambitious, building enormous facilities and assuming an outsize presence in the media. Clearly, they all take their meaning from the intersections of particular historical circumstances that are judged to be significant. These might be defined in terms of family and morality, immigration and the transformation of the American population, economic opportunities and catastrophes, the growth or contraction of public domains—though how these are interpreted varies considerably. A gospel of wealth drives the popularity of some of these churches, while others assiduously avoid what they view as the moral corruption of rampant consumerism (Bielo 2011). What makes all of these movements important in the context of the study of TFAM is a pattern of reliance on religion and spirituality in moments of social unease (Hartman 2015). Such patterns appear to have distinctly American forms, as they are linked both to the religious history of the United States and to the unique concatenation of political, social, and economic conditions that characterize particular historical moments (Anderson 1979).

It is somewhere in the interstices of these diverse literatures that my work on TFAM finds a conceptual home. Fellowship congregations are making audacious claims to elements of their spiritual heritage that others would deny they have a right to possess. While for many, worship in a Fellowship church is a reclamation project, for some others, it has the attributes of "conversion." Some of these members may have been unchurched, and others may have worshipped in non-charismatic traditions, but even for those who are returning to the practices of their youth, the very exercise of recuperation has much of the spiritual intensity of conversion—in this case, the discovery that their sexual/gender identity or presentation has not disqualified them from being children of God. This understanding has the force of revelation, as shame is stripped away and the full person is embraced by the Holy Spirit.

Filled with the Spirit

I have argued elsewhere that LGBT community life is not usefully conceptualized as a closed system that is tightly bounded, but that it is rather a porous and fluid site where interactions and identities move back and forth depending upon context (Lewin 2009). The Fellowship is a setting in which LGBT, black, and Christian identities all converge upon one another, further enlarged by commitments to progressive political action and community service, which are amplified by understandings of Christianity as requiring a deeply interpretive process that demands education. As I indicated earlier, the object of study is never "just" LGBT, any more than it can be limited to Christianity, African American culture, or churches as the engines of political mobilization. Identities shift and ramify depending on circumstances and context, a process that is further encouraged by the doctrine of radical inclusivity, a commitment that assaults boundaries of all sorts. As we shall see, "radical inclusivity" gives this notion of permeable boundaries new urgency and meaning.

I argue in the following chapters that the Fellowship brings together two missions in a manner that moves beyond its commitment to its core constituency—black, LGBT Christians. I situate the formation of the Fellowship in the context of the long history of the black church and its relation to the continuity of black community and to the solidification of black identities. I present accounts that detail the experiences of rejection that LGBT people have suffered in the black church. These are not monolithic accounts. Some lived through regimes of "don't ask, don't tell"; some chafed at the invisibility of themselves and their families. Others spoke with disgust about pastoral hypocrisy, as some preachers who inveighed fervently against homosexuality were known to pursue same-sex partners on the "down low." In other cases, individuals who revealed their identities or were "outed" by others found themselves expelled from their churches. These were experiences that sometimes led them to stop attending church altogether or to migrate through a succession of more liberal alternatives, until finding the Fellowship. This chapter also details the formation of the Fellowship and its precursors, commenting on its intersections with other churches with specific outreach to LGBT people.

Its connection to Pentecostal worship has deep historical roots and is heartfelt, but also at least conceptually conditional, as no TFAM leaders claim that this is the only acceptable way to praise God. Still, by using expressive African American worship as a starting point, TFAM can attempt to make those who were despised in traditional churches whole again, citizens of their faith in the fullest sense, able to embrace memory and nostalgia without reservation. At the same time, TFAM's adherence to the complex set of ideas called "radical inclusivity" means that the constituency of the Fellowship is potentially never static, able to expand to meet the ever-changing challenges presented by the diversity of the real world.

In line with this reality, *Filled with the Spirit* takes up the process by which members and leaders in TFAM tack back and forth between their histories and roots—or what they believe these to be—and a commitment to be open to change and flexibility, as the only route to achieving the more expansive notion of radical inclusivity that increasingly animates its institutional existence. Even in the context of this openness, TFAM offers a Christian worship experience that is unapologetically grounded in the black church, and that draws its power from deploying the expressive style of worship that is characteristic of the denominations that make up the black church and in which most of its members were raised.

The book will also consider Bishop Flunder's charismatic role and the ways in which her persona drives how TFAM is structured and how its leaders imagine its future. The Fellowship grew directly out of Bishop Flunder's personal experience and vision, and it would be difficult to overstate the regard in which she is held or the awe that worshippers feel in her presence. At the same time, however, we will see that her charisma draws not only on her ability to perform the attributes classically associated with charismatic leaders, but also, perhaps paradoxically, on her resistance to some of these attributes—her lack of pretension, her insistence on trying to replace herself, in short, her refusal to be wholly defined by her charisma. Bishop Flunder's charisma is another of the elements of TFAM that rests firmly on the shaky ground of paradox. Besides the fierce loyalty that TFAM members have for Bishop Flunder, however, other leaders have emerged in the coalition, including (as of this writing) one bishop who is designated as Bishop Flunder's episcopal assistant, four bishops who oversee particular US regions, and one whose responsibilities center on global ministry and especially on work in Africa. Still, Bishop Flunder's persona has a particular resonance in TFAM that makes it difficult to imagine how the coalition will operate when she eventually steps aside.

Central to the spiritual quest of Fellowship members is their understanding of what "coming out" means and why it is important. In the stories they tell, the political rationale for coming out—long axiomatic and indeed virtually mandatory in the LGBT rights movement—takes a backseat to the spiritual benefits of acknowledging one's "authentic identity." For some members, failure to take this step impedes inhabitation by the Holy Spirit and hence prevents the individual from achieving spiritual wholeness. Discussions about coming out, couched in terms that have to do with wider concerns with spiritual health and authenticity, suggest that in the Fellowship calculus, transcendent spiritual experience cannot occur unless space that can accommodate the Spirit is accessible.

Essential to this process is the centrality in TFAM of the worship practices, music, and language that recall the shared histories of black Americans. "Old-time" is a descriptor that I often heard when a particular worship style or message is worthy of approval or is deemed particularly authentic. Such styles often draw on mention of the past, particularly in the South, using images of food, weather, grandmotherly wisdom, slavery, and African roots to unite worshippers in the contemplation of cultural memory and presumptions of shared histories. The use of historical metaphors and of key worship elements (e.g., language, music) that can be understood to be "traditional" assures participants that their experience in an LGBT-affirming church is the "real thing." In other words, nostalgia can be used to establish the authenticity of the Fellowship experience, a key challenge in the constitution of LGBT cultural forms.[6]

I also give close attention to the ramifications of radical inclusivity for the mission of TFAM and the directions taken by congregants (often called "saints") in choosing ministries inside and outside the church and in deciding to pursue seminary training. The Fellowship is, to put it mildly, big on education, constantly exhorting active members to take courses or to pursue certifications or degrees at divinity schools and Bible colleges. Not all of those studying in seminaries intend to take up pastoral positions, though some do (or may later decide to take such a path). The push for education reflects the interpretive inclination of the Fellowship as members are taught—often in direct opposition to what they may have learned in other churches they have attended—that the Bible is a historical document written by people who composed texts that reflected their cultural and social circumstances. The message is that the Bible is not sacred per se and certainly not an object to be worshipped. It is an interpretive and interpreted artifact, a narrative crafted by people with specific standpoints who lived in particular times and places; further examination is demanded by the fact that it has been translated from original languages, a process that may have distorted the intentions of the text. This method for understanding the Bible is constantly reiterated in the Fellowship, with the goal of bringing congregants a level of basic religious literacy that will enable them to study further and to rebut homophobic readings of Scripture.

Similarly, the importance of public engagement is stressed in the Fellowship as a key element of the "radical inclusivity" message that unifies the coalition. If members are to reach out to persons who have been marginalized and stigmatized in the world, and perhaps in other churches, they will have to leave the comfort of their congregation and take their work to the streets. While public engagement and political activism have been key foci of many black churches, some denominations have long been suspicious of too much involvement with the world, fearing its corrupting influence. In particular, the Church of God in Christ (COGIC), the denomination in which many Fellowship members grew up, tends to oppose political involvement, even discouraging members from voting. The Fellowship actively supports political outreach, but how members choose and sustain particular pathways must be inspired by the Holy Spirit.

This sense of a spiritual and political mission is animated directly by the complex meanings that circulate in the doctrine of "radical inclusivity." On one level, radical inclusivity speaks to the organization's mandate to reach out and embrace the most marginalized and despised of people, to draw them into Fellowship churches, and to lead them to understand that God loves them just as they are, supporting them as they move toward healing whatever misfortune afflicts them. Church members hope to accomplish this without formal evangelism; indeed, the notion that nonmembers would be exhorted to join (or that members would try to convert a certain anthropologist) was greeted with laughter. Conversions are the work of the Holy Spirit and cannot be "made to" happen. That radical inclusivity extends beyond boundaries of race, class, gender, sexuality, and so on is understood as a fundamental truth in the Fellowship.

But radical inclusivity also speaks to the embrace not only of individuals of all types, but to the future direction of the Fellowship as an organization. This ecumenical impulse, most visible at the level of the national coalition, opens up potential contradictions with the dedication of the Fellowship to spiritual union with Jesus Christ. How is radical inclusivity symbolically enacted at Fellowship events, and what does this tell us about the possible directions that the coalition will take in coming years? Will radical inclusivity have limitations on its expression or organization—that is, can TFAM not only embrace worshippers from outside the traditions of black Christianity, but expand to include Euro-Americans or non-Christians in a meaningful way? I can only interpret the way I was embraced by TFAM members as a family member and invited to join in all aspects of the various churches' activities as inspired by a particular dimension of radical inclusivity. Indeed, as I indicated earlier, my arrival at the first Fellowship church I attended seemed to have been understood almost as predictable, evidence of the reach of radical inclusivity, and my identity as anthropologist fit into this recognition. Not being black and not being Christian seemed to have enhanced the welcome I received, perhaps because it spoke to the truth of radical inclusivity.

Most importantly, in this book I take up what has been either a missing or an unarticulated element of current discussions of race, gender, and sexuality by adding close attention to spirituality and faith. As I shall argue in later chapters, scholars who are interested in the intersections of race, gender, and sexuality have tended to ignore the spiritual needs of the people they study, and thus to assume that the "queer" subjects who are mostly the focus of their attention are wholly concerned with how their identities are enacted in the material world, and how that material world gives their subjectivities meaning. I will contend that this approach neglects the ways in which these people's identities are shaped by far more than the impact of observable phenomena, as they also are deeply concerned with their spiritual well-being and with their connections to the unseen, the ineffable forces of the sacred. The powerful experience that the Fellowship offers speaks to the continuing importance of the yearning for spiritual wholeness and rectitude that LGBT people share with other people in the United States and elsewhere.

ONE

"I've Been 'Buked": The Double Consciousness of Being LGBT and Black

"George Howard" grew up in a Pentecostal church in the Deep South in the 1970s. He had been aware of his homosexuality since his childhood. Arriving in Chicago, he found a far more open and accepting world, a place with Gay Pride celebrations, lots of gay bars, and an energetic drag scene. He still wanted to be part of a church family, but for a long time he had no success finding a suitable congregation in Chicago. He explains his struggle to find a church home:

I didn't go to any churches here because they were either too large or they were gay bashing from the pulpit and had a huge choir full of homosexuals and a congregation with even more and then you know you hear all this agreement from the masses and I just could not see myself being a hypocrite. Not in that way, not in the sanctuary, I was not going to stand up and say, "Amen, Pastor, that's right!" and I don't believe it. My belief is that God knows all of us, better than we know ourselves, and that he made all of us just as we are. I came to the conclusion for myself that if I keep asking God to change me, then you know I'm telling him that he messed up, that he did wrong. So that's what made me say to myself, accept it and be done with it. I used to fast and pray early in life, especially before I turned twelve because turning twelve was that age where there was a heaven or hell for you. Before twelve, you know God would probably forgive you and you could go to heaven. But at twelve, you could make your own decisions and there's a heaven or a hell for you. I used to fast and pray, you know, "Please take this away from me."

Despite the greater acceptance LGBT people have experienced across American society since the 1970s, African American communities have been described as particularly inhospitable to homosexuality and to be especially antagonistic toward people with non-heteronormative gender or sexual identities in religious settings (Anderson 1998; Bates 2005; Douglas 1999; Griffin 2006; Johnson 2008). Like other black Americans, many LGBT black people hunger for a religious home and a spiritual center, historically located in the black church. In this chapter, I will detail the history of the black church and outline the particular challenges faced by LGBT people who yearn for acceptance in what they often describe as a "church home."

The Black Church in America

To understand the stories of Fellowship members that will be told in these pages, we must begin with the almost immeasurable importance of the black church and religious belief for most African Americans (Frazier 1974 [1964]; Lincoln and Mamiya 1990). Speaking broadly of the many denominations that constitute the black church, scholars have described its significance as going back to the days of slavery, when Africans who had been transported to North America struggled to survive not only the physical hardships of captivity but the threats that servitude presented to their sense of the order of the material and supernatural world. Slavery generally entailed close interaction among people of disparate African origins, who often spoke unrelated languages and came from diverse religious backgrounds. While disputes about whether slaves were able to preserve elements of their African cultural heritage or were utterly cast adrift and forced to invent new creeds have preoccupied scholars for generations (Frazier 1974 [1964]; Herskovits 1990 [1941]), most were exposed to Christianity from their early days in North America—whether intentionally or obliquely (Raboteau 1978). Even as this occurred, there was vigorous debate in the antebellum period over whether Christianity might be used to make slaves more compliant or whether it would arouse rebellious feelings among them grounded in a sense of equality with slaveholders as children of God (Genovese 1972). In any case, some rejected the new religion, but many others either found elements of Christian doctrine compatible with their earlier beliefs or discovered specific features of Protestant practice that were appealing (Mintz and Price 1992 [1976]; Raboteau 1978). In particular, scholars have argued that the emphasis on direct experience of the Holy Spirit that characterized Baptist and Methodist evangelism in the antebellum period was attractive to slaves as it offered a compelling translation of African beliefs in the dynamic world of spirits and the ability of individuals to have transformative contact with them (Battle 2006).

Some research indicates that elements of African religions figured prominently in the spiritual activities of slaves, sometimes providing the foundation for resistance to the degradations of captivity (Young 2007). Biblical stories offered compelling examples of how embattled Hebrews survived assaults on their spiritual practices and managed to sustain themselves as a people, and many of these offered slaves images of redemption that, if not close at hand, could at least be imagined. As historian of religion Albert Raboteau explains, the accounts of God's interventions on behalf of biblical Israel helped "slaves to assert and maintain a sense of personal value—even of ultimate worth" (Raboteau 1978: 318). Even during slavery, Christianity sometimes presented slaves with opportunities to preach or lead worship, that is, to achieve positions of leadership or esteem in their communities. But in many cases, worship was carried out in secret, constituting an act of rebellion against the constraints of slavery. Taking a different approach to this discussion, folklorist John W. Roberts urges his readers to pay close attention to the African foundations of African American culture, resisting the impulse to label discrete elements as "Africanisms." He proposes, instead, what he calls an "Afrocentric perspective," one that would see African and American traditions in a "dynamic relationship" (Roberts 1989: 9). Following this approach, Roberts traces such folk hero figures as the trickster and the conjurer to African precedents, and also argues for strong African influences in the form and content of spirituals.

While slaves were often baptized or otherwise "Christianized" soon after they arrived in America, it is of lasting significance that Christianity made a major impact on slaves during the First Great Awakening around 1740 (Raboteau 1978) and later during the Second Great Awakening in the early nineteenth century.[1] During both of these periods of intense religious fervor, white evangelists for the Baptist and Methodist denominations were especially active in the South, converting both slaves and masters. These denominations worshipped in a manner that was notably expressive and emotional (at least in comparison with other religious practices brought to America from England) and engaged directly with Scripture and evangelism. Raboteau (1978) suggests that slaves probably found the practices of the Catholics, Congregationalists, and Episcopalians, which may have been the denominations of their masters, less appealing because of their more restrained style of worship. He also points out that the Baptists and Methodists welcomed clergy regardless of education, thus clearing the path for slaves and later free blacks with little if any formal education to make their way into the clergy. He explains:

> A converted heart and a gifted tongue were more important than the amount of theological training received. If a converted slave showed talent for exhorting, he exhorted, and not only to black audiences. The tendency of evangelical religion to level the souls of all men before God became manifest when awakened blacks preached to unconverted whites. (Raboteau 1978: 133–34)

Theologian Horace Griffin argues that the affiliations of black people with what have now coalesced as conservative Protestant denominations have important implications for present-day religious thinking. White members of these churches are theologically orthodox as well as firmly conservative on social issues such as the family and homosexuality, but since a more substantial proportion of black people are members of these and other traditionalist denominations, such views are even more prevalent among them (Griffin 2006). One of the ironies of this history is that these (white) churches often used biblical authority to defend slavery in a manner that Griffin argues is echoed today in their approach to homosexuality. Griffin explains that black Christians tended to support a markedly sex-negative version of Christian tradition, probably responding to racist demonization of black sexuality as excessive. Their efforts to achieve respectability after emancipation generated a strikingly puritanical approach to sexuality and the body, one that E. Franklin Frazier also remarked on in *Black Bourgeoisie* (1957). According to Frazier, creating and maintaining an image of the black body as chaste was one cultural strategy that blacks used to try to attain a respectability based on control of their "savage instincts" (Griffin 2006: 59).

As black feminist theorists have observed, sex negativity in black culture can be traced to the toxic sexual myths that are foundational to racism, circumstances that rose to the surface in a particularly dramatic manner during the 1991 confirmation hearing for Clarence Thomas's nomination to the Supreme Court. Anita Hill, a law professor who was a former employee of Clarence Thomas at the Equal Employment Opportunity Commission, testified to his having sexually harassed her, even specifying the vulgar language he used on these occasions. These allegations laid bare persistent sexual stereotypes of both black women and black men, and led many African Americans to repudiate Hill's decision to make her experience public as an unfortunate instance of "airing dirty laundry" (Morrison 1992). That African Americans are typically viewed as hypersexual, with appetites that exceed the "normal" sexuality of white people, penetrates every aspect of black political and social experience, as Patricia Hill Collins has persuasively argued (Collins 1991, 2004). Given the pervasive reach of these malicious stereotypes, the defensive strategies intended to disarm them permeate black religious observance, which in turn serves to stigmatize behaviors or identities deemed to be problematic as black people struggle for respectability.

Besides its significance as the site of religious observance, in which worship enabled slaves and later emancipated African Americans to express their yearnings for freedom and dignity, the church has long provided key resources that have furthered the ability of besieged communities to survive. As early as 1849, abolitionist Martin Delany stated that "among our people generally, the church is the Alpha and Omega of all things. It is their only source of information—their only acknowledged public body—their state legislature" (quoted in Glaude 2003: 338). With the end of slavery, the "invisible institution," established under slavery and the institutional churches built by free blacks, grew and morphed along diverse denominational lines and "provided an organization and structuring of Negro life which has persisted until the present time" (Frazier 1974 [1964]: 37). As Frazier explains, the church regulated marital and family relationships, fostered economic cooperation, provided education, and served as the crux of political life. Even more important, the church offered refuge to blacks struggling to survive in an unremittingly hostile world. Religious scholar Eddie Glaude Jr. enumerates other activities that were housed in black churches: mutual aid societies, athletic clubs, libraries, insurance companies, and many different kinds of social events, as churches usually provided the only large public spaces to which black people had access both before and after emancipation (Glaude 2003). Indeed, historian Evelyn Brooks Higginbotham makes clear that churches were the primary means through which African Americans interacted with the state and other racially constituted institutions. She calls this "the public dimension of the black church, not the religious dimension of the public realm" (1993: 9).

Churches offered spaces where blacks could criticize racism and white society and could gain access to status and esteem away from sites where they were belittled and humiliated. Long ago, W. E. B. Du Bois noted the centrality of the church not only to the black community in a physical sense, but as "peculiarly the expression of the inner ethical life of a people in a sense seldom true elsewhere" (Du Bois 1994 [1903]).

CHAPTER ONE

> For African Americans, long excluded from political institutions and denied presence, even relevance, in the dominant society's myths about its heritage and national community, the church itself became the domain for the expression, celebration, and pursuit of a black collective will and identity. (Higginbotham 1993: 9)

Expanding these multivalent social and cultural roles, the church has also often served as the source of political mobilization—most notably in the mid-twentieth century as the cradle of the civil rights movement (Baer and Singer 1992; Harris 1999).

But beyond the many instrumental roles the church has taken in the lives of American blacks, religious participation and particularly access to the expressive worship style of the various denominations that constitute the black church mean something more than religious observance alone: they stand for blackness perhaps more strongly than any other symbol of cultural affiliation (Battle 2006).[2]

The centrality of the church continued after emancipation. Free African Americans established themselves in the South and were able to maintain the religious associations they had during slavery; as many moved north and west during the Great Migration, beginning around 1916, they established churches on the model of those they had left behind (Wilkerson 2010). As Isabel Wilkerson and others who have documented the pathways of the Great Migration have shown, denominations and styles of worship that were central to African American life in the South made their way north and west with the migrants, as did food, music, and other ethnic markers (see also Best 2005; Lemann 1991).

Sharing cultural traditions and preserving the history of African American culture loom large for many American blacks today. Anthropologist Faye Harrison recounts the "grounding for the sense of cultural tradition" that is enacted in down-home family reunions in the South, whose participants include both those who remained in the South and those who migrated away from their ancestral roots. These events, which usually include both sacred and secular ritual components, constitute "an ancestor-focused pilgrimage" that accentuates the continuing meaning of "old-time" customs and stories (Harrison 1995: 35). Accounts such as Harrison's highlight the importance of continuity and tradition in the ongoing vigor of the black church, as well as enduring nostalgia for the various southern locales to which African Americans outside the South trace their origins.[3]

These ties to religious heritage are strong among African Americans, even those who have moved outside the South and prospered economically. The Pew Forum reports that regardless of education and other class markers, the vast majority of black Americans continue to be members of historically black churches such as those affiliated with the National Baptist Convention or the African Methodist Episcopal Church (AME), with a smaller percentage affiliated with other (mostly evangelical) Protestant churches (Pew Forum on Religion and Public Life 2009; Sanders 1996). As one might expect from these statistics, belief in God and both faith and observance figure prominently in African American life. Even considering the high levels of religiosity that typify Americans in general, as compared with Europeans (Caplow 1985; McLeod 2007), black people's involvement with religion, especially with Protestant Christian observance, is far more central to ordinary life than it is for other racial/ethnic groups (Taylor, Chatters, and Levin 2004). Indeed, an article from 2011 in the *New York Times* reported that black people who were both gay and didn't believe in God found it easier to "come out" to parents about their gayness than about their atheism (Brennan 2011; see Pinn 2014 for an extended personal statement on atheism by a prominent black religious studies scholar). Black people attend church at higher rates than the general population; report more intense belief in the afterlife, miracles, and other divine phenomena; and are more likely to engage in regular, even daily prayer. They are also somewhat more likely than people in the general population to hold negative views of homosexuality and same-sex marriage, though their views on a variety of political issues are far from uniform and are evolving as the national discourse on these topics shifts in the wake of judicial support for marriage equality (Pew Forum on Religion and Public Life 2009).

Women in the Black Church

But LGBT identities are not the only basis for feelings of exclusion and rejection in US black churches. As is true in many religious communities, regardless of their racial composition, women have long functioned as the heart of black churches, though their roles as leaders were often covert and highly constrained by gender. Higginbotham details the complex roles of US black Baptist women (1880-1920) who remained in the background and avoided taking on explicit leadership roles. As members of an educated female elite, these churchwomen particularly focused on conveying cultural standards to the masses of church members. As discussed earlier in this chapter, they crafted what she calls a "politics of respectability," seeking to instill poor black people with bourgeois standards of behavior. They tended to understand racism as being exacerbated by the improper behaviors of African Americans, and thus urged black people to exercise restraint in their public demeanor, avoiding such possible offenses as gaudy or immodest clothing, the use of snuff, and playing baseball on Sunday (Higginbotham 1993: 15). But they also constituted a powerful force that worked tirelessly to improve the standard of living of black people, to provide opportunities for poor blacks to improve their access to education and employment, as well as energetically opposing racist abuses, particularly lynching.

While intense controversy has long raged about whether women could serve as clergy, with many churches regarding preaching as beyond the limit of women's appropriate role, scholarship on the history of black church life makes clear that women often occupied prominent positions outside the clergy and were honored for their contributions (Wiggins 2005). Some black churches did allow women to preach or to act in other kinds of publicly sanctioned leadership roles, including musical performance, but others drew the line at ordination, insisting that such forceful women remain in support roles without the benefits of ordination or other formal insignia of pastoral power. Holiness and Pentecostal denominations (both white and black) present a varied picture with respect to the ordination of women, with some granting women the right to preach and others enforcing restrictions on preaching or exercising formal authority in other contexts (Chaves 1997).

The Church of God in Christ (COGIC), the largest black Pentecostal denomination, has been particularly strict in barring women from preaching, making a careful distinction between "teaching" and "preaching," even as these two roles sometimes overlap in ways that make them functionally, if not formally, indistinguishable. As historian of religion Anthea Butler explains, this distinction highlighted "the difference between helping people to learn the Word and actually proclaiming the Word" (Butler 2007: 35). Accordingly, COGIC women took a major role in teaching people how to achieve sanctification or purification through the Holy Spirit. Women whose deportment met denomination standards could become church mothers and take on assignments in COGIC's Women's Department. In the absence of the right to ordination as elders, pastors, and bishops, Butler shows, women in COGIC used other means to achieve leadership.

> There is the power of ordination, but there is a greater power in controlling the ordained, which is what COGIC women did. . . . By using their charismatic authority

and their organizational position that was outside, but alongside, the Episcopal structure, COGIC women were able to become power brokers both inside and outside the church setting. (Butler 2007: 6)

Even with these powers, however, many women in COGIC and other black denominations who experienced the call to preach or evangelize felt thwarted by the limitations imposed on them. Once they had the opportunity to become leaders in the civil rights movement and came under the influence of the emergent feminist movement in the late 1960s and 1970s, however, staying in the background, no matter how much actual power that afforded, was no longer a viable option for many women. As recent scholarship on the civil rights movement has shown, women often took decisive roles in the struggle, but watched as their contributions were minimized, forgotten (Olson 2002; Ransby 2005; Stockley 2005), or even ridiculed, as in Stokely Carmichael's famous suggestion that the position of women in the movement (the Student Non-Violent Coordinating Committee [SNCC]) should be prone. With that comment and other dismissive attitudes in mind, many black women became feminist or womanist leaders, forging a movement that largely operated separately from the predominantly white Second Wave groups that most (white) people think of as *the* feminist movement (Collins 1991; Walker 1983). With this growing feminist awareness as a foundation, no matter how deep their attachment to the churches in which they'd grown up, the limitations imposed on their spiritual (and political) growth felt confining and unfair (Roth 2003).

Struggling with Identities

Despite attachments to the black communities from which they trace their heritage and the churches that symbolize that heritage, LGBT people who are black find themselves enmeshed in painful struggles over the legitimacy of their place in these very communities, a situation exquisitely encapsulated in W. E. B. Du Bois's famous statement about double consciousness: "One ever feels his two-ness,—an American, a Negro; two souls, two thoughts, two unreconciled strivings, two warring ideals in one dark body, whose dogged strength alone keeps it from being torn asunder" (Du Bois 1994 [1903]: 2). While Du Bois was trying to explain the conflicts experienced by black people as they struggle to establish a sense of personhood in a culture that devalues them, his words could easily apply to the efforts of black LGBT people to define their place in African American communities.

CHAPTER ONE

As political scientist Cathy J. Cohen has argued in her work on black community institutions, struggles for acceptance generate disputes over whether an LGBT person can be considered authentically black. Cohen examines the issue from the perspective of public and community responses to the AIDS epidemic, which may have life-threatening implications for persons suffering from the disease.

Contestation over identity, in this case indigenous racial identity, has tangible effects, influencing the distribution of resources, services, access, and legitimacy within communities. (Cohen 1996: 365)

In particular, Cohen challenges the ways that members of black communities have invoked a notion of *"the* black experience" as the basis for scholarship, community organizing, and political mobilization, arguing that this conceptualization is deeply essentializing and fails to fully consider the many sources of difference that also inflect "blackness."

This means that for African American LGBT people, the matter of rejection and homophobia, coming from the church or from other sources, is easily transformed into a challenge to identity.[4] Thus, while they still experience the responses that come with being viewed as black, especially by those of other racial backgrounds, the problem of identity has to do with authenticity and presumptions about loyalty.[5] Cohen (1996) points out that the importance of maintaining their membership in the black community has thus been a priority that shapes how gender/sexual identity are managed. Thus, black gay men and lesbians have long felt they had to remain silent presences in their communities because of their need for support against the pressures of racism. In a similar vein, in *Talking Back*, cultural critic bell hooks describes how black gay people in the community where she was raised shared the fate of others who lived under the constant pressure of poverty and racism.

Sheer economic necessity and fierce white racism, as well as the joy of being there with the black folks known and loved, compelled many gay blacks to live close to home and family. That meant however that gay people created a way to live out sexual preferences within the boundaries of circumstances that were rarely ideal no matter how affirming. In some cases, this meant a closeted sexual life. In other families, an individual could be openly expressive, quite out. (hooks 1989: 120–21)

Even with the amount of individual variation hooks describes, she reports that a double standard prevailed by which gay men had avenues through which they could achieve regard and respect, particularly if they became economically successful. Lesbians, however, suffered more undiluted homophobia and accusations of being unnatural. At least in part because of the pressure on all women to have children, lesbians often accepted these standards, in some cases seeking to assert their authenticity as women by becoming mothers. Perhaps counterintuitively, she explains in *Salvation*, gay people often had a protected status in the black church (as they also did in the arts) in segregated communities where "the church was a safe house, providing both shelter and sanctuary for anyone looked upon as different or deviant, and that included gay believers" (hooks 2001: 193).

The erasure of gay identities has been especially egregious in representations of leading black cultural figures, though a number of recent studies have begun to counter longtime omissions, particularly in reference to the Harlem Renaissance (Carbado, McBride, and Wiese 2011; Dickel 2012; Schwarz 2003; Thomas 1997; Wilson 2011). Historian John D'Emilio's (2004) important biography of Bayard Rustin documents the ways in which discomfort with Rustin's gayness undermined his visibility in the civil rights movement as well as his portrayal in later accounts of the period. And historian Kevin Mumford (2016) chronicles the role of gay men in the United States from the March on Washington to the AIDS crisis. Of course, much of this invisibility parallels the broader amnesia about gay and lesbian cultural figures that was routine in American society until the very recent past. Except for those whose homosexuality was so conspicuous that it couldn't be ignored (Gertrude Stein and Alice B. Toklas, for example), lesbian and gay writers, artists, political leaders, and so on didn't have to do much to "pass"; others did it for them. For those who were financially able or were located in major cities, gay bars, urban enclaves, and summer resorts allowed some relief from the pressure of passing (Kennedy and Davis 1993; Newton 1993; Read 1981).[6] An examination of the politics of LGBT identities, however, in these periods must be informed by awareness of the changing meanings of terminology and identity itself, as today's "gay" may not be a category that can be simply imposed on earlier ways of life.

For African Americans, these conflicts seem to have played out even more starkly. Many African American LGBT people have written about the significant challenges they face in managing what they often experience as two conflicting—even oxymoronic—aspects of their identities. An article by Gregory Conerly with the provocative title "Are You Black First or Are You Queer?" (2001) lays out some ways of conceptualizing the dilemma. Citing 1982 research on black gay men by J. M. Johnson, Conerly argues that blacks who are gay or lesbian are compelled to choose between racial and sexual identities, possibly leading them to gravitate to white communities and prefer white lovers, thereby becoming "gay-identified" blacks. For those who are instead "black-identified," maintaining primary ties to the black community may mean having to "hide their sexual identities to appease heterosexist black communities" (Conerly 2001: 13) and becoming distanced from lesbian and gay political struggles.[7]

Similar dilemmas are reported in the reflections of black lesbian writers Barbara Smith (1983) and Jewelle Gomez (1983), who describe the struggles of African American lesbians to feel at home in their own racial communities. Audre Lorde, too, approached the issue head-on, famously describing the problem as she encountered it after coming out in the 1950s.

> During the fifties in the Village, I did not know the few other Black women who were visibly gay at all well. Too often we found ourselves sleeping with the same white women. We recognized ourselves as exotic sister-outsiders who might gain little from banding together. Perhaps our strength might lay in our fewness, our rarity. That was the way it was Downtown. And uptown, meaning the land of Black people, seemed very far away and hostile territory. (Lorde 1982: 177)

Along similar lines, in the introduction to the collection of writings that he edited in 1986, Joseph Beam wrote:

> Because of our homosexuality the Black community casts us as outsiders. We are the poor relations. The proverbial black sheep, without a history, a literature, a religion, or a community. Our already tenuous position as Black men in white America is exacerbated because we are gay. We are even more susceptible to the despair, alienation, and delusion that threatens [sic] to engulf the entire Black community. (Beam 1986: 17)

The predicament voiced by African American gay men and lesbians recalls Du Bois's famous invocation of the "two-ness" of Negro subjectivity, quoted earlier in this chapter. Both personal narratives and research derived from a number of disciplines suggest that being gay, lesbian, or transgender may be experienced as inconsistent with membership in the black community, possibly even as intrinsically opposed identities. For example, in his ethnographic study of gay black men in Harlem, William Hawkeswood acknowledges that men who are both black and gay may live in either predominantly black or white areas of New York City, but he distinguishes between two populations based on which identity shapes daily life more directly. Like Conerly, he defines "black gay men" as those who are dispersed throughout the city and travel in circles that include gay men of all races; in other words, they have established themselves in "mainstream gay social life" (Hawkeswood 1996: 13). On the other hand, the "gay black men" who are at the center of his book make their identity as black men primary. They choose to live in Harlem, to remain connected to their families and churches, to participate in the gay scene in Harlem, and to seek out other black men as sexual partners and lovers. By referring to one another as "family" or as "children," Hawkeswood argues, they use language that evokes multilayered definitions of kinship as embracing statuses based on blood or in-law relationships, those that indicate shared sexual identities, and the recognition of the importance of being black in how they define themselves.

Sociologist Mignon Moore's study of black lesbian couples and their children, *Invisible Families*, makes related points about how the women she worked with conceptualize their identities. Recalling Cathy Cohen's observations, she reminds us that gay black people who make their homes in black communities must sometimes contend with perceptions that they are not authentically black. Early in her discussion of how black lesbian families understand their identities, Moore emphasizes that the black church and African American religion more generally are no less central in the lives of black lesbians than among other community members. Discourses of respectability have constrained black lesbians' efforts to affirm their sexuality, which means that black lesbian couples must craft "their own representations of Black respectability" (Moore 2011: 13). Her book details how class position inflects black lesbians' approaches to managing respectability; these strategies may vary, but they allow women to preserve their autonomy as lesbians even as they make compromises to remain in African American communities. The pressures of enacting respectability and the need to preserve community ties have particular impacts on how individual black women come to accept their same-sex attractions and form gay identities, and Moore shows how different racial and economic contexts also affect these processes. Explaining her approach to understanding the identity management strategies of the families she studied, she writes:

Given the structural inequalities that have historically been associated with race, gender, and sexuality for this population, my subjects cannot entirely stop thinking about or escape from categories. . . . *Identity* is represented in this work not as a settled status but as a lived, continuous project. (Moore 2011: 4; emphasis in original)

CHAPTER ONE

Moore examines these issues from a somewhat different perspective in her account of how black LGBT people in Los Angeles interacted with their neighbors during the 2008 controversy over the anti-same-sex marriage initiative, Proposition 8, which was widely supported by the African American population and especially by black clergy (Abrajano 2010; Ghavami and Johnson 2011; Powell et al. 2010). In urging their neighbors to vote against the measure, one of the most important tasks facing black LGBT people was to affirm their membership in the community, counteracting assumptions that gay people don't live in South Central (a predominantly black area), but are an alien species found only in West Hollywood or some other gay ghetto. Speaking of those black LGBT people who affirmatively remained in black neighborhoods, Moore explains that community acceptance was something they hoped to negotiate, though many no longer were willing to conceal their sexual identities to accomplish this.

> They remained because they trusted in racial solidarity and racial group membership. They also remained because they had less confidence that they would ever be fully accepted as members of other identity groups such as those based solely on sexuality. . . . But the move from gay sexuality as a primarily private activity or behavior, to the open expression and insistence on acknowledgment of it from family, community residents, and even church parishioners, often comes at a price. Openly gay people might have to temporarily forego full acceptance from family and friends. This is a price many are willing to pay in order to nurture their racial group affiliation. (Moore 2010: 209)

It is clear that Moore deals with a multilayered paradox in her work. Who is invisible and where is this invisibility enacted? The black lesbian families that Moore studied are not literally invisible: they live in either predominantly black or racially mixed communities and cannot be said to actively conceal their sexual identities or their family status. At the same time, they must constantly make decisions about how to deploy these features of their lives among relatives and members of their racial communities. On another level, these families are largely absent from the broader LGBT literature that has posed sexuality as the source of a stigmatized master identity that erases or trivializes all other allegiances (Goffman 1963). However, Moore reveals a different aspect of the identity paradox in her work on blacks in Los Angeles. Those who lived in black neighborhoods had to struggle against an erasure based in assumptions about who gay people are and where they would be found. To the extent that local residents assumed that there were no gays or lesbians in their communities, they couldn't see them even when their presence was unconcealed.

African Americans with LGBT identities then had to work especially hard just to make themselves legible as both LGBT and black.[8]

How the Church Distances LGBT Members

Discrimination against those with non-heteronormative gender/sexual identities may take several forms. On one level, black churches have long resisted acknowledging the presence of members of their congregations who have non-heteronormative gender or sexual identities. Such persons might be made to feel unwelcome through a succession of slights, even if they are not explicitly expelled from the church. Maintaining their membership in such congregations might require LGBT persons to endure homophobic diatribes in sermons or other public speech, and to be marginalized when the families of other congregants are recognized and celebrated. The expression of disdain might extend to vituperative sermonizing about the sinfulness of homosexuality; the abusive language and vilification that may accompany sermons in black churches on the sinfulness of homosexuality tend to be especially zealous. In some instances, individuals who reveal their non-heteronormative sexual or gender identities are banned from performing important roles in their congregations (such as leading the choir). An even more total rejection involves being expelled from the congregation, or "disfellowshipped" in the language of some denominations.

Many observers report a less dramatic form of exclusion in their home churches, a sort of "don't ask, don't tell" convention (Douglas 1999; Griffin 2006). A more covert rejection of LGBT people may even appear, for instance, in seemingly liberal churches that offically welcome gay people but refuse to recognize fully their relationships and families. Under these conditions, LGBT persons can inhabit these settings even when there is implicit knowledge of their identity and when their worship style allows them to perform non-heteronormative gender behaviors (as wearing a robe to sing in the choir might), but explicitly naming LGBT identities or seeking recognition for them violates an unspoken rule of which all are aware. Any breach of these expectations can entail being distanced not only from the church but from the black community as well, a bitter expulsion that appears in many personal narratives on the difficulties of enacting both black and LGBT identities (Conerly 2001; Johnson 2003, 2008).

Performance studies scholar E. Patrick Johnson has evoked the intense dilemma faced by LGBT African Americans when he offers the narrative of

Chastity/Charles (Chaz), a pre-operative transgendered person living in a small North Carolina town. Chastity "lives 'her' life as a woman Monday through Saturday night and 'his' life as a man on Sunday in order to sing tenor in the mass choir at . . . church" (Johnson 2008: 15). As Chaz narrates his story, he grew up going to a Pentecostal (Fire Baptized Holiness) church, where singing in the choir allowed him an opportunity to express his creativity. "And I could be somewhat flamboyant with the guise of being spiritual," he explains (345). The congregation accepts Charles as long as he doesn't insist on talking about his identity. He observes limits he understands to be firm, by not "crossing the lines being, openly gay, in a quote/unquote heterosexual church. . . . Because according to men's standards and the way that the Bible is versed, homosexuality is known to God as an abomination. . . . And when you are very flamboyant, when you are very showy with your mannerisms and with your beliefs in church, that's when you begin to cross that line" (362).

The story told by Chastity/Chaz exemplifies strategies adopted by many LGBT black people, even those whose gender presentation is quite unconventional. The key elements are the lifelong commitment to church and to loving the Lord, the awareness of having a sexual or gender identity that is not acceptable, whether that is learned directly or not, and the belief that the church as an institution is inherently "heterosexual," and thus isn't a suitable place to present a transgressive sexual or gender identity. Persons who find themselves in this situation may use various strategies to reconcile it. In Chastity/Chaz's case, there was a progression of solutions: not going to church at all, going to church but dressing in a particularly outrageous way, and going to church while agreeing to a "don't ask, don't tell" arrangement. All of these are problematic in various ways, though each solution may be adequate for meeting certain goals—pleasing parents, feeling that one is able to be close to God. Of course, finding a church that allows one to worship and achieve spiritual wholeness while also having one's unconventional gender/sexual recognized and valued is another strategy, but one that eludes many LGBT people.

A variation on the "don't ask, don't tell" strategy is revealed in the research of sociologist Richard N. Pitt. Using Festinger's theories of cognitive dissonace, Pitt argues that some black gay men can maintain a belief in positive interpretations of gay identity even while worshipping in conservative and explicitly homophobic black churches (Pitt 2009, 2010). By focusing on the inherent imperfection of churches and members of the clergy, men in this position can neutralize the shame that threatens to make them outsiders in their churches, and thus manage to remain in settings that are otherwise stigmatizing. Like the black lesbian churchgoers with whom Krista McQueeney (2009) worked, the men Pitt studied found ways to reconfigure ideas about goodness and Christian virtue so that it would not be difficult for them to be included, and hence entitled to worship in these congregations.

AIDS Enters the Picture

In many instances, churches' responses to homosexuality have been, perhaps inevitably, inflected by reactions to the arrival of HIV/AIDS as a critical health issue in the mid-1980s, with many churches being especially unwelcoming to persons with HIV/AIDS in their midst, a category often conflated with sexual orientation (Cohen 1999; Constantine-Simms 2000). Even when community leaders have spearheaded efforts to provide services for people suffering from AIDS, they rarely have strayed from the homophobic rhetoric characteristic of their approaches to those who were (or were perceived to be) gay (see Harris 1986 for an evocative example of how this may unfold at a funeral for an AIDS victim). These biases had particularly toxic consequences at the height of the AIDS epidemic when many churches either refused to care for members suffering from the disease or to acknowledge those deaths that were the result of AIDS. Cathy Cohen reports that "a number of black ministers, even as they started AIDS ministries, still preached against what they believed to be the 'sinful' behavior involved in the transmission of HIV." One prominent Baptist minister, for instance, "stated that while the church has a 'divine responsibility' to those who live with AIDS, drug addiction and homosexuality are still 'against the will of God'" (Cohen 1999: 101).

Although the epidemic's reach has eased with the introduction of antiretrovirals and drug cocktails, there continue to be community members who are either long-term AIDS survivors or newly infected, so the needs in this area remain significant.[9] The plight of persons who are HIV-positive or suffering from AIDS is amplified, of course, by other misfortunes that disproportionately afflict black Americans—poverty, incarceration, homelessness, and drug dependency among them. In other words, these are community members whose needs are acute, so their marginalization or rejection by the institution that has traditionally dispensed both spiritual and material assistance to black people can be particularly devastating.

Adding to the injuries suffered by LGBT worshippers might be the knowledge that the very pastor who is vigorously moralizing about the sinfulness of being gay or about adultery might be engaging in these very behaviors on the "down low." Such scandals are not rare, the 2010 case of Bishop Eddie Long of the New Birth Missionary Baptist Church in Atlanta being only one of the most publicized stories that has emerged in recent years (Severson and Brown 2011). Still, not all such instances of pastoral hypocrisy get attention in the press. In some cases, congregants may choose to ignore indications that their pastor is not being honest; in other instances, the very gay people who hear themselves accused of depravity on Sundays may be invited to commit the very same "sins" at other times with the pastor himself.[10]

All of these injuries led Bishop Flunder toward the eventual formation of the Fellowship, later renamed the Fellowship of Affirming Ministries (TFAM), a coalition of like-minded churches that developed at the start of the twenty-first century. TFAM's trajectory parallels the evolving story of how black LGBT people have struggled with the hostility of their churches and their need to find ways to worship God in a comfortable environment. TFAM has resisted pressures to constitute itself as a denomination, that is, an administratively distinct branch of Christianity that marks boundaries between itself and other groups that define themselves as denominations. Denominations have the ability to discipline the exercise of spiritual practice within the confines of their authority and thus can constrain experimentation and local autonomy.

Creating Church Homes for LGBT People

Despite the profound suspicion many religious bodies have held about non-heteronormative gender and sexual identities, some churches and other religious organizations in the United States have made efforts in recent years to accept and even welcome LGBT members into their midst. In other cases, churches that cater specifically to LGBT worshippers have sprung up across the country, providing what some perceive as a safer environment for gay people seeking a church home (Gorman 1980; Shallenberger 1998; Shokeid 1995; Thumma 2005; Wilcox 2003).

A number of predominantly white mainline religious bodies have a long record of supporting LGBT equality. The Unitarian Universalist Association (UUA) began to take public stands in this regard in 1970 when its General Assembly passed a resolution to end "Discrimination against Homosexuals and Bisexuals."[11] Another denomination that took an early stand on accepting LGBT members and clergy was the United Church of

Christ (UCC), which called for non-discrimination in employment, volunteer service, and membership policies in 1985, and followed this resolution with others supporting transgender persons and the struggle for marriage equality.[12]

Implementation of such policies has been more controversial in many other predominantly white Protestant denominations, with struggles erupting that have threatened to split them in ways reminiscent of the divisions in American churches over slavery (Goodstein 2017; Moon 2004; Noll 2006; Stein 2001), though some commentators argue that open and affirming policies might generate growth for mainline denominations that have seen declining membership in recent years (Goodstein 2012; Thumma 2006). In some cases, individual congregations have supported various measures that support LGBT members, such as welcoming LGBT congregants, accepting LGBT persons as clergy, blessing same-sex unions, and speaking out in support of LGBT public issues, such as the treatment of persons with HIV/AIDS, marriage equality, and the right to serve equally in the armed forces, even when their national leadership has not approved such policies for the entire denomination.[13]

Still, the stances of most churches were historically so hostile to LGBT people that some felt they would never be able to worship in a welcoming environment unless they formed their own congregations. The first such major effort, which has now coalesced into the largest LGBT-focused denomination, is the Metropolitan Community Church (MCC) (formally known as the Universal Fellowship of Metropolitan Community Churches [UFMCC]).[14] Its founder, Troy Perry, had been a preacher since he was young and had struggled over the years with his same-sex desires. Although he had grown up Baptist, he joined the Pentecostal denomination Church of God in his youth, married a woman he met there, and was called to pastor a church in Illinois. Someone with whom he'd had a liaison informed church officials about his homosexuality, and he was excommunicated from the Church of God, eventually losing his marriage and the next church in which he pastored.[15] In 1968, after a failed suicide attempt and having witnessed the humiliation of a friend who was arrested at a gay bar in LA, he began to pray intensely, trying to discern what God intended for him.

With God's help and understanding, I became convinced that He was moving me to a mission, that a vision of that mission would be revealed to me. When it came, I would never look back; I would never have to. My journey would be forward. My course would be clear. (Perry 1972: 126)

As he continued to pray for a revelation, his mission became clear. "God wanted me to start a new church that would reach into the gay community, but that would include anyone and everyone who believed in the true spirit of God's love, peace, and forgiveness" (Perry 1972: 128; see also Arnold 2002; Tobin and Wicker 1972). His friends were skeptical, one inquiring whether he really imagined that "a bunch of queens" would willingly commit themselves to any sort of religion. He placed an ad in *The Advocate*, a monthly gay magazine, and began holding services in his living room in Los Angeles. Twelve gay men attended the first week. By the end of the service, when Perry served communion, everyone was in tears. Each week, more people came, and soon the fledgling church had to seek larger spaces for its services. Within three years, the church had grown to the point that it was able to dedicate its own building, and growth of the denomination continued to explode in subsequent years.[16]

The formation of the MCC spurred the emergence of other groups in mainline churches that focused on outreach to LGBT persons, a pathway that has been pursued even in denominations that do not officially accept non-heteronormative worshippers (Warner 1995). Dignity, an organization that has served LGBT Roman Catholics since 1969, reaches out to those who want to maintain Catholic ritual practice, holding mass and other worship in non-church locations, and Affirmation performs a similar role for LGBT Mormons. Similar organizations exist in virtually all mainline Protestant denominations, and among the more liberal denominations—such as the Methodists, Presbyterians, Lutherans, and Episcopalians—the existence of openly LGBT congregants has been accompanied by an openness to the ordination of LGBT clergy and the blessing of same-sex marriage. Still other groups have taken up the more targeted mission of providing Pentecostal or Apostolic worship to members of sexual minorities, and since about 1980 a movement to create LGBT-affirming Apostolic or Oneness Pentecostal churches has generated a number of church alliances.[17] These organizations vary considerably in terms of their racial composition.[18]

While joining a mainline church that welcomes LGBT members or an MCC (or similar) congregation may be viable options for African American LGBT people, the actual extent to which any particular religious organization does more than merely tolerate the presence of LGBT worshippers is quite varied. And additional complications may present themselves. Many African Americans are ill at ease worshipping in majority-white congregations, suspecting that the welcome they receive may not be sincere or secure. Beyond their fears of racism, whether overt or covert, there is the very important matter of how worship is conducted. The mainline liberal denominations that have sought to be open and affirming are also characterized by a restrained style of worship. Shouting, dancing, and other expressions of inhabitation by the Holy Spirit are not typical of such churches, nor are they encouraged. Thus, the worship experience in such congregations is profoundly different and may be largely unsatisfying to those coming from black churches where call-and-response worship, manifestations of being filled with the Holy Spirit (ranging from calling out encouragement to the preacher, shouting and stomping, to dancing, to speaking in tongues and collapsing, i.e., falling out or being slain in the Spirit) are customary. Services at black churches following these traditions tend to be longer than those in mainline white churches, and the role of these churches in communities, as we have seen, can be far more penetrating than for white churches. As I indicated above (see p. 189, n. 16), MCC churches vary considerably, and while some may provide a Pentecostal form of worship, the small number of African American celebrants in most congregations doesn't necessarily reassure black worshippers that they are truly welcome, or that their familiar, expressive styles of worship will be appreciated.

At the same time that these developments in majority-white denominations were ongoing, gay-identified pastors began to organize churches with specific outreach to black gay and lesbian Christians. In 1982 Pastor Carl Bean—a black gay man who was a Motown singer known for his early gay rights hit, "I Was Born This Way" (1977)—founded the Unity Fellowship Church of Los Angeles in 1982 (UFCLA), with an explicit outreach to gay and lesbian African Americans. The Unity Fellowship Church Movement (UFCM) later coalesced into a denomination and spawned the Minority AIDS Project (MAP) in 1985, an organization in Los Angeles that provides a broad range of HIV-related services to a minority clientele. Now archbishop, Bean continues to lead the denomination, which currently includes seventeen member churches around the United States (Bean 2010). Unity Fellowship espouses a theology based on Christianity but that also expresses respect for all spiritual traditions; it is officially open to people of all races and sexual identities, and seeks to eliminate male domination[19] (see also Bates 2005; Leong 2006). Although Unity grew out of Pentecostal and Baptist traditions, observers have noted that it has blended other elements into its theology, particularly drawing on psychotherapy and spiritualism (Leong 2006).

Another early pioneer in black LGBT religion, James S. Tinney, explained the need for black gay churches by recalling how both the black church in America and mostly white gay churches were created. In both instances, these churches emerged in response to the exclusion of their members from full participation in other churches. He recalled how the African Episcopal Methodist Church (AME) was formed because of the experience of free blacks in the late eighteenth century who were barred from full participation in worship at a white church.

> Other churches have come into existence precisely because the Christian church was not fluid and dynamic enough to be comfortable with pluralism. Black churches as a whole were created because white churches excluded Blacks from equal participation and leadership. . . . White gay churches have . . . come into existence under circumstances related to the oppression of sexual identity that parallel the circumstances related to oppression of Black identity. (Tinney 1986: 71–72)

In other words, Tinney argued that a reasonable response to the hostile behavior of either white churches toward blacks or of black churches toward LGBT members has been to create a place of worship where all of one's identity will be respected and embraced. In 1982 Tinney—a Pentecostal who was excommunicated from the Church of God in Christ when he revealed his homosexuality—founded Faith Temple, a predominantly black lesbian and gay church in Washington, DC. Despite Tinney's death in 1988, the church has continued to operate as an independent entity.[20]

City of Refuge and TFAM: The Emergence of Radical Inclusivity

The Fellowship of Affirming Ministries grew out of the vision of (now) Bishop Yvette Flunder, who currently serves as presiding bishop of TFAM. The church that she established in San Francisco in 1991 grew out of her early work with the HIV/AIDS epidemic and the social service agency she created, Ark of Refuge. Her inspiration for beginning her own church, after some years of association with the Love Center, a progressive independent Pentecostal church in Oakland, came directly from her feeling that despite Love Center's tolerance for its gay and lesbian (or same-gender-loving) members, its embrace of them was not as total as it needed to be to fully support them in all respects.

TFAM's mission is animated by the complex meanings that circulate in the doctrine of "radical inclusivity." On one level, radical inclusivity speaks to the mandate to reach out and embrace the most marginalized and despised of people, to draw them into Fellowship churches, and to lead them to understand that God loves them just as they are, supporting them as they move toward healing whatever misfortune afflicts them. The Fellowship's website explains the concept of radical inclusivity as a special mission to serve those at the margins of society, "especially women, same-gender-loving individuals and their allies, transgendered persons, persons in recovery, the recently incarcerated, the economically disenfranchised, and persons infected and affected by HIV/AIDS."[21] Radical inclusivity extends beyond boundaries of race, class, gender, as well as sexuality, and so is understood as the guiding principle of the Fellowship.

On another level, radical inclusivity speaks to the embrace not only of individuals of all types, but to the future direction of TFAM as an organization. Bishop Flunder often speaks of the coalition as providing the template for a "new Reformation," whereby people, whether Christian or not, will see the error of exclusionary practices and biases based on sex, race, gender, and other factors, and seek to open themselves to all kinds of people. She grounds this interpretation in the history of the Azusa Street Revival (1906–9) that launched Pentecostalism in the United States, emphasizing that it was an assemblage of worshippers that upended the hierarchies traditionally attached to race and gender (Alexander 2011). Her concern with history places TFAM squarely in what Bishop Flunder sees as the real message of Azusa Street.

The Azusa Street Mission grew out of the Holiness revival movement that flourished in nineteenth-century America, particularly among Christians from the lower classes who became disenchanted with the growing elaboration of mainline churches and with what they saw as the impiety that accompanied it, and sought to restore "the vitality, message, and form of the apostolic church" (Blumhofer 1993: 13). Over decades, these doctrines were elaborated in various movements first in Britain and then in the United States, and served as the inspiration for the Great Awakenings of the eighteenth and nineteenth centuries. Historian Robert Mapes Anderson characterizes the exponents of the Holiness movement as the "disinherited" who rejected what they saw as the worldliness—really sinfulness—of the more middle-class Protestants in the mid-nineteenth century, including those who made up the Social Gospel movement (Anderson 1979: 31–32). Also known as Christian perfection, entire sanctification, or baptism of the Holy Spirit, this quest is derived from the teachings of John Wesley, the founder of Methodism, and focused on zealous attention to commandments, deep faith, and earnest prayer (Anderson 1979; Blumhofer 1993; Dieter 1996). Because of the increasing gulf between middle- and lower-class adherents of Methodism, the Holiness movement crystallized as a protest against class privilege as well as being opposed to preoccupation with the "worldly" matters that were the central focus of the Social Gospel movement (Anderson 1979: 31).

William Seymour, the black preacher who spearheaded the Azusa Street Revival, had been a member of Charles Parham's Bible school in Houston, Texas, where he became a believer in Baptism of the Holy Spirit, glossolalia, and other gifts of the Holy Spirit as evidence that a person was saved.[22] As described in the Invocation, he felt called by the Spirit to go to Los Angeles, where he started the Azusa Street Mission, the radically egalitarian revival that is widely seen as having launched Pentecostalism in America, building on its roots in earlier religious movements. The racial and gender equality that marked the revival, however, eventually yielded to social pressure, and believers moved back to or reestablished racially segregated and patriarchal churches; the basis for an effective religious critique of gender and racial hierarchy collapsed, and the churches that the Revival created or transformed (COGIC, Assemblies of God, among others) lost a major component of their inspiration. By the 1920s, racial animosities had intensified and definitively split the movement into white and black denominations, with some of the white Pentecostals joining forces with racist organizations, including several that were not only hostile to blacks, but anti-Semitic, anti-Catholic, and sympathetic to the Klan. According to Anderson (1979), disputes between oneness and Trinitarian Pentecostals also contributed to these rifts.

This was a blunder, Bishop Flunder asserts, and TFAM's mission is to return to the promise of Azusa Street and bring back the radical inclusivity it had portended; despite the Fellowship's desire to weave different strands of Christian practice into its worship, its unifying doctrine—radical inclusivity—has even broader aims. As outlined in the Invocation, radical inclusivity concerns both the mission of the Fellowship, in terms of who it sees as its intended constituency, as well as in terms of its vision of growth and progressive political outreach.

The Fellowship of Affirming Ministries is made up of two strands. First there are the member churches and congregations, local ministries across the United States, and now abroad as well, that seek to provide the kind of accepting environment that even mainline affirming churches struggle to attain. The basis of these congregations is a form of worship that draws its inspiration from the historical black denominations, but that reaches out not only to LGBT worshippers, but to all kinds of people who are stigmatized, underprivileged, and marginalized from mainstream communities. While most members are African American, persons of any race are welcomed, as are persons whose religious backgrounds may diverge from the tradition that inspires most worship. It is not entirely clear what prevented Bishop Flunder from seeking to attach her movement to one of the existing black churches that reached out to LGBT worshippers. She has told me that the organizational form of Unity wouldn't allow for clergy to be credited with their earlier experience, but geographical distance may also have been an element of her decision to create her own autonomous church. Her opposition to TFAM constituting itself as a denomination, rather than a coalition, probably plays a role as well, as Unity is organized as a denomination, which may make it less open to the great range of doctrinal and worship practices that she hopes to foster in TFAM.

Though the number of affiliated congregations fluctuates, according to a 2014 congregational roster, TFAM has between thirty-five and forty member churches and ministries in the United States along with member congregations in Mexico, Africa, and Southeast Asia. Some of these congregations are large and stable, while others are small and ephemeral, but a core group of TFAM members participate in national convocations (every other year in odd-numbered years) and regional meetings (every other year in even-numbered years). Bishops oversee each of the US regions—East, South, Midwest, and West, each of which has approximately ten member congregations—and the Fellowship Global, which operates mainly in Africa, where Bishop Joseph Tolton and Reverend Ann Craig are most active in Rwanda, Kenya, the eastern region of the Democratic Republic of Congo, Uganda, and Côte d'Ivoire. Their work involves both bringing existing Christian congregations into TFAM and helping to support the formation of LGBT-affirming congregations. All of the regional bishops have the assistance of other clergy in their area.[23]

In an effort to make TFAM even broader in its reach, persons and organizations from outside the original boundaries of the Fellowship have been invited to join the new Fellowship of Affirming Ministries, with progressive clergy from some non-LGBT and non–African American churches offered affiliations, along with non-Christians. The UCC and the MCC are the most visible members of this broad coalition, but it also includes representatives from Religious Science/Spiritual Living/New Thought.[24] This ecumenical impulse, most visible at the level of the national coalition, is intended to provide the foundation for collaboration and to offer TFAM a group of potentially influential allies. While the embrace of diverse religious organizations is authentic and fundamentally linked to the larger interpretation of radical inclusivity, it coexists with the Fellowship's foundations in African American worship traditions, a partnership that may not be as attainable in local congregations as it is at national convocations.

The emergence of the Fellowship represents a very particular moment in the ongoing story of the engagement of LGBT people with the wider African American community, as it does in the evolution of religion in early twenty-first-century America. Not all black people who are LGBT will find a home in TFAM, nor does TFAM provide a solution to the cultural rifts that often assume that religion and gender/sexual freedom cannot avoid irresolvable conflict. No matter how committed TFAM members are to the promise of radical inclusivity, it seems unlikely that all persons—regardless of race, class, gender, sexual orientation, and religious background—will find in it a solution to their spiritual needs. But it does offer a location that is broadly welcoming and that, by seeking to embrace all who come within its congregations, can provide a place many will find feels like home.

As I have argued in this chapter, while the Fellowship takes its inspiration from the confluence of a number of recent historical, sociological, and political developments, it is also firmly rooted in a religious history that gives the positions it takes particular legibility. Thus, TFAM is both old and new, and we will see in the chapters that follow that its management of these seemingly contradictory origins shapes its practices and has potential consequences for the directions it takes in the future. TFAM hovers on the knife edge of tradition and innovation, both embracing an expanded notion of history, and struggling against it. It is this struggle I will document in the chapters that follow.

TWO

"Lead Me, Guide Me": The Charisma of Bishop Flunder

The evening service at the TFAM Midwest Regional meeting had ended, but worshippers were lined up in the aisle to be blessed and touched by Bishop Flunder. One by one, they approached her to listen to the soft words she spoke and then to experience her physical blessing. Each person had two people waiting behind her for the expected falling out, as Bishop's touch would predictably lead her to collapse backward into the arms of her companions, who slowly lowered her onto the floor. Some fell into a state of rapid spasmodic movement, while others seemed to be asleep or unconscious. The trance state lasted only minutes for some worshippers, while for others, the time on the ground continued for ten or fifteen minutes. Arising from the floor, some began to weep, others to smile broadly, and some continued to be caught up in a kind of trance state, dancing in the quick two-step characteristic of Pentecostal churches, or speaking in tongues, swaying from side to side, and sometimes unsteady on their feet. Companions tended to those in this state, moving furniture out of their path, bearing towels and water and following them around. I asked my friend Vickie whether those on the floor were actually unconscious or asleep, and she said, "I've been watching this all my life, but I've never done it, and I really don't know." Her comfort in admitting that she had never fallen out, despite having grown up in a Pentecostal church, was similar to others who either were not

CHAPTER TWO

inspired to this behavior or refrained from it consciously. There was no implication that their connection to the Holy Spirit was any less fervent or meaningful.

Responses to worshippers who entered an ecstatic state were protective but casual. Their condition did not arouse great interest, except among those in their immediate vicinity, and once the trance had ended, both the person who had been in an ecstatic state and those assisting her returned to their seats or prepared to leave. While these states occurred at many of the worship services I attended at TFAM churches regardless of who was leading the service, their connection to Bishop Flunder's presence was clear: worshippers were eager to be blessed by her, and many seem to have come to the service with the expectation that they would experience a transcendent state and be filled with the Holy Spirit. While the blessings of other clergy were also powerful, it was only Bishop Flunder who seemed to have the instantaneous effect of altering many congregants' spiritual condition. This form of charisma is frequently found in churches, both Pentecostal and not, with founding clergy occupying a special role, but I will argue that Bishop Flunder's power has a more complicated foundation. It reveals both continuities with the traditional black churches that TFAM members came from, what Bishop calls "Metho-Bapti-Costal," and the ways in which TFAM is vastly different from those institutions.

Bishop Flunder's Journey

Yvette Flunder grew up in the Church of God in Christ (COGIC), the largest black Pentecostal denomination in the United States. Indeed, she is descended from generations of well-known preachers who migrated to San Francisco from Texas and can count herself as a member of the elite of the church. Her grandfather and two uncles were bishops, and her father and stepfather were pastors of a prominent church in San Francisco. Early in life she knew that she had a calling to preach.

> BISHOP FLUNDER: I knew myself to be called to full-time ministry.
> EL: How did you know that? If I can ask that.
> BF: Well, because it started to evidence itself in my life. [I was] one of those kids that if I walk down the street and I look behind me, there are ten or twelve people walking behind me. Because, there was a certain charisma, maybe give it that name, that I think was a part of my gifting that I felt myself called to

gather people. . . . Everywhere I went, people would come and say, "Tell me more." It was that kind of experience.

EL: Even people you didn't know?

BF: Even people that I didn't know before. "Tell me more" happened, you know? And that was just a part of what I knew was the charisma that came with my gift.

Now the presiding bishop of the Fellowship of Affirming Ministries (TFAM), Bishop Flunder and her partner, Mother Shirley Miller, sat down with me one early evening in a Thai restaurant a few blocks from City of Refuge, the church she founded in San Francisco. Over spring rolls and curry, I asked her about her journey. Bishop Flunder explained that as she was growing up, she knew that her gift could not be realized within the confines of COGIC because she was female. Her mother was also a gifted preacher, with a following in the COGIC community, but never was eligible to receive the official recognition that would have come with ordination. Bishop Flunder felt constrained and frustrated in COGIC, but her commitment to the church led her to struggle for some years before deciding to leave the denomination.

She describes her conflict with COGIC in terms of three major issues that eventually led her to withdraw from the church. The first part of the story was her realization that she was called to preach and the fact that there was no way she could pursue the dream of taking the same path as the men in her family. But the matter of ordination wasn't the only problem Bishop Flunder saw in COGIC; in fact, ordination was only a part of what she identified as a larger, more pervasive obstacle to her remaining in the church.

[Another] departure I think for me from the Pentecostal church had to do sort of with the patriarchy. You know? The ways in which the church forced male dominance in every area. Not just around ordained ministry but just in every area. Now they catered to men and didn't require them to make the same preparations that women had to make for much less, which was very troubling to me, you know?

Although Bishop Flunder was never directly involved in the women's movement, she was inspired by a woman teacher she'd known at Saints Academy, the COGIC boarding school she attended for high school. This teacher was highly educated and articulate, and was respected by male church leaders. Her example led Bishop to understand that her gender didn't have to hold her back from guiding others to spiritual fulfillment.

CHAPTER TWO

The third element of her estrangement from COGIC surfaced when Bishop Flunder came to terms with being "same-gender-loving" (SGL). She had begun to realize that she was attracted to other women when she was in her early twenties, but felt that this was a sinful inclination that she had to overcome. Her marriage to the gay man who fathered her daughter was an effort at "reparative therapy" for both herself and her husband. Laughing, she tells me:

I figured that I could get married, I could marry the gay away, you know? And, uh, it didn't work. For him or for me for that matter. But I did try.

Once she came to understand herself to be a lesbian and solidified her relationship with Shirley Miller, now of over thirty years' duration, she grew even more disillusioned with COGIC and gave up on her call to preach, which seemed hopelessly impeded. Instead, she used her spiritual foundation to intensify her commitment to various social justice causes and became a social service administrator, aided by the training she'd received at Heald College, a San Francisco–area business college. She worked with troubled youth and the elderly, and eventually moved into AIDS services and prevention, finding enormous satisfaction in serving poor and disenfranchised populations. "I felt that doing social work was enough church for me," she said, recalling that period of her life.

Bishop Flunder's experience resonates with many of the stories that I heard from leaders and lay members in the Fellowship, the church coalition she created in 2001. These interlocutors told me about their struggles to reconcile non-heteronormative sexual or gender identities with their place in black communities and especially churches. Women described feeling trapped by their gender, often being told that they could best realize their ambitions by marrying a preacher. Men told stories of being appreciated for their musical abilities, serving as choir directors and music ministers, for example, while knowing that they could never expect their gender or sexual identity to be accepted. This was a world of "don't ask, don't tell" in which everyone understood the rules and tolerated indignities in order to preserve their place in a treasured institution. It was also a world where gender determined one's ability to follow one's calling.

The story Charla Kouadio told me exemplifies this experience on many levels. Charla grew up in a Baptist church in Florida and had felt the call to preach since she was young. At the time I interviewed her, she was the pastor of a Fellowship congregation in a New England city, finally realizing what she has always felt God wanted her to do.

I remember being young and feeling called to ministry, to preaching, and like thirteen years old talking to my pastor and saying I want to do that and him saying, "Baby, maybe if you're lucky, maybe you'll marry a preacher."

Charla's entire family was involved with the church they attended, serving as ushers, singing in the choir, doing whatever was asked of them. When Charla was in her late teens, however, she realized she was a lesbian.

[The church] was my whole life until I started wrestling with my sexuality and suddenly that didn't have any place. . . . So how does that fit in to all the things that I've heard because I've heard all those negative things about being gay and God not loving [gay people].

Charla stopped going to church for a while, but then returned, going back to the same church she had formerly attended where the pastor had preached vituperative sermons denouncing homosexuality. She explained:

I think it's interesting that when I decided to go back to church, that's the church that I went to. So it's almost like I like the black God, if I'm going to be engaged in a relationship with God, then I've got to get used to the black God because that's all I knew.

When she got involved with her partner, Theresa, who had moved to Florida from a northern city for a job and had a similar background in the Baptist church, it was immediately clear that they would go to church together. Theresa had been attending an Episcopal church, but Charla found the pastor boring. So they went to Charla's Baptist church. Theresa explains:

Charla hated that [Episcopal] church because she said the preacher was really, really boring, and then we went to her church and they were talking about faggots and sissies, and I said, "Well, not there!" And we found a Baptist church that we really loved. It's vibrant worship, but it was kind of "don't ask, don't tell," and that wasn't good enough for my kids to hear. Because I don't want any problems with my kids. I spent a lot of time raising them to love Jesus and so we can't have them against me because I'm a lesbian, and so we went there for a while and an acquaintance told Charla about this great new church in "Orangeville," and you have to go and it's "Peace Center" and Pastor Bonnie is the founding pastor and she and Pastor Sylvia, and so Charla went to check it out to make sure it was okay and that was our church.

CHAPTER TWO

This turned out to be a Fellowship church, which was both women's introduction to the coalition. Their move to New England, some two years before we spoke, was inspired by Charla's reengagement with her call to preach and her realization that she would need more education than her bachelor's degree to be effective in a pastoral role. She enrolled in a seminary in the Boston area, convinced that God had told them where to go even though it took some time for all the details to work out.

Charla's story resonates with that of Bishop Flunder and repeats itself over and over in the accounts of other TFAM clergy, especially among women. But this is a story that makes worship in the Fellowship compelling for many of those who have become involved in TFAM churches, whether they are clergy; have taken up calls to be deacons, elders, or ministers; or are lay congregants. The need to be part of a church that fulfills one's spiritual needs and also recapitulates key elements of one's religious heritage is one that worshippers share with Bishop Flunder.

The Fellowship

By the time Yvette Flunder began to think about the problems of LGBT black people who longed for a spiritual home, the options described in chapter 1—welcoming mainline churches, MCC, and black-oriented churches like Unity Fellowship—already existed. But none of them seemed quite right to Flunder. Now in her early sixties, Flunder embarked on a three-decade journey from the Church of God in Christ (COGIC), through other churches and community work, and finally to her current position as the presiding bishop of the Fellowship of Affirming Ministries (TFAM). She describes the process that led her back to church.

And then, one day I was driving my car, and I had this epiphany on the road . . . that what I needed to do was combine a social ministry with a spiritual ministry because one needed the other. One was the yin to the yang of the other, you know? . . . When you're working with people around their personal needs, I think part of the health of the individual is their spiritual needs as well. However they define the divine in their lives. Sort of what the originators of the twelve-step program found out. That having a higher power or believing in a higher power of some sort helps people to reach for something you know that [is] above and outside of themselves. And so, I ended up making that combination happen. So I went back to church.

Bishop Flunder knew better than to return to the deeply patriarchal orthodoxy of COGIC, so she joined Love Center in Oakland, an independent Pentecostal church led by Bishop Walter Hawkins, who was also a well-known gospel singer (and a cousin of her partner, Shirley). He had also grown up in COGIC, but Love Center had a much more progressive agenda. Bishop Flunder and Shirley, both of whom already had national reputations as gospel singers, began to sing with Hawkins's renowned gospel choir and to record gospel music. She also was involved with Love Center's outreach to people with HIV/AIDS, called the Ark of Love. She worked there for some ten years and describes the church as having many same-gender-loving members.[1] But despite the progressive environment at Love Center, there were limits to acceptance for these members.

There were a lot of same-gender-loving people around. But not affirmed in the way that our relationships and unions were celebrated. And we were warmly tolerated. But not celebrated; we couldn't celebrate. So when we celebrated relationships, it was always straight people, it was never same-gender-loving people. And so it's not that we were on the down low—it's just that we were just not really celebrated. And I felt like it was dichotomous, unfair, that I started talking about it. Then I realized I was trying to live out my vision in somebody else's church. And I just responded to the call. I came to San Francisco. I had about fifteen people from various places in the Bay Area and when we started in our family room . . . in August [1991] or so, by the time we got to November, we had to find a place to worship.

City of Refuge—the church Bishop Flunder founded several years after she started the Ark of Refuge, a social service agency that focused on HIV and AIDS—started meeting in her home. But, as she describes, it quickly became larger and larger, moving from one rented location to another until it bought a building in the South of Market area of San Francisco and finally, in 2013, moved to a much larger and better-equipped facility in Oakland. At first, she didn't feel that she needed to get a divinity degree; with her long history in the church and the business background she already had, she felt fully prepared to lead a congregation. But then she was invited to the Pacific School of Religion to help develop a Certificate of Ministry program, a bridge for people who were already preaching to get into seminary.

Long story short, we designed the CMS program, the Certificate of Ministry Studies, and we decided to go through it ourselves, sort of as a pilot. And then I had a friend of mine, an MCC pastor that I had been knowing for years, and he sat down next to me one day on the campus and he said, "Well, you ought to go on and do that master's program." And I said that I don't need to do that. I been in church all my life; I just don't need it. And he said, "Well, if you don't, people will always think of you

CHAPTER TWO

as a para-preacher." And I got so mad at him. I was so mad at him I stayed up most of the night. I said, "A PARA-PREACHER! He did not say that to me! A para-preacher!" And then the next day, I signed up. I got my master's at the Pacific School of Religion. . . . And I just loved it. I love the discipline of reading and writing, organizing my thoughts. You know, that's what school really did for me. It helped me to organize my thoughts, the stuff that's already in there. Give some language to it. Do some research and see what other people have thought about these things. Then add my ideas to the existing cadre.

Bishop Flunder went on to earn a doctor of ministry degree at the San Francisco Theological Seminary in San Anselmo, California, and now serves in visiting faculty positions at seminaries around the country. Although she had good friends in the Metropolitan Community Church (MCC), she explained that it didn't feel comfortable as a place to worship.

[I] didn't think of MCC as being culturally appropriate because it was predominantly European American. My people were predominantly African American, emerging from strong Fundamentalist backgrounds. So, it wasn't until later on that we all began to see the connections between our churches, you know? And started working with greater intensity now to make that happen.

The Fellowship (now TFAM) gradually emerged as people in other parts of the country heard about City of Refuge and wanted to replicate the model that had been established in San Francisco. As it grew, Fellowship leadership forged connections with the UCC and the MCC (Bishop Flunder is ordained in both), but they have also sought to expand in ways that will help to enhance the Fellowship's influence and visibility. This has meant forming alliances with other affirming churches and groups, whether they are predominantly LGBT, African American, or not. The more inclusive entity, the Fellowship of Affirming Ministries (TFAM), was created in 2011 to accommodate levels of participation other than forming constituent congregations. The connection with the UCC was formed at the point when Flunder decided that City of Refuge (and subsequently other Fellowship churches) needed the backing of a national denomination if they were to continue to thrive. As Bishop explains, City of Refuge went "denomination shopping," looking at the African Methodist Episcopal Church (AME), the United Methodists, and the UCC, before settling on forming a relationship with the UCC. She credits this decision largely to the high level of congregational autonomy that City of Refuge required, with the UCC turning out to be the only denomination that she believed would assure such independence. The connection with the UCC has proven durable. Some other congregations in TFAM are also part of the UCC, and UCC representatives regularly attend TFAM regional and national events. Indeed, the UCC once attempted to recruit Bishop Flunder to serve as its president, but accepting that position would have demanded that she relinquish her leadership of TFAM, so she declined.

Although the Fellowship maintains cordial connections with the smaller Unity Fellowship Church Movement (UFCM), founded by Carl Bean (see chapter 1), at the time she was forming City of Refuge and later the Fellowship, Bishop Flunder found the organizational structure of Unity too constraining to be a possible anchor for her church and its coalition. Among other issues, potential pastors who had preached in other churches were required by Unity to start over at the beginning, usually as deacons, rather than getting "credit" for past experience.

As of this writing, TFAM member congregations and ministries vary from substantial churches with steady membership, some of which own their own buildings, to smaller and sometimes transitory ministries struggling to establish themselves. Besides the four US regions (East Coast, West Coast, Midwest, and Southern), each headed by a bishop, there now are member churches in Tijuana, Mexico, and Africa, as well as an orphanage supported by the Fellowship in Zimbabwe. The most recent area of growth has been in Asia, with new churches forming in Hong Kong, mainland China, and Thailand, largely through the efforts of Paul Lucas, a graduate of the Pacific School of Religion who is affiliated with TFAM. TFAM also has what Bishop Flunder describes as "covenantal agreements" or affiliations with other religious organizations: the UCC, the MCC, Centers for Spiritual Living, and the churches presided over by Bishop Carlton Pearson and Bishop Jim Swilley (as of this writing).[2] These affiliations continue to expand, and in each case have defined particular guidelines for the kinds of projects on which TFAM and the other organizations will collaborate. TFAM regional conferences are held every other year (in even years) and national convocations in the alternate years. As I will discuss later, many active members in local congregations are encouraged to take courses or pursue divinity degrees at various institutions, which Bishop Flunder sees as providing the foundation for the future leadership of the Fellowship.

Roots of Female Preaching in America

Although Bishop carved out a space to be a preacher after experiencing the intense opposition to women taking on such roles that was pervasive in COGIC, the history of women serving as preachers and religious leaders in America shows that the path she took is not totally novel. This is not to say that achieving prominence in the churches they served has been without significant obstacles, but the strategies women have used to secure some sort of authority and visibility are instructive. Women struggled to have their voices heard in both black and white churches of various denominations even before they could become ordained, and the forms of power they were able to assemble depended heavily on circuitous forms of influence they were able to exert (Butler 2007; Dodson 2002; Gilkes 2001; Higginbotham 1993; Wiggins 2005). Their roles in education and evangelism, as well as in providing key material resources and other forms of support to their churches, have all meant that their importance far outstripped whatever formal positions they were able to achieve. In particular, women exercised their spirituality and served God in many different arenas, both within the boundaries of the church and outside in their families and communities (Frederick 2003).

Women were central figures from the earliest days of Pentecostal worship at the Azusa Street Revival, which demolished social distinctions of race and gender as all kinds of people found themselves able to speak in tongues, prophesy, testify, and otherwise contribute to the service as the Spirit moved them. Agnes N. Ozman (later Mrs. LaBerge) had the Spirit fall on her at Charles Fox Parham's Bethel Bible School in Topeka, Kansas. After Reverend Parham laid hands on her, she began speaking and writing in "Chinese" and was unable to speak in English for three days, an event commonly described as the first evidence of speaking in tongues and as the beginning of the Pentecostal movement (Synan 1971). Later at Azusa Street, Jennie Moore (the future wife of William Seymour) began to play the piano and sing in what observers thought was Hebrew (Synan 1971). Other leading Pentecostal women leaders, among many, were Florence Louise Crawford, a disciple of William Seymour who took the movement to the Northwest, and Aimee Semple McPherson, who founded the Foursquare Gospel church (White 1989: 198).

Catherine Brekus's (1998) exhaustive study of both black and white women preachers in the United States over the span of the first two Great Awakenings offers some perspectives on the kinds of challenges Bishop Flunder has confronted. The women who were able to carve out a place for themselves as evangelists and itinerant preachers occupied positions at odds with the usual situation for women in their period, especially in terms of gender expression. Ann Lee, the founder of the Shakers—which began in England and became an important utopian community in the United States beginning in the 1770s—was an illiterate who claimed to receive her inspiration directly from God. The Shakers, which began as an offshoot of the Quakers, believed in sexual equality and flourished for a time in the United States despite the commitment its members made to celibacy. "On the surface, Lee's richly 'feminine' descriptions of herself as the bride of Christ and the mother of the elect elevated women's ordinary experience of marriage and childbirth to cosmic significance. Instead of trying to justify her religious leadership by denying her biological womanhood, Lee transformed it into the foundation of her spiritual authority. Not only did she reject the common wisdom that women's experiences of pregnancy and childbirth made them weaker than men, but she insisted that those experiences linked them to the divine" (Brekus 1998: 109). In this she differed dramatically from Jemima Wilkinson, whose preaching career occurred in the same time period as Lee's. A leader of the Public Universal Friends, Wilkinson insisted that she had transcended her biological sex and dressed in androgynous garments that most observers characterized as "masculine." Her demeanor was also taken as masculine because of her commanding style. Each of these early white American women preachers had to make sense of the conundrum of gender and sex, and each coped with it differently, with Wilkinson's solution being to repudiate femaleness as burdensome.

The ability of women to claim spiritual authority was embedded in their understanding of themselves as having been chosen by God to spread the gospel and, indeed, as having received their authority to preach directly from the Holy Spirit. Such nineteenth-century black women Methodist preachers as Zilpha Elaw and Jarena Lee, for example, made it clear that they had no choice in the matter of becoming preachers. Like many male preachers, they were self-effacing, describing themselves as reluctant to take up the call to preach, but that as instruments of God, they had no ability to reject what God had demanded of them. But while they described themselves as passive instruments, they also laid claim to having received divine inspiration (Brekus 1998: 193).

Before Bishop Flunder answered the call to preach, other black women had made names for themselves as pastors of well-known churches in Chicago. Wallace Best (2005) documents the stories of Elder Lucy Smith and Reverend Mary G. Evans, both of whom led African American congregations in Chicago during the 1920s and 1930s. Chicago churches experienced enormous growth in this period owing to the Great Migration, which brought many thousands of blacks to Chicago (and to other cities in the North and the West). Migrants arrived from the South with few resources, skills, or connections, but they did have religious backgrounds in the expressive forms of worship with which they'd been raised and the need to continue to worship in their new homes. The proliferation of storefront churches in Chicago and other cities during these years speaks to the desire of these new arrivals to re-create the churches they had left behind. But the arrival of migrants in such numbers created a crisis for the established black churches, particularly AME congregations, which had long disparaged shouting and other such spiritual excesses as primitive and undignified. Once the deprivations of the Great Depression took hold, there was an even greater demand for churches to assist impoverished congregants, and black churches assumed myriad functions akin to social work along with their spiritual mission. Given the practical challenges faced by worshippers, pastors had to prove themselves not only as spiritual leaders, but in the arena of management, establishing charitable programs and generally rising to the challenge of assisting poor and working-class migrants from the South (Best 2005; see also Sernett 1997).

Elder Smith pastored All Nations Pentecostal Church and was also a pioneer in the emergence of church services being broadcast on the radio. Reverend Evans had left an AME church that wouldn't support her call to preach, becoming pastor of the Cosmopolitan Community Church, and Elder Smith established her own church in response to having been barred from preaching in the Church of God in Christ, which prohibited women from leadership roles. In different ways, both deployed images of motherhood in establishing their authority, but even as their congregations were dominated by women worshippers, neither challenged the patriarchal assumptions of conventional Christian belief; for example, Best reports that they both seemingly accepted the image of the Holy Ghost as masculine. Both took steps to deflect attention from their female bodies; Lucy Smith weighed over three hundred pounds, and Mary Evans, who was suspected of being a lesbian, wore androgynous clerical robes for public appearances and photographs. Still, even in the patriarchal world of black religion, both women achieved significant prominence. When Elder Smith died in 1952, her funeral was one of the largest in the history of black Chicago, with sixty thousand people coming to view the body and an estimated fifty thousand lining the route taken by the funeral procession. In a departure from the practices of other African American churches, her All Nations church drew not only black worshippers, but whites and members of ethnic minorities, a reprise of the early Pentecostal experience at Azusa Street, and perhaps a precursor to the radical inclusivity espoused by TFAM (Best 2005: 174).

Stories that resemble those told by Bishop Flunder also appear in the accounts assembled by folklorist Elaine J. Lawless (1988) of white women Pentecostal preachers. Working with small-town and rural preachers in

Missouri, Lawless provides detailed descriptions from the women about how they came to preach and evangelize. Their roots are located in Pentecostal churches that disparage women's ability to preach, often banning them from preaching altogether or only allowing them to do so on insignificant occasions, such as weekday worship. In most instances, these obstacles completely prevented women from assuming regular church assignments, although some of the women Lawless interviewed managed to become the primary pastors of their churches. But others could only work as itinerant preachers who traveled to revivals but were not affiliated with established congregations.[3]

Like Bishop Flunder, the women Lawless observed and interviewed emphasized the agency of God in bringing them to the pulpit. In other words, they avoided making claims to having special powers or ambitions, but explained that God had demanded that they take up preaching, typically recalling an instance when "the Lord dealt with me," and that they had no choice but to do as God wished. One woman, for example, had set aside her preaching and then fell on the ice and injured her hand; she understood that episode as meaning that God was giving her a warning, demanding that she return to preaching (Lawless 1988: 29).

Running through all of these accounts is the conviction that becoming a preacher is the outcome of a call from God, one that perhaps can be postponed, but which cannot be permanently resisted. Women preachers found support for their vocation in the precedent of the prophetess Deborah in the Hebrew Bible's book of Judges and the importance of Mary Magdalene as the first person who testified to Christ's resurrection, according to all four canonical gospels. The Pauline epistles, as well, offer numerous named examples of women pastors, teachers, and church leaders (Fiorenza 1993; Klein 2000; Russell 1985). Still, even as contemporary Pentecostal churches continue to relegate women to secondary roles outside the ministry, a number of women preachers and televangelists have gained international prominence in Pentecostalism in recent years, including Joyce Meyer and Paula White, both of whom are white, and Juanita Bynum, who is African American. Besides their engagement with the gospel of prosperity, their preaching puts forward a unique message that anthropologist Marla Frederick calls a "gospel of sexual redemption," in which they speak to the sexual vulnerability and abuse experienced by themselves and by many other women (Frederick 2015: 89). Their ability to attract enormous audiences is grounded in signs that they are called to ministry. In these cases, as in examples of women whose charisma can be discerned in the responses of others to their message, various kinds of life experience as well as seemingly innocuous events—accidents, coincidences—line up to tell a person, white or black, that she is called to preach the word of God (see also Kwilecki 1987; Walton 2009). Thus, when conditions are right, women do have the possibility of gaining attention from their churches as powerful preachers and prophets.

Charisma

As the story that opens this chapter illustrates, there is no way to examine the special role of Bishop Flunder without taking note of her personal charisma, that is, her ability to elicit expressions of awe and admiration among worshippers. Charisma is a quality that scholars of both religion and politics have examined, as leaders in both arenas are often understood to have qualities that mark them as charismatic, and many features of these scholars' analyses help us understand Bishop Flunder's powerful persona.

The word "charisma" comes from the Greek, and literally means "gift of God's grace" as used in Paul's epistles, where it was first elaborated (Potts 2009). The idea of charisma is well-developed in the New Testament, providing the foundation for Pentecostal worship practices (e.g., Corinthians 12:8–11, Romans 12). This means that the term "charisma" has multiple meanings in the context of TFAM, referring both to the state of grace and its gifts that all worshippers aspire to achieve, and to the individual qualities of leading clergy. Pentecostalism glorifies and elevates spiritual experiences that evidence grace or qualities that are sometimes called "gifts of charisma" or "spiritual gifts," and the quality is dispersed among members of the congregation in the course of worship. But beyond this, the fact that Bishop Flunder describes her gift or her calling to preach as "charisma" is strikingly on target, but in a different sense than Paul's intended meaning. Rather, she radiates the qualities that Max Weber defines as charisma:

A certain quality of an individual personality by virtue of which he is considered extraordinary and treated as endowed with supernatural, superhuman, or at least specifically exceptional powers or qualities. These are such as are not accessible to the ordinary person, but are regarded as of divine origin or as exemplary, and on the basis of them the individual concerned is treated as a "leader." (Weber 1968a: 241)

Weber's discussion of charisma brought the term into contemporary usage in a sense very different from that used in the New Testament. In his definition, actual manifestations of divinity are not necessary for a person to possess charisma; it resides rather in the response of others who believe the person to be endowed with these qualities. Nor do charismatic individuals need to believe themselves to be divinely inspired; they act decisively on their environment and their connections to other people in ways that mark extraordinary and powerful individuality (Shils 1965: 200). Charisma, then, in this reading, is a dimension of individual personality that has a powerful impact on those with whom one interacts. It is not universal, of course, as particular cultural contexts locate charisma in specific kinds of individuals (Willner 1984). As political scientist Ann Ruth Willner details in her study of political charisma, for example, Gandhi had qualities that constituted charisma in the Indian context, but these qualities would not have been likely to resonate elsewhere; in the same fashion, Franklin Roosevelt's charisma must be understood as part of a specific historical and cultural milieu. Once the term "charisma" was revived and elaborated upon by Weber, it moved into the general lexicon, used to refer not only to powerful religious and political figures, but to celebrities from various milieux—entertainment, sports, and media—where it seems merely to refer to some compelling personality characteristic (Potts 2009).

Willner enumerates qualities, any one of which may constitute charisma. These include first, prescience, or the ability to foretell the future; second, a capacity to read the minds or intentions of others; third, an ability to heal (or harm) in unorthodox ways; and fourth, a cluster of qualities that amount to invulnerability (Willner 1984: 22). Anthropologists have paid close attention to such attributes as they have emerged mainly in religious contexts (Lindholm 2013), but some anthropologists and other scholars, especially political scientists, have focused on how the phenomenon may appear among political leaders, including many who also might be classified as demagogues (Lindholm 1990).[4]

Psychologist Len Oakes uses the term "prophet" to designate a person who radiates charisma, defining such a person as "one who (a) espouses a message of salvation that is opposed to conventional values, and (b) attracts a following of people who look to him for guidance in their daily lives" (Oakes 1997: 2). He examines many different contemporary and historical examples of charismatic religious leaders, explaining, "Of all the prophet's talents, his social insight is the most remarkable, verging at times on the paranormal. The ability of charismatic figures to read their audience, to say precisely those things which strike a chord, and to see into the hearts of others gives rise to tales of telepathy" (Oakes 1997: 18). Although his main concern is with the leaders of cults, he does not make the error of attributing all of the prophet's appeal to his followers and their needs. Indeed, Oakes is careful to make clear that the "magic" that emanates from the prophet is real, quoting anthropologist Weston La Barre, who spoke of charisma as "streaming" from the shaman, a reflection of her "psychological voltage" (La Barre 1980: 52). And, echoing Weber (1968b: 254–55), the authenticity of the prophet's charisma is that it is unremunerated, often exerted in support of social reform rather than as a way to glorify the prophet herself.

Bishop Flunder in the Pulpit

Everyone I spoke to in the Fellowship agreed that Bishop Flunder is a charismatic figure. Although members of TFAM do not locate Bishop Flunder's charisma solely in her oratory, no one disputes the fact that she is a powerful preacher. As mentioned earlier, services in TFAM churches generally follow the form that typifies worship in African American churches. Theologian Henry H. Mitchell characterizes such worship as following two principles: "The first is that one must declare the gospel in the language and the culture of the people—the vernacular. For some this involves resistance to a temptation to sound learned and 'proper.' . . . The second . . . is that the gospel must speak to a person's current needs" (Mitchell 1990: 20). Beyond this, interaction with the congregation is a vital element of black preaching, including interjections from the worshippers ("Amen," "Praise the Lord," "Well," etc.) and appeals for support ("I'm preaching good now," "Do you hear me?" "Tell your neighbor"), or acknowledgments that the sermon has been lengthy ("I'm almost finished") (Mitchell 1990: 100–101), which imbues it with a kind of urgency. The sermon must also appear to be spontaneous, even if the preacher has a prepared text on paper or an electronic device, and the argument that drives the sermon should seem to be constructed more out of passion than logic (Mitchell 1990: 114). Of course, the preacher may depart from her prepared text as the Spirit moves her, and responses from the congregation may shape the direction the sermon takes.

Bishop Flunder, like other pastors I heard preach in TFAM congregations, adheres to these basic principles, using vernacular and allusions to common experiences in black American life to make the sermons entertaining and engaging, to make worshippers feel that they are the intended audience for the comments. It is particularly vital for the sermon to address issues of concern to the congregation and not to get mired in theological abstractions. Folklorist Gerald Davis (1985) also notes that sermons favored by the three black congregations he studied in Oakland, California, had qualities worshippers identified as "southern." This meant that these were sermons that were "preached from the Spirit," seemingly spontaneous, and did not appear to be filtered through "university training," evoking a style that even congregants long removed from the South identify as being embedded in their "roots" (Davis 1985: 8-9). Davis also identifies circularity as an organizing principle of African American sermons, as it is of other performative genres in black culture. That is, a central motif is presented and then strategically repeated, with innovations characterizing its successive reiterations, much in the way that a jazz performance is organized. That achieving a final synthesis using a motif may take considerable preparation ought not to undermine the extent to which the sermon appears to be wholly spontaneous.

The power of Bishop Flunder's sermons derives, then, not from their originality of form—they are indeed classic examples of African American church oratory (homiletics)—but from the far-reaching scope of her message. The sermons are calls for the congregation to take action, to refuse to allow their religiosity to temper the necessity of their engagement with the world. They also protest cultural forces that have degraded and abused congregants whether through racism, sexism, homophobia, or other forms of bias. She departs from traditional themes to invite the congregation to move toward some sort of activist engagement.

In the summer of 2015, Bishop delivered a sermon at TFAM's national convocation in Oakland, California. The sermon questioned religious orthodoxy of all sorts, interrogating fundamentalist certainties that regularly are put forward by clergy. Her examples ranged from religious responses to the Black Plague, to periodic predictions by various religious figures that the world was about to end, to the hysteria that arose around the millennium when technical failures were expected to be catastrophic, to the pressure put on women to exhibit the holiness that would keep the whole group safe, to the way that racism is facilitated by dehumanizing the group being viewed as "other." She freely admitted that she no longer feels she has a single answer to any theological question, even after having grown up in an environment that insisted that one could discover such unambiguous answers.

I have discovered that the longer I live, the less certainty I have about things. Where I used to have one answer, now I have seven or eight. Or nine or ten. To the same question. And it sort of depends on the day of the week, how I'm feeling, what I'm reading, what is shifting me, how I'm shifting. Because I've given myself permission

CHAPTER TWO

to have theological fluidity. I'm not interested in being absolutely certain about absolutely everything. It doesn't do anything to my faith and it does not disturb my walk with God.

This ready acceptance of the ambiguity of religious doctrine and the situational nature of what are touted as scriptural certainties means that she also feels able to question the notion that God alone is behind everything that happens, that human beings have no agency. She brings up environmental degradation, racism, and disease, among other issues, and asks her audience to accept the notion that they must take responsibility for some of these misfortunes.

Here is what I propose: People of all faiths and lands and countries . . . decide that we are going to both enact and pursue an active campaign to change this predictable response from religion that comes at a time of crisis. We are in crisis. Again, stop blaming God. The earth is mad because we made her mad. Stop blaming God. People are warring with one another because we don't know how to love one another. Stop blaming God. Somebody said, Why would God let this happen? God is asking, Why would YOU let this happen? Stop blaming God. Where were you when people were hungry? What are YOU doing about it? People are incarcerated illegally and immorally. What are YOU doing about it?

Bishop Flunder here makes a major departure from the kinds of sermons most Pentecostal preachers deliver. She is asking her congregation to take responsibility for what happens in the world, to let go of the notion that God or Jesus will take care of their future. In doing so, she emphasizes the notion that all people in the world share the need to address the political, environmental, health, and social justice issues that continue to plague not only black people, but everyone.

These attributes all seem to be present, in various measures, in Bishop Flunder, though other congregants or clergy may also display some of these qualities. It is not unusual to meet members of TFAM congregations who understand themselves to be prophets or prophetesses, and who are recognized as such by other worshippers in their churches. But worshippers have special feelings about Bishop Flunder. They associate her touch with a kind of healing or transport to a level of spiritual transcendence amply illustrated in the blessings worshippers seek out at the end of services. Worshippers seem to hope for her to be inspired to heal; it doesn't happen at every service, but it seems that if she is sufficiently inspired, Bishop can transmit the power of the Spirit to the congregation. A sign that such healing is imminent can thus be discerned by her behavior during the service: if she begins to dance or speak in tongues or display other evidence that she is experiencing charismatic gifts, it is likely that such spiritual transcendence will be transmitted to the congregation.

I witnessed Bishop Flunder's charisma emerge on many occasions when she seemed uniquely able to understand what a person approaching her needed or was thinking. At the sunrise baptism service held at the 2013 national convocation in Las Vegas, Bishop and several other clergy positioned themselves in a small pool, all clad in white robes, about waist-high in the water. Worshippers descended into the pool one at a time, each one's demeanor different. In each case, as the person approached, Bishop Flunder looked intently at the person and then murmured something comforting, usually about what she perceived that person to need, drawing her knowledge from her reading of the person's appearance and behavior, as told to her by the Holy Spirit. "I know why you're here, baby," she would say before telling the person what she discerned. Many were so moved by this that they began to cry. The baptisms themselves took different amounts of time, depending on the emotional state of the worshipper. Spectators surrounded the pool, many going into states of trance themselves, dancing and speaking in tongues. Still others watched without being visibly transported, but still closely following the proceedings. There seemed no ranking of these behaviors; both were acceptable.

Bishop Flunder's magnetic qualities inhere both in her behavior and her appearance. First, she is strikingly attractive, with a particularly warm and compelling smile, and she is always smartly dressed. In 2013 she lost a large amount of weight, and this only added to her appeal, though some members of TFAM churches who hadn't seen her since she began her diet worried about whether she had been ill. She eased their concerns at the 2013 convocation when she talked very explicitly about her weight loss, inspired by her doctor's prediction that she was risking serious threats to her health if she didn't lose weight. She managed to speak about the importance of taking care of one's health without sounding at all judgmental of the many TFAM congregants, especially women, who are overweight.

Bishop Flunder's gifts seem to resemble those that Weber described as characteristic of the "ethical" prophet. As explained by Oakes, such a prophet seeks "to create a realm of blessedness upon the earth, purged of violence and hate, fear and need . . . [and has] a divine ethical mission. . . . His aim is not to become like God but to become God's instrument and to be spiritually suffused by the deity" (Oakes 1997: 29; see also Weber 1968b: 275). But her qualities do not seem to correspond to the ones that Oakes

CHAPTER TWO

details for many of those he studied, in that she seeks to nurture similar gifts in her followers and does not seem to desire a personal exalted status for its own sake. Like the followers of prophets described by Oakes, charisma is constructed in important ways by the audience or, in this case, congregation; members of TFAM "actively seek a vehicle for the expression" of the works they hope to achieve (Oakes 1997: 129). As Weber emphasized, charisma draws on qualities of a leader but needs to be recognized by others in order to become manifest.

I argue here that while Bishop Flunder's demeanor exhibits some of the qualities that Weber and other scholars have specified as typical of charismatic leaders, she also displays qualities that sharply differentiate her from classic exemplars of charisma. First, many congregants describe her as down-to-earth and approachable, a person with whom one can easily converse or in whom one can readily confide. Second, while she is aware of her stature as an important and influential public figure, she seems uninterested in achieving the kind of prestige that would elevate her above her congregants and members of her community. Her efforts to train future leaders speak to her determination to avoid having TFAM be all about herself. She is also unique in that she calls on worshippers to apply their spiritual powers to engage with the world, a message far removed from traditional Pentecostal doctrine, especially as conveyed in COGIC.

Bishop Flunder's Unusual Charisma

Anthony Sullivan—a longtime Fellowship member, now the pastor of a United Church of Christ congregation in the Chicago area—explains what TFAM members see in Bishop as a leader: "Other people see her as this powerful preacher, or this singer, or this activist, or this advocate, or they see her as this person who hobnobs with the president [Obama]. And she is all of these things." But what makes her important to him is that he feels a connection with her on a much more human level. "What makes her a good leader for me is that she is both authentic and touchable. What I mean by authentic is that she is not a person who is so well put together that they are artificial. She is a person who puts on her pants the same way I do." He goes on to discuss Bishop's struggle with her weight, a problem shared with many people in TFAM. As he puts it, "For lack of a better word, we have a lot of fat people in the Fellowship. And in the early years of the Fellowship, it was quite evident that Bishop Flunder also struggled with weight issues. But when it got to a place where she was right at the cusp of being declared diabetic, she realized that she had to do something about that. And seeing her go through the process of taking ownership of her health made her authentic to me."

Pastor Anthony's comments resonate with those of others in TFAM who acknowledge Bishop Flunder's exceptional rhetorical talents, but understand her charisma as emanating from other dimensions of her being. Andrea Vassell—a New Yorker who has put her career as a nurse on hold while she studies full-time for a master of divinity degree at Lancaster Theological Seminary in Pennsylvania—first refers to Bishop Flunder's experience in COGIC as the source of her unique ability to lead TFAM. She notes that Bishop had grown up in the center of COGIC and knew the world of charismatic and Holiness worship intimately, giving her a special bond with most of those who worshipped in TFAM congregations. This applies not only to African Americans, but to Latinos and white people, who often also come from churches with these particular traditions. "She can think not just the things about [these churches] that are uniquely wonderful, but she can speak to the things about them that are problematic if not malignant, and do so from a place of personal knowledge and not from a place of 'Hey, I read a book.' She also came out of the leadership of the COGIC church. She has seen and heard way more than most people ever will." But after saying this, Andrea quickly moves to pointing to Bishop Flunder's dedication to preparing herself for her work. "She was already a very smart woman, and she took the time to prepare for her profession, in ways that, along with whatever she had before, give her a handle on the theology that is beyond what she was taught at the feet and knees of her grandmother and her father. It's also the learned piece, the formal learning piece, she has taken the time to engage in that."

She then explains that Bishop Flunder's example served as an inspiration to her as she decided to further her own theological education.

What [Bishop Flunder's leadership] has done is also serve as an inspiration [to] the number of us who had gone ahead and engaged in theological learning and education formally and are continuing to do so from the baccalaureate program all the way up to the doctorate level. . . . I must say that it is directly related to who she is and how she has shown up in community and how she has demystified that whole thing. There used to be this cloud, this wonderful white cloud over the pulpit, where women were not allowed, and the seats of power were among the men who were doctor this and doctor that, and they held those places. She demystified it. She basically said, "If you want one, go get it. There's nothing to it. If you do the work that people ask you to do, remain consistent, and do the work."

CHAPTER TWO

Andrea explains that many Holiness and Pentecostal churches traditionally harbor suspicions about clergy who have too much education, fearing that advanced academic training might cause one to lose one's anointing, but that Bishop Flunder's example stands in sharp opposition to this position. In other words, while Bishop Flunder's power as the leader of TFAM draws on her history in COGIC, her rejection of major components of that heritage also stands as a key element of her personal power. She inspires members to pursue further education, in her view vital to making sure that TFAM will have future leaders prepared to continue the work she has begun. To do this effectively, she works to demystify the process of gaining further theological training, thus essentially undermining the specialness of her own status.

Pastor Vanessa Brown, who leads TFAM congregations in New York City and Newark, talks extensively about Bishop's intellectual leadership, her ability to share her experience as a leader, and her efforts to remind everyone that it is never too late for them to get in touch with their own skills and strengths. She's inspiring, knows how to motivate pastors, Pastor Vanessa explains, and she "knows how to start a fire and keep it going." Bishop considers education very important so that people in the LGBT community know how to interpret the text, how to liberate themselves through the Word. "She's been anointed and chosen by God. . . . She has this way about her, she's a mother and so the nurturer in her comes out. People need nurturing. People have been abused. There's something about her. There's not just one thing about her; there are several things. . . . It's boundless, limitless. Bishop hasn't put any boundaries on it. You don't have to understand everything. I know that what God has shown her is greater than who she is and that's a pretty great thing." In line with this emphasis, Pastor Vanessa is studying for a master of divinity at the New York Theological Seminary, even while pastoring two congregations.

Others speak of the feeling that there is a special quality of holiness that surrounds Bishop Flunder. Charla Kouadio, pastor of a TFAM congregation in Massachusetts, explains, "There's like a holy presence. You feel if you're close to her, you're closer to God." Her partner and co-pastor, Theresa Coley-Kouadio, adds:

I think she presents herself as your friend and your ally. It's interesting because we've seen her in various functions. We've seen her at the Fellowship and we've also seen her at UCC things. And it's amazing, even to people who say the most foolish things, she has found a way to connect to them. And to connect to either their pain, or their concern, or their goals in a way that they feel encouraged after the interaction. And it's just amazing to watch how people just flock around her and sit at her feet. . . . When she talks to you, you have her complete attention. Like there is nothing else that she is thinking about. There's nothing else on her plate. That your time with her, there is no place she'd rather be in the whole wide world than sitting in front of you listening to what you have to say.

Pastor Charla continues, explaining that the charisma is not primarily conveyed in Bishop's preaching:

I think she's an excellent preacher, don't get me wrong, certainly that. But she's able to make that personal connection that you feel like she's preaching to you. . . . Especially if there's hundreds of people there.

Pastor Theresa expands on what this means, when I ask how Bishop Flunder is able to make a personal connection with a large number of congregants, she exclaims: "I don't know! There's a Holy Spirit kind of connection. She'll say something and you'll say, 'Oh, that's what I was thinking about.' And I don't know how that happened, but it will make sense." When I ask Pastor Charla how she thinks this is accomplished, she speculates:

You think about the Billy Grahams and all those kinds of people, people who are able to move a whole crowd, there's something in more than what they're saying: It's the way their bodies move. It's the way they seem to be looking at you even though there's thousands of people. And I don't know what that is. Maybe that's what you hope? You hope that she's looking at you? Or maybe it is that gift she has that God has given her that she is able to give that perception.

Alvis Ward, an active member of City of Refuge, describes "being floored" the first time he heard Bishop Flunder preach. When I ask him what impressed him, he tells me it was "the transparency and the honesty, the authenticity of it." He continues:

She was refuting many of the concepts of the traditional church, what I heard as damnation theology. She was countering that. . . . And it floored me. I thought here is someone who is not afraid, among her contemporaries, to speak truth to power. . . . She was sharing her personal growth and interactions along the journey that got her to the place as she often said of free people. I fell in love with it. It was authentic. It was warm and welcoming. You found no reason not to be a part of something real.

CHAPTER TWO

Alvis has participated in many different kinds of worship experiences and sees his own perspective as "universalist." He doesn't define himself as gay, refusing to accept what he considers narrow or confining identity categories.

I've never wanted to choose a box. And I've always known that, because people have always tried to pigeonhole me, to keep me nicely nestled for their convenience or for their comfort.

Instead, he describes the lure of City of Refuge as being

the people, because they came from all walks of life. I was happy to see heaven on earth in one environment. You had Asian people, black people, female, trans, mental health, non–mental health, you had homeless, you had able-bodied, everything that you could think of that was a part of the right now and the creation story. And some things that were not part of the creation story were there. I remember when the church changed the restroom to a unisex restroom. Bishop had this whole communication about living in the house, you and your brothers, everyone sharing the same restroom, and how one person would be on the commode, and another person would be in the shower. You go in to do what you need to do, and then you go about your business. It was easy to take down the male and female signs and make it the-whosoever-will restroom. I thought that was powerful because it made sense. You could see that in your past and in envisioning forward. It was simple.

Alvis situates Bishop Flunder's power as a leader not in her preaching, however, or her ability to question taken-for-granted assumptions. He explains that the source of her leadership is to be found in what he calls "her remembrance."

She remembers her ancestors' journey, she remembers her journey, and the visions for the journey that is yet to come. And she brings all that to this time and this moment. She knows how to homogenize and compile all of that information from past, present, and future for now. And that's what I find powerful, how she . . . authentically engages for others to empower themselves, to empower others.

When I ask what qualities make her able to have this impact, he says:

With her truth. With her study. Because you can only come by that ability, I know that she can only come by that ability by faith. Definitely hands-on. You know, she's not a bystander. She's always in it. That's what I think makes her a great leader. Because of all that, at City of Refuge, I ask why am I here, why do I keep coming here? Yes, I like the participation in the choir. Yes, I like other auxiliaries that I'm a part of. But it's the teaching moment that makes her a great leader. She studies and she brings the study, not haphazardly, to the table. And you want that, you want to live in it, you want to share it with others. My whole vocabulary was upgraded to include a whole Flunder-ism dictionary that I impart to others daily in my walk alongside that vocabulary that I learned through my schooling. Sometimes there are no words in the English language that I find can convey feelings and thoughts, and I draw directly from the Flunder-ism dictionary to clarify.

Alvis locates the impact of Bishop Flunder's leadership in a combination of vision and knowledge, as well as in her ability to question traditional categories and make new ideas real and compelling.

There's none like her. She is unique. . . . She's on a path where you really have to be able to engage everybody and make everyone feel welcome at the table. So many things are set up based on sex, based on male-female roles. I love how she dismantles the roles. Because you can get past the roles, then everybody is equal. I think that's the last frontier, dismantling the roles.

His assessment, then, of Bishop Flunder's unique abilities draws on a range of capacities that she can impart in worship and other contexts. She conveys both something located within herself, "authenticity," that is inspiring in itself and speaks to her abiding faith. But her quality of engagement is also part of what makes people want to follow her, not being a "bystander," in his words. These capacities are amplified by her studies, through which she introduces new ideas to her congregation. But at the same time, she has an ability to frame ideas that are grounded in common sense as profound and transformative. By establishing unisex restrooms at City of Refuge, for example, she made clear that the church is like a family, where everyone uses the bathroom as needed and there is no need to allow gender conventions to inhibit routine activities.

As was clear when Bishop Flunder related her personal journey, she understands herself to have a gift that can be described as charisma. When I ask her to explain her own charisma, she says:

I think that in my understanding, the Greek word *charismata* has to do with a certain magnetism, a certain draw, something that folks would call anointing, where a person is enabled. It's a gifting to do certain things. It's not just skill—skill helps—but it has to do with the gifting to do what it is that I am called to do. I am called to do certain things. And I have what I believe is the accompanying charisma to do those things. I think that's what comes from God. It would be a poor God to call you to do something and not enable you to do it.

I press her to explain how she knows that she possesses this gift.

BF: I'm absolutely certain that God called me to it, because of the fruit.
EL: Meaning the results?
BF: Yes. Precisely.
EL: Do you ever hear God telling you to do this work?
BF: Well, I think that in terms of me hearing an audible voice that speaks English with an African American accent—no, I don't hear that. What I do hear are signals, what some people might call coincidences. But I call them "witness." When it's something that I am really supposed to do, I believe that the circumstances line up to enable me to do that thing. That's what I believe. And that has been my experience that the circumstances do line up that enable me to do what I am called to do. The circumstances being the opportunity, the people, the finances, you know, things line up. If God wants you to do something, it's in God's best interest to make it possible.

"What happens," I ask, "when you want to pursue some course of action that doesn't work out? Does that ever occur?" She says that it does, often.

So I know that it's not the thing to do. The agency to do it. I've wanted to do a lot of things, and the agency to do it never came. And I've learned to just move on to the next thing. . . . There's just been a lot of things that seem to be a good idea that just didn't materialize, and some of them still will. Sometimes you can get the want, but you don't have the wind right, and you have to wait for the rest of it. I tend to think because I've been talking to God a long time, that when I inquire about something that is still in my heart and in my mind, and it keeps coming up, then I want to know when is this supposed to happen? Why am I reminded of this so often? And oftentimes, there are things that come to pass at this time in my life that I saw years and years ago. And they're just now coming to pass.

Even as someone whose belief system and experience are both far from what TFAM members bring to church, I have experienced Bishop Flunder's remarkable ability to fill those with whom she communicates with inspiration and hope. This happens both in her sermons, which adhere to African American styles of preaching but which also ask worshippers to expand their imagination of what they can do with the insights she offers, and in conversational interactions outside worship services. Bishop Flunder focuses on anyone with whom she is speaking with an intensity that makes that person feel exceptional and important. Her absolute attention makes the recipient of such a connection feel that her/his problems outweigh anything else Bishop Flunder might have on her mind. But even as her focus is serious, her affect is leavened with a quality of informality and humor that puts the person with whom she is talking at ease. When Pastor Anthony speaks of her "putting on her pants the same way" that he does, he alludes to a lack of pretentiousness that makes anyone who interacts with her feel that achieving spiritual clarity such as she possesses is possible.

Bishop Flunder's sermons, and the music that accompanies them, bring many of the worshippers to be slain in the Spirit, to dance, to sing, and to move around the sanctuary. In July 2013, at the convocation in Las Vegas, she spoke to the congregation about the plans for City of Refuge to move from San Francisco to a new building in Oakland, which would also serve as the national and global headquarters for TFAM, emphasizing the way that God intervened in the process at every step. As the sermon progressed, Bishop Flunder spoke more graphically about how God had made this happen, had made the old building on Howard Street sell for much more than it would have the previous year, and to allow them to obtain the building they wanted in Oakland, a facility with 31,000 square feet, explaining how God intervened in the context of escalating real estate prices in the Bay Area.

I want you to know that while you're here taking care of God's business, God is taking care of yours. If you haven't already gotten the word, expect it here. Expect a phone call. Expect a text. Expect an e-mail. God is making a way! Finances are coming! People are coming! Resources are coming! . . . Let me read the Scripture and then I'm going to sit down.

While Bishop prepares people to hear her message, she puts the matter of communication with God in terms that are strikingly ordinary. She also plays on a constant theme of being "almost done," something that underscores the spontaneity and urgency of the message, suggesting that she didn't plan to say what she ends up saying, but that God gave her the words.

How are we going to do our "what's next"? How is it going to happen for us? First of all, we're going to have to have the courage to move when the Lord says move. Twenty-two years we've been in San Francisco. Twenty-two years, and we said we'd

CHAPTER TWO

never go to Oakland. Because Oakland is over-churched. I said, We'll never go to Oakland.

But God spoke to our spirit and said that there is work for us to do. I said, Well, how about Emeryville? God said no. I said, How about Vacaville? God said no. I said, How about Hayward? God said no. How about Alameda? God said no. I said, Okay, we're going to make preparation in San Francisco. You don't get the whole of it until you obey what God says. Because what God intends you to do is move on the thing that God says. And then the rest will come when you move on what God says. Tell your neighbor, the rest will come when you move on what God said.

Once it was established that City of Refuge must move on what God was telling them, the practical details needed to be considered. How much was the building worth? Would the financial part of the puzzle work out?

And I said, What will they want for the church? It cost us a million five fifty to buy it. What will they give us for it? It might be worth three million by now, but let's put it out there and see what will they give us for it. And someone came by and said I think this building is worth four or five million. I said, What? I said, Four or five million dollars? They said yes. I said, Let's ask five million. We put it out there for five million, and within two weeks, we had four or five offers for five million. . . . I need you to hear what I'm saying. All right. We got five million dollars for a building I thought was worth three. But the dot-coms had come back to South of Market, and they pushed the price up. Had we sold the building last year, we probably would have gotten three. But we waited on the Lord. Don't get uncomfortable in your waiting. Wait. Because God has got something prepared for you, that somebody else built. So while we were waiting on the Lord, and struggling to keep the building going, it went up by two million dollars.

While some might attribute the rapidly rising price of the building to business interests, particularly the return of dot-com businesses to the area, Bishop explains it as God having told them to wait until a more auspicious time to sell the building.

Then we said, We want to buy a building in Oakland that will give us parking. That's all we said to God. We're tired of being landlocked in San Francisco. We went to see a building, [and] it had a gate. And we went around the back, and the whole back of it is a parking lot. One hundred twelve parking places. It was a union temple. We talked to the union. They had another buyer. They said, We got another offer and, well, we're sorry. And Charlene [the music minister] came over to see the building. And she hadn't heard that. And she walked up on one of the union men. She said, Don't I know you? And he said, Yes, I know you. You're the one who taught me how to sing and play the piano. And she said, Well, you know, we want this building. And he said, Are you the ones we have the offer from? Well, no, I understand somebody else has put an offer on the building. He said, Give me a few minutes. Am I telling the truth? He went in and talked to the plumbers and the ironworkers and the painters and the roofers. Twenty-one unions. And when he came back, he said, You all don't worry about it. Come back to a meeting next week at eleven o'clock and bring your plans with you. I'm going to talk to them between now and then.

Long story short, we rolled up, about twelve of us, to a room full of union men. And me. I'm five foot two. There's nothing I can do about it. When we came in the room, they had union man chairs, set me down in a union man chair. Can't hardly see over the top of the table. They said, Tell us what you're going to do in this building. And we told them about our dream and our vision and what we believed that God would do. And they told us to go out for a minute. And we came back and they said, Present us an offer. We presented them an offer. Listen to me. And while they were deciding our offer, the other offer fell out. You know it did. Here's the third and last principle, whatever is for you, whatever is for you, whatever God plans in your what's next—tell your neighbor, Stop thinking small—thirty-one thousand square feet of space. Tell him, Stop settling for less than God shows you. Stop settling for less than God revealed to you. If you don't have it yet, WAIT on it; it's coming. Because when God said it, it's true.

It's clear that God wanted City of Refuge to get this building because everything was put in place to make it happen, from the fact that one of the union men had studied music with Minister Charlene, to the sudden collapse of the earlier offer. Bishop Flunder gives the story lots of flavor, describing the image of her small self sitting in a huge chair intended for a "union man," presenting the church's offer, and telling the men what City of Refuge has planned for the building.

This brings her to the Scripture reading and the larger point of the sermon, the theme of how working together is essential if one is to achieve one's dreams.

Now listen to this passage, and I'm going to stop. Ecclesiastes, four, ninth verse. It says, Two people are better off than one, for they can help each other succeed. If one person falls, the other one can reach out and help. But someone who falls alone is in real danger. Two people lying close together can keep each other warm. But how can you be warm alone? Ask your neighbor, How can you be warm alone? A person standing alone can be attacked and defeated, but two people standing back to back, BUT TWO PEOPLE STANDING BACK TO BACK, tell your neighbor, tell your brother or sister, I've got your back. I've got your back. Tell your brother or sister, I've got your back. When you get your building, we're coming to shout. When God

CHAPTER TWO

blesses you with a new program, we're coming to shout. I said, When you need an offering, we're coming to lift it for you. When you need money, we're coming to raise money for you. When you need to build an addition on your building, we're coming to help you! Because we got your back. And three are even better than two, because a triple-braided cord is not easily broken. I'm going to stop. God's got something planned for it, but if we're going to do it, bishops, we've got to do it together. If we're going to do it, preachers, we've got to do it together. If we're going do it, we're going to do it together.

> This leads Bishop back to the matter of the building.

And I want you to know that when City of Refuge went out and looked at that building, one of the first things we said was, Now we can establish a leadership center for the entire Fellowship. We can create a headquarters. Say headquarters. We are twelve years old and we got us a headquarters. Say headquarters. . . . We have us a HEADQUARTERS! I said, We have somewhere we can go and establish the offices for our local and global ministries. If God be for you, what shall we say to these things? If God be for us, who can who in the world can be against us?

> She then returns to the theme of togetherness and mutual concern.

My baby grandson said this, his godmother bought him a full drum set, all the drums, and the whole thing, and he gets his sticks. And his auntie Titi, Prophetess Twanna, she got him new sticks. And he gets on the drums, and he goes bam, bam, bam, bam, until your whole head and your liver and everything inside—bam, bam, bam—and then he stops and he says, Grandma, I want to play the drums for somebody. Essentially, playing the drums is no good when you're playing by yourself. He said, essentially, I'm ready to take my drums down to the church so I can play my drums for somebody. I want to say to all the dancers, it's not a good dance until you dance for somebody. To the singers, it's not a good song until you sing for somebody. I want to say to the prophets, it's not a good prophesy until your prophesy [is] with and for somebody. Here's the deal. We're in this together. I want you to find at least three people, and I'm through with this, and tell them, I'm in this with you. Tell them, I'm in this with you! We're on our way together. We're on our way to our promise together. We're on our way to our "what's next" together. And I declare to every pastor in this house, if God did it for Refuge, God did it for Bethel [the TFAM church in Washington, DC], God will do it for you! I said, God will do it for you! God will do it for you! God will do it for you! Your labor is not in vain in the Lord. Trust in the Lord. With all your heart and all your mind and all your strength. And this is the last thing I want to do before I sit down, because we got work to do tonight. I want you to praise God like it's already happened. Praise God for us in San Francisco and

1   Bishop Flunder preaching (photo by Veronica Jordan).

Oakland. Praise God for our headquarters for the Fellowship of Affirming Ministries. Praise God like you've already seen it! Give God that kind of praise. Give God that kind of praise. Give God that kind of praise.

While she has been preaching, the music has become more insistent, pulsating, and many in the congregation are dancing in the aisles and shouting. Some are running around the perimeter of the sanctuary.

Give God that kind of praise. Now, clap your hands in the sanctuary, and shout unto the Lord with the voice of triumph. We are the head and not the tail. We will be lenders and not borrowers, God will give us more than enough. Tell somebody, MORE THAN ENOUGH! Tell somebody else, MORE THAN ENOUGH. That is the promise of God.

Bishop is now moving with the Spirit, as the congregation becomes more animated and the music plays rhythms that support being filled with the Spirit. Bishop sings some of the lines of her sermon.

You may take your seat if you can. Hallelujah. I feel preaching in this house. You may have your seat if you can. Tell your neighbor, More than enough. We have some bishops to consecrate. I want the bishops to know that GOD IS GOING TO GIVE YOU MORE THAN ENOUGH. Turn and tell somebody, Your struggle is over. Turn and tell

CHAPTER TWO

somebody, Your struggle is over. I'm going to stop. I'm going to stop. I feel praise in this house. God bless you. Under these robes, we struggle too. Yes we do. Trying to figure out how to take care of it all, and get the bills paid, and take care of our families, and manage our households. I want you to hear me say, Our struggle is over. Our struggle is over!

Bishop shifts her message to affirm the reasons for God's support for City of Refuge and TFAM.

Somebody says why is God going to do this for us? Tell somebody, It's our vindication. You didn't hear what I said. I said, It's our vindication, because we dared to include everybody. Because we dared to love everybody. It's a new day. There's a brand-new new coming. I'm all off script. I can't even find my script.

Here she emphasizes the spontaneity of the message, the fact that it comes directly from God.

God's going to take care of it! God's going to take care of it! Don't you worry about it. Don't you worry about it. God's going to handle it for you. Give God the glory for it. God's going to take care of it for you! You got to hear my spirit. Don't worry about your life! God's got a plan for your life, a plan for your ministry. What shall we say to these things, if God be for us—and I declare to you, God is for us. Amen.

The congregation is now fully engaged. Many are falling out, while their neighbors move furniture out of their way, fan them, and bring water and towels to assist them. Others are dancing in place, doing the characteristic rapid two-step that indicates being filled with the Spirit. Still others are moving around the room, often being followed by someone with a towel and water in preparation for a possible collapse onto the floor.

Somebody just got a glimpse of it. It won't be like it's been. Tell your neighbor, It won't be like it's been. It's a new day. I've seen heaven open up. I've seen it with my own eyes! I've seen heaven open up and the glory of God, hallelujah, falling on God's people. It's our turn. It's our turn. Some of you, God had you back behind in the desert. I said, God had you back in the desert until you got over Egypt. And you thought the desert was your home. It wasn't your home. God had you back there, waiting for you to get over Egypt. Tell somebody, I'm over it. I'm not a slave to anybody or anything. I'm over it. Now God is moving you to Canaan. Because you're ready. Tell your neighbor, You're ready, ready, ready, ready. Tell your neighbor, You're ready, ready, ready, ready! You're ready. Egypt taught you something. It had a purpose. But you're ready now. Move on into your promise. God can trust us with great things, because God has done great things for us.

Tell your neighbor, The desert taught me something. I said, The desert taught me something. It wasn't a useless time in my life. The desert taught me something. I got changed in the desert. Something happened to me in the desert. I'm not the same girl I was. The desert taught me something. I got God spoke to me out of a burning bush. He said, Don't worry about it, Yvette.[5] I am who I am. I'm all you need me to be. Now go back and tell Pharaoh I said, Let my people go. God is going to send you home with a word in your mouth. Forgive me. I know the time. But I feel deliverance in this room. Help me, Bishop. Hallelujah. And when the Lord gets ready, I said, when the Lord gets ready, you got to move, you got to move, you got to move, you got to move. So cut the people loose that are holding you and making you think you can't do better, and you can't have better, go out there in nothing, step out on nothing, and declare to you that if you do, God will put something up under your feet. You've got to move, you've got to move when the Lord gets ready.

This part of the sermon moves to more general themes of aspiration and merit. It reminds worshippers that they are entitled to want more from life, but that they can only succeed by following God's signals, being patient, and accepting the meaning of whatever adversity they have suffered. The theme of Egypt and freedom offers, of course, a particularly compelling model of the resilience of the human spirit, and its ability to rise above even such extreme hardship as slavery.

By the time Bishop Flunder has finished the sermon, and the congregation has been asked to rise and hold hands with those standing nearby, many of the worshippers are either still filled with the Spirit or recovering from its inhabitation of their bodies. She has made a number of crucial points, some having to do with practical matters—specifically the sale of the old building and the purchase of the new headquarters in Oakland—but others returning to key themes in African American worship. She has introduced the notion that God will communicate directly (by e-mail or text!) and that believers will learn what they are supposed to do next, and the notion that God will smooth the way to whatever is desired if it is also what God thinks is appropriate. The way one discerns God's desires is by following the path he lays out, and if obstacles are too onerous, one must conclude that God didn't intend one to take that particular direction. All of this goes back to the redemption of the Exodus from Egypt and God's embrace of his people when they were suffering under slavery.

Bishop Flunder's explanation of all of these processes is uniquely convincing because the congregation fervently believes that she has a special connection with God, that her charismatic gifts open the way for God to speak through her to his people in TFAM. The urgency of the message she is delivering is mediated by music and by the actions of the congregation, as well as by the implication that it is not fully under her control. She's "almost done" several times and explains that she can't find her "script," which doesn't seem to have been in evidence at all. While the scriptural reference is brief, it does confer authority on the sermon in a manner that is typical of African American sermons.

How TFAM Is Different

Bishop Flunder and TFAM depart from COGIC and the other Pentecostal denominations in embracing the idea of salvation through God's grace, the belief that faith alone leads to salvation and that such salvation is not conditional on avoiding sin, a key Baptist doctrine. Many TFAM worshippers grew up in various kinds of Pentecostal churches, but it is important to note that a large proportion of worshippers came from Baptist churches, including Primitive Baptist and Missionary Baptist. Bishop Phyllis Pennese explained to me that Baptists believe that all human beings are condemned to sin, but that God has provided salvation because of his love for mankind. This means that the Pentecostal notion that salvation can only come from avoiding sinful behavior and being committed to praising and worshipping God, and the related conviction that salvation is conditional and may be lost because of sinful behavior, is largely absent from or downplayed in TFAM congregations. TFAM not only embraces congregants regardless of their personal histories but constantly reiterates that they are loved by God no matter who they are. In adopting this dual theology, of course, TFAM reflects the backgrounds—mostly Baptist and Pentecostal—of the core of its worshippers.

TFAM congregations continue, nonetheless, to engage in the forms of worship that are characteristic of Pentecostal churches, including the laying on of hands, holy dancing, speaking in tongues, and other expressions of charismatic gifts. What emerges is an amalgamation of Pentecostal and Baptist doctrine that allows worshippers to experience the kind of expressive, fervent devotion to God that reminds them of the churches they once attended, but to be assured that God's love for them is complete and unconditional.[6]

Nevertheless, Bishop insists that the foundation for leadership in TFAM must rest on solid theological training, drawing on her refusal to be classified as a "para-preacher." It should be noted that this requirement is related to the emphasis she places on understanding Scripture as historically and culturally specific rather than as infallible. TFAM members are urged to be aware that what the Hebrew Bible and the New Testament say about sexuality, to mention the key area of contention for most members, cannot be interpreted without a knowledge of the time in which these texts were written as well as an appreciation for the vagaries of translation from the original Hebrew and Greek into English, a task that was carried out under differing historical conditions (Gomes 1996; Helminiak 2000 [1994]; Metzger 2001). This position serves as a strong foundation to the challenge that TFAM poses to the toxic positions taken by so many churches against their LGBT members. Sufficient education will allow one to dismantle the conventional renderings of the Hebrew and Greek texts. Once that has been accomplished, the systematic disparagement of people with nonconforming gender or sexual presentations (or those who are different in some other way) cannot be sustained.

What Follows Charismatic Leadership?

Bishop Yvette Flunder possesses qualities that mark her as charismatic, both in the social and spiritual sense of that term. She has a captivating personal demeanor that puts even skeptics at ease, but while those who hear her speak may move into altered states and exhibit the charismatic gifts of the Spirit, their reverence for her is tempered by her insistence on presenting herself as a fallible human, not necessarily sure of the answers to all questions. Still, the question of what will happen if Bishop Flunder dies or retires hovers in the air with no clear resolution in sight. Some church members locate their devotion to City of Refuge and TFAM in her charismatic presence and can't imagine sustaining their involvement if she was no longer the head of TFAM and the pastor of City of Refuge. Others insist that there are other powerful leaders who will be able to step up to the challenges of leading TFAM, even though they are not prepared to name the person (or persons) who will step into the breach.

Bishop Flunder possesses the qualities that Weber and other scholars have identified as definitive features of charisma. Yet her impact on church members also depends on her refusal to be cast as an extraordinary figure who stands above her adherents. This is, indeed, part of her charismatic appeal—the fact that she doesn't embrace the trappings of incomparability and willingly seeks important leadership and spiritual capacities in those around her. She radiates a kind of charisma that paradoxically resists its own authority and is perhaps even more commanding for that reason.

It seems that the combination of her ordinary, prosaic humanness and her extraordinary ability to perceive the needs of others—conveying knowledge in a way that makes it applicable to understanding the dilemmas of daily life—are what endow her with charisma. How TFAM will manage when she eventually steps down is unclear. Certainly, encouraging clergy and lay members to get seminary education is part of a larger plan to develop future leaders. But whether they will have the unique combination of simple humanness, authenticity, and gifts that she traces to God's plan for her remains to be seen.

THREE

"Just as I Am": Revealing Authentic Selves

Pastor Troy Sanders, now the leader of a congregation in Atlanta that is part of TFAM, told me the story of his long struggle with coming out as gay.

> I had an encounter with God, a very literal encounter with God. I went away to pray, which I would often do. And in this time, I said, "Well, why won't you deliver me? Like, if you don't deliver me, just let me die." And I remember hearing the Lord ask me a question, "When have I ever asked you to change?" And I thought to myself and I started naming all of the times that I've heard sermons in my mind like "Of course you were that word, that bishop and that pastor." And the second voice, the second question was "When have I ever asked you to change?" And the second part of that question I remember was, "When have I ever stopped using you, knowing who you are?" It was a real—we call it a "coming to Jesus" moment.

Pastor Sanders had long understood that he was gay but had feared that this would make it impossible for him to continue to be a preacher, an identity that he had held since his teenage years. He had carefully guarded the secret, but this encounter with God convinced him that he could no longer conceal his sexuality. He explains how this came to pass.

> I heard it from a place that was not from my audible ear but from deep within my being. . . . And the questions, they weren't just like hearing things in the wind. But it . . . resonated in me. It shook my core. And the result of it was very clear that there had been, it was

something more than just something I conjured up in my mind. And so I started the process to come out. And I went back to my therapist. . . . And I started. I called my family; I came out to my mom. My grandmother had passed by that time. And I started to walk in truth, and I took a really hard hit for it. But for me, my integrity would not allow me [to lie any longer].

"Don't ask, don't tell" is a mandate that once applied not only to lesbian and gay participation in the US military, but that has long been a way of life for gays, lesbians, and transgender members of African American Christian churches. As we have seen, black churches typically attempt to deny the existence of LGBT people in their community. But, on the other hand, many accounts by black lesbian, gay, or transgender people speak to a long tradition of congregations ignoring often blatant departures from heteronormativity as long as these congregants refrain from explicitly articulating their identities.

Of course, the problem of recognizing the presence of LGBT congregants is hardly confined to black churches. As I noted earlier, it has not been uncommon, to say the least, for LGBT Christians to make significant contributions to their churches—participation in the choir or as organist, for example—with the (spoken or unspoken) proviso that they need to tone down their appearance when performing their duties in the church. Scholars who have studied the experience of LGBT Christians have provided abundant evidence of the painful dilemmas faced by those who want to maintain a religious affiliation, but can do this only at the price of secrecy and shame. For some, affiliation with a particular church is embedded in personal and family history, linked to a hometown, to lifelong social connections, and to cherished memories. In some other cases, life experience, including the intense self-reflection occasioned by the coming-out process, opens up a need for a spiritual home, with a religious institution functioning as a refuge from the pressures of the world. Even when that is so, however, continuing participation in a church might be obtained at the price of unrelenting pressure to be more "normal," to move through life transitions, including heterosexual marriage, on the same trajectory as others in the congregation (Shallenberger 1998). While some choose to endure the discomfort of continuing to worship without revealing their identities, attempts to "solve" the problem may include curtailing religious observance altogether, finding a tolerant mainstream congregation, or joining an alternative religious organization that makes a specific outreach to lesbian, gay, and other members of sexual or gender minorities (Barton 2012; Gorman 1980; Shallenberger 1998; Shokeid

1995). For some, managing two identities that are apparently contradictory involves a constant struggle.

Sociologist Richard N. Pitt (2009, 2010) has written compellingly of how gay black men devise strategies that will enable them to remain in apparently unwelcoming churches. Along similar lines, Krista McQueeney (2009) explains that lesbian church members engage in something she calls "oppositional identity work," reversing Christian language and beliefs that define homosexuality as sinful to craft "good Christian identities" (152). The strategies McQueeney describes, particularly in the predominantly black, working-class church where she conducted research among lesbians, include "minimizing, normalizing, and moralizing" sexuality. Minimizing involves foregrounding racial identity, allowing black lesbian congregants to continue to define themselves as good Christians (157–59). Normalizing is achieved by highlighting adherence to monogamy and fidelity in their relationships, thereby distancing themselves from the promiscuity assumed to be central to the gay world and also by accentuating their commitment to such key feminine institutions as motherhood (159–66). Finally, moralizing emerges when some lesbian worshippers assert that their sexual identity is actually a "blessing," something God had entreated them to assume as part of a special calling (166–69), and thus neither sinful nor indicative of some sort of curse.

Still, for many, such strategies are not workable or cannot overcome the stigma their church membership conferred on them. This might mean exclusion from a home church, sometimes going as far as a kind of excommunication or expulsion known as "disfellowshipping," to be described later in this chapter, which presents many black (and often white) LGBT people with a serious dilemma if they are to remain true to notions of moral responsibility that they have absorbed Sunday after Sunday in their churches. The possibility of experiencing marginalization in or exclusion from the church puts pressure on LGBT worshippers since it opens the door to total removal from a world that they value deeply. On one level, black LGBT church involvement highlights issues of identity management that recall the performative maneuvers that Erving Goffman (1963) described being pursued by persons with stigmatized identities. For some blacks who are LGBT, the tension leads to a permanent rift with the church; for others, as I've indicated, remaining in the church may be possible only at the cost of honesty and personal dignity. For still others, finding a religious community that welcomes LGBT members (such as the Metropolitan Community Church [MCC] or some mainstream churches like the United Church of Christ [UCC] and the Unitarian-Universalist

Association that have declared themselves open and affirming) offers a solution; in this case, the presence of other queer parishioners alleviates the isolation they face in most churches, though the liturgical style may not resemble that of the black church and thus not meet their needs for expressive worship. As Episcopal priest Horace Griffin (2006) points out, some black LGBT Christians may fear encountering racism in predominantly white churches, a justifiable source of anxiety, given the history of racism among white LGBT people, even if they share a sexual orientation with the other members. They must reach a decision about how to balance threats of homophobia and racism, a choice that offers no easy solution.

Coming Out

Gay rights advocates have long argued that coming out—acknowledging one's non-normative gender or sexual identity to oneself, but most critically to others—is beneficial to the mental health of LGBT people and also foundational to political mobilization in support of gay rights agendas. Coming out has been celebrated, elaborated, demanded, and sometimes imposed on the unwilling. The stories that LGBT people tell about the experience of coming out are structured around the risks individuals face when they decide to take this step. Indeed, the "coming-out story" is a genre that has specific features—usually a claim that LGBT identity is an innate characteristic, that revealing it is essential to achieving optimal mental health, but that coming out may also be dangerous, threatening the individual with being ostracized from non-gay circles—whether these be made up of family, friends, coworkers, or fellow church congregants. Coming-out stories depend in large part on a narrative of essence and coherence, with a basic plot line involving discovery of one's "real" identity, a revelation that then demands a course of action that will allow that identity to flourish (Weston 1991; Zimmerman 1984). For many, the discovery leads to moving to a location deemed more "gay-friendly"; for others, particularly those who lack education and financial resources, such geographical relocation is impossible, so they must devise strategies that will make being gay more manageable in their home community (Gray 2009).

Telling one's coming-out story is a kind of cultural performance, often an almost ritualized part of getting acquainted with new LGBT people, but sometimes also demanded by non-LGBT acquaintances. "How did you figure out you were gay?" is a typical kind of question non-LGBT people may ask, assuming that this aspect of one's identity has a self-conscious history attached to it. Coming out is understood to have a structure not expected for the unmarked process surrounding heteronormative coming of age; being lesbian or gay, in other words, demands an explanation, and the explanations that are given are usually predictable and culturally conventional. It's a given in the popular understanding of coming out that revealing one's sexuality may lead family members to reject a person or that even in the absence of outright rejection, some estrangement and distancing is apt to occur. In fact, LGBT people who report familial acceptance rather than rejection are treated as rare icons of a bright future, their parents and other relatives effusively showered with gratitude (Weston 1991). I observed similar patterns in lesbian and gay wedding ceremonies I studied, as family members who attended were treated as heroes (Lewin 1998), though given the greater visibility of non-heteronormative people in recent years, one can expect this pattern to have diminished and to have been replaced by at least partial acceptance.

As Kath Weston has shown (1991), coming out has sometimes been equated with rebirth after death, with the period of being in the closet understood as a kind of spiritual death. In many instances, the very experience of recognizing one's homosexuality or discomfort with one's assigned gender bears the imprimatur of revelation. Its authenticity—the discovery that one was "always" this way but couldn't admit it or understand it—seems to flow from ineffable sources. For a religious person, then, the logic is that if one's basic nature is given by God, then one's homosexuality or non-heteronormative gender identity is especially sacred, and refusing to acknowledge it requires one to reject God's plan and to be dishonest in God's sight. Anthropologist Mary Gray documented such sentiments in her book on LGBT youth in Appalachia, where most families attended fundamentalist or evangelical churches, which we might expect to be unreflectively rejecting (Barton 2012). Still, one mother expressed her support for her child's transition from female to male as follows: "'Well, in my book, God don't make trash.... [M]y child is my child. ... I can't understand any parent rejecting their child for how they feel'" (Gray 2009: 162–63).

Similar perspectives come up in TFAM sermons when pastors say something along the lines of "God doesn't make mistakes." The notion that one's personhood is the result of God's intention is essential to these interpretations; each of us was made in the image of God even as these images are almost indescribably diverse (Moon 2014). In seeking to legitimate the desire of same-sex couples to marry, Episcopal Bishop John Shelby Spong explains, "Homosexual orientation is a minority but perfectly natural characteristic on the human spectrum of sexuality" (Spong 1988: 198). Similarly, Troy Perry, the Pentecostal preacher who founded the Metropolitan Community Church, describes his discovery of the importance of coming out: "We homosexuals must all learn to rid ourselves of the sense of shame that we have been conditioned to accept from the heterosexual world.... How could we go on being ashamed of something that God created? Yes, God created homosexuals and homosexuality. It [sic] exists throughout history, and all over the world" (Perry 1972: 3). Catholic priest and theologian Daniel Helminiak puts it this way:

> According to faith, it is God who creates us. Divine Providence forms us as we are. Our genes, our temperaments, our time and place in history, our talents, our gifts, our strengths and weaknesses—all are part of God's inscrutable and loving plan for us. So somehow God must be behind the fact that some people are homosexual. Then why should God's word in the Bible condemn homosexuality? There must be a mistake in the reasoning somewhere. (Helminiak 2000 [1994]: 26–27)

Sociologist Jodi O'Brien describes this process as "transforming a discourse of shame and silence ... into a narrative of pride and expression ... based on a belief that homosexuality has a place in God's plan" (O'Brien 2004: 194).

The Politics of Coming Out

Scholars of LGBT life have long been interested in coming out as either a psychological or political phenomenon. The psychological approach emphasizes the mental health benefits to be gained, presumably, by refusing to conceal one's "true" identity. An early consideration of these issues was offered by Barry Dank (1971) who examined the process by which individuals realize that they are homosexual. Other investigations attempted to delineate stages by which homosexuals come to terms with their identity and, presumably, accept it and integrate it into their social lives, distinguishing in many cases between its private and public dimensions (Cass 1979). Not surprisingly, a central focus of many of these inquiries has been identity formation among homosexual youth (Savin-Williams 2005) and in recent years has examined how changes in the public status of sexual minorities have affected this process, presumably ameliorating some of the more painful aspects of recognizing that one is LGBT.

Anthropologists have taken somewhat different approaches to this issue. Gilbert Herdt (1992) examined the coming-out struggles of young people in Chicago and tried to show that their process took the form of a classic rite of passage. In other work on youth in Chicago, Herdt and his coauthor psychiatrist Andrew Boxer (1993) described the support offered at a gay community center that helps young people find their way through the coming-out process. In her research with LGBT youth in Appalachia, Mary L. Gray (2009) detailed how young people used the Internet to locate others with whom they could identify and resources that might help them resolve continuing conflicts with family and community. Research on ex-gay groups has taken a different angle of approach, documenting the difficult process of moving from being gay to straight and showing that most who participated in a particular ex-gay group in fact land somewhere in the middle (Erzen 2006; Gerber 2011; Wolkomir 2006), as neither definitively straight or gay, but rather "ex-gay."

As gay and lesbian people have struggled to achieve more social legitimacy and to gain access to a variety of civil rights, coming out has come to count as a kind of political move that demands visibility (Weeks 1979). Because of this political emphasis, the phenomenon of "outing" persons who deny or conceal their homosexuality, especially when such persons are culturally or politically prominent, came to the fore in the 1980s. This articulation of revealing a person's identity meant that secrecy was equated with a kind of social cowardice, evidence that one had given in to the homophobic pressures of the wider society by refusing to acknowledge one's gay or lesbian self. This was understood not only as harmful to the individual, but as a move that compromised the position of other LGBT people or brought more social opprobrium down on visible gay and lesbian people (Gross 1993, 1999, 2001; Signorile 1999).

But some scholars have questioned the continuing utility of the political impulses that fueled the early gay rights movement. Indeed, a major theme in some recent queer scholarship has been to resurrect and embrace gay and lesbian shame as a way to resist incorporation into regimes of what Lisa Duggan (2003) has called "homonormativity." These approaches, then, read shame not primarily as painful but as courageous, a perspective that drives most of the contributions to the volume *Gay Shame*, edited by David Halperin and Valerie Traub (2009). As sociologist Barry Adam notes in his essay in the Halperin and Traub volume, gay shame might be considered the antithesis of gay pride, but rather than embracing pride, he criticizes it as the foundation of what he sees as a trend to commercialize gayness. He argues that a resurgence of shame would move some back to a pre-pride world in which commercial interests and "homonormativity" had not yet surfaced and meaningful community formation was more possible (Adam 2009).

None of these approaches considers the situation of people of color who are also LGBT and for whom shame might have other resonances than those embraced by contributors to this volume. Racism inflects these stories in ways that white queer people don't generally take the time to imagine; sexuality among African Americans, in particular, collides with ascriptions of shame and disgrace in ways that go beyond the particular meanings of non-normativity (Collins 2004).

Racial Complications

As pervasive as the preoccupation with coming out is, a number of black gay scholars have questioned how such concerns have come to dominate accounts of how gay and lesbian people manage their identities. Marlon Ross (2005), for example, has called our attention to rarely noted parallels between ideas about recognition of the gay body and discourses relating to race as they emerge in American culture. Citing the work of feminist American studies scholar Robyn Wiegman on the politics of visibility (1995), Ross points to the ways in which coming out has been linked to progress narratives that highlight the experience of white middle-class gay and lesbian subjects and virtually erase how class and race may intersect with "coming out." For example, he asks us to consider the extent to which narratives of gay migration do or do not resemble stories of the Great Migration, pointing out that the motives and contours of the latter are unlikely to be similar to the former. And he emphasizes the ways in which coming-out narratives seem to preclude the primitive qualities still clinging to understandings of racial difference (see, for example, Baker 1998), as they depend on notions of progress toward modernity. In other words, narratives of queer migration to cities have been assumed to constitute a form of progress, while other stories of movement (or lack thereof) have received little attention (see also Gray 2009, on how young, low-income queers from small towns in Appalachia deal with the challenges of crafting identities when migration is neither feasible nor necessarily desired). Ross argues persuasively that the dominant account of coming out and indeed of the gay body offered by Foucault and his followers resolutely summons up a white middle-class image (Foucault 1990; and following him, such scholars as Sedgwick [1990] and Halperin [1995]).

Both C. Riley Snorton (2014) and Jeffrey Q. McCune Jr. (2014) take up the much-debated matter of the "down low" (DL) as a designation for black men who have sex with men. McCune, for example, has linked the DL to broader, and very necessary, practices that have evolved among black people for concealing their true feelings, particularly in the arena of sexuality. Following Darlene Clark Hine's analysis (1989) of how "a culture of dissemblance" protects women from potentially dangerous scrutiny of their sexual lives, McCune urges us to understand the DL, and the wider arena of what he calls "discretion," as part of a general pattern of secrecy, rather than as a unique and dishonorable expression of shame.

Snorton uses some of the same approaches but gives especially close attention to the production of the DL in the environment of the black church. He points in particular to the seeming paradox of gender nonconformity in the deportment of choir members and the pretense that none of these men are gay. His reading of the 2010 Eddie Long scandal focuses on the varied responses generated by the revelations that Bishop Long, who had long been vociferous in opposing gay rights, was in fact leading a secret sex life on the DL. In much of the copious publicity that attached to the stories, Bishop Long's misdeeds—both having sex with men and being a hypocrite—were cast as representative of black men and the black church, what many already believed even before the scandal erupted. Both McCune and Snorton are essentially theorizing the accounts offered by black gay men in their personal narratives, most of which illustrate the pressures to dissemble and the consequences of failing to do so successfully. In doing so, they develop themes that appear in the stories offered by E. Patrick Johnson in *Sweet Tea* (2008), and also extend some of the concerns that animate personal narratives such as those by Keith Boykin (2005) and Kai Wright (2008), also echoing some of the contributors whose accounts appear in Joseph Beam's classic *In the Life* (1986).[1]

Other scholarly work has attempted to move the question of coming out into a context that depends on an understanding of intersectionality—in other words, that coming out might not have the same meaning in communities of color or among immigrants. Following this logic, Latino studies scholar Carlos Decena (2011) has argued for a more fluid understanding of identity that challenges the all-or-nothing reading of coming out. Not unlike the contributors to the Halperin and Traub volume, he links the widely accepted emphasis on coming out to the normalization of a particular kind of gay and lesbian identity. "Given the growing legitimacy of predominantly white and middle-class lesbians and gay men in this country and of models that presume and uphold individual decision making, refusals of speech, pride, and visibility have been generally interpreted as suspect, as evidence of denial or internalized homophobia, or as outright pathology" (Decena 2011: 18). Decena further claims, "Instead of being the beginning of a project of social transformation—as coming out was understood in the early days of gay liberation—

individual self-realization through speech has been severed from collective social change. Today, one comes out not to change the world but to be a 'normal' gay subject" (18). His critique draws on his examination of the lives of Dominican gay men living in the United States, where he finds that coming out can be superfluous for subjects whose sexuality is already tacitly understood, "neither secret nor silent" (19). In Dominican families, the implicit agreement to not talk about particular topics is part of an ethic that situates sexuality as private and not an appropriate topic for discussion. In this context, according to Decena, formal acts of coming out are redundant and produce needless stress.

Taking a different approach, anthropologist Elizabeth Kennedy (1996) has evocatively described the subtle ways in which lesbian identity was both secret and hidden in early twentieth century Deadwood, South Dakota, an arrangement that allowed lesbian women considerable freedom from surveillance. Her close reading of the life history of a lesbian who lived in Deadwood in this period suggests that rather than discretion being necessarily oppressive and productive of shame, it allowed lesbians to combine full integration into the wider society with the formation of woman-centered spaces. While the external pressures to conform to societal norms—for example, to marry men—persisted through this period and often interfered with lesbian social life, the valorization of coming out that followed the increasing visibility of lesbians later in the twentieth century depended on a rigid "dichotomy between heterosexual and homosexual [that became] hegemonic" (Kennedy 1996: 39). Such an inflexible categorization didn't necessarily meet the needs of lesbians who did not wish to be isolated from the wider society.

The approaches to mandatory coming out that have been taken in queer and cultural studies are noteworthy for their lack of relevance to the experiences of TFAM members, particularly vis-à-vis the quest for spiritual fulfillment that Fellowship worshippers seek. Queer scholarship has rarely engaged with the spiritual dimensions of LGBT experience; indeed, it considers virtually every aspect of LGBT life *except* for spirituality. Importantly, shame has a very different meaning in the context of religion than it has in the abstracted calculus of cultural studies. For those who were raised in the judgmental worlds of most Christian churches, shame has to do with losing a chance at salvation, to being doomed to suffer in the eternal fires of hell, and to being thrust out of the embrace of one's church family. This means that it is vital for TFAM members to overcome the onus of shame and banish it from their lives, and thus to feel that they deserve to receive God's love. Resisting the impulse to promote shame as productive of a form of cultural transgression means regaining access to

God's love and restoring the basis for claims to full membership in one's family and church. This sense of entitlement may not match the treatment one receives from the family or the church, but if a person feels certain that she deserves to be regarded as worthy, it may be easier to endure rejection and disparagement.

Coming Out and Religion

Coming out may also have spiritual dimensions that lead individuals to rethink their involvement in religious institutions, sometimes intensifying their need to be in conversation with God. The experience has sometimes been compared to a conversion experience, in that the "truth" of the newly discovered or acknowledged identity appears with blinding clarity, prompting a reexamination of old assumptions. Those who have recently come out may rethink their religious and spiritual needs, and rededicate themselves to a more personally authentic worship practice. They may come to see their old practices as steeped in hypocrisy, reevaluating their spiritual mentors and intensifying their efforts to lead spiritually fulfilling lives. They may also repudiate feelings of shame they may have long experienced before finding the courage to come out, either to themselves or to others. TFAM members I spoke with consistently linked their belief that they must conceal their sexual orientation to alienation from the spiritual benefits of church attendance.

For persons who have strong religious attachments, their connection to church (which many call their "church family") may take on a role in coming-out narratives that resembles stories of revelation to family. An individual's pastor may figure as a close adviser and mentor, and bonds with other members of a church community not infrequently take on the contours of kinship, particularly as they are often linked to long-term personal histories. But in this context, coming out, as necessary as it seems to be, may be seen as dangerous on many levels: a person not only may be cast out of her/his blood family, but also runs the risk of being expelled from one's spiritual home. Even if one believes that God demands honesty, the rejection by one's church carries implications of intractable sin, of isolation from the exultation to be achieved through collective observance of religious practices and, especially for African Americans, exclusion from a historical source of support and identity affirmation. This is the conflict that emerges repeatedly in the stories of TFAM congregants.

I characterize finding a queer-friendly church or one that welcomes

CHAPTER THREE

LGBT members as a *social* solution to the problem of gender and sexual difference in the context of religious observance. Such solutions promote a sense of comfort and safety, of course, as joining a welcoming church allows a continuing involvement with Christian worship and reduces the pressure to "act straight" on Sundays. But while the struggle to balance seemingly incompatible identities is an important part of the story of black LGBT Christians, as it also may be for white LGBT Christians, it cannot be resolved solely by the existence of a friendlier environment. As I've indicated, particular liturgical practices are the hallmark of the black church, something social solutions do not, in and of themselves, fully facilitate. What TFAM members are looking for, in contrast, is something far greater than a safe social environment; they want access to a source of profound spiritual inspiration that will allow them to experience inhabitation by the Holy Spirit and the gifts that come from being filled with the Spirit.

Thus, in the calculus of TFAM, as I will show, coming out takes on a new meaning, as does finding and joining a church that is not only safe, but likely to bring oneself closer to spiritual fulfillment. It becomes a religious or spiritual obligation, indeed, a central element of worship, and thus a first necessary step toward spiritual cleansing and being filled with the Holy Spirit. The necessity of declaring oneself, of seeking and sharing an authentic self, then, is no longer only a personal achievement or a social obligation. It is, instead, an absolute requirement in the quest for spiritual wholeness and communion with God. Coming out in this context erases the contradiction between identities: one is simply a whole person who wishes to allow the Holy Spirit into her life. Thus, communion with the Holy Spirit both demands and enables coming out, allowing congregants to achieve more authentic identities through direct communication with Jesus and to do so in a context that draws on the expressive worship style of the black church.

The theme of coming out was at the heart of the major ceremonial event at the 2009 national Fellowship convocation, the celebration marking the twenty-fifth anniversary of the presiding bishop, Yvette Flunder, and her partner, Mother Shirley Miller.[2] Dressed in formal attire, some two hundred celebrants filed into the hotel ballroom for a sit-down dinner and entertainment honoring the couple. Several members offered musical tributes to the deep love shared by the two women, while others made short speeches about what the example of their relationship meant to them personally. Many of the speakers began with accounts of having been ostracized from the churches and communities in which they had been raised because of who they loved. Some spoke of the kinds of problems that come up in relationships, or about their own difficulties sustaining commitments. In each case, the love of Bishop and Mother was invoked as a model that not only can inspire the members of their home church and the Fellowship, but that can serve as a spiritual foundation for the coalition.

The most intimate comments about the relationship came from Bishop's daughter, who spoke at some length, and with considerable humor (and some tears), about growing up with Bishop and Mother, who began their relationship when she was six years old. She was always told to refer to Mother as "Auntie Shirley," and neither she nor Auntie Shirley's daughter, also a part of the household, understood the nature of the relationship for many years. "We did not know that they were together for many years, which is how 'Auntie Shirley' came about." The whole family eventually moved to their own house together, but the two women concealed their relationship, as they were still active members of the Church of God in Christ, which demonized their sexuality and left them no language for describing their love.

All this secrecy, as she tells the story, was a strain on the family, with the two girls feeling confusion and anger until they finally confronted their mothers, who confirmed what the teenaged girls had come to suspect. She emphasized that having to make sense of this information while attending a church where sex is "just not talked about"—that is, with no organized support—created a situation that was very difficult and affected all the family relationships. Even as these remarks emphasized comical incidents and the tragic ironies of her mother's (and as it turns out, her father's) closeted behavior, she returned repeatedly to the ways in which secrecy had at least temporarily crippled her relationship with her mother and the ways in which it could have—but ultimately didn't—undermine the bond between her mother and her partner. Not only did Bishop and Mother's union survive this long period of secrecy—some ten years—but their commitment to God never wavered. The story concluded with a description of the ceremony the two women had to celebrate their marriage, clear evidence of their triumph over the closet. In her remarks following this tribute, Bishop Flunder summed up the nature of their achievement as a lesbian couple: "We came out together. If you can come out in the Pentecostal Church, you can do anything."

Beyond acknowledging the negative impact of the closet in the lives of church members, however, through personal testimonials like that of Bishop and her daughter, preaching at church services frequently takes up the theme of the spiritual dangers of being closeted. At one service I attended in San Francisco, a church member came forward to offer testimony about her encounter with Jesus. She began her comments wearing a mask that covered her entire face and explained that this is who she was before she came out: she couldn't even have recognized herself if she'd looked in the mirror. She spoke compellingly of making bad sexual choices, abusing drugs, and other behaviors that undermined her ability to have an honest relationship with anyone in her life. When she finally came out as "a same-gender-loving woman," the mask came off—she removed the mask as she explained this—and she was able to absorb the message of the Holy Spirit that worship at her church made possible.

Coming to Jesus

It is clear that TFAM members trace their ability to reveal their identities to particularly powerful spiritual encounters. Pastor Troy Sanders, who now occupies a leadership position in TFAM, began preaching in an Apostolic church while still a teenager, knowing that he had a calling. He told me a story of deep commitment to the church, followed by despair when he realized he was gay.

> **PASTOR SANDERS:** I knew that I was gay, I knew I was same-gender-loving but had no context around being affirmed, and so I grew up with this dualistic dichotomy going on.
> **EL:** So were you scared that this made you, that this was sending you to hell or that you were a sinner?
> **PS:** I think, Ellen, . . . the principal feeling was not that of fear but of . . . disappointment, in some way that I disappointed God by being gay. . . . [T]he earliest feelings that I can kind of connect with are the fear of Hell. Everybody in the church, in the Pentecostal church, was scared of going to hell! You was scared of going to hell for eating too much. You was scared of going to hell for not paying tithes. You was scared of going to hell for everything. If you didn't fast if you were sick. If you didn't dance in a couple of Sundays, you might be hell bound. You know, the idea of hell . . . was very prevalent but it wasn't the determination for me. The church . . . taught me that homosexuality was wrong but my life had been in the church. From a child, I'd given my life. And I just didn't understand how this God who I had loved would not deliver me. So there was a sense of deep-seated disappointment.
> **EL:** Did you want to be not gay anymore?
> **PS:** Oh, certainly, certainly. I went through the process in the beginning [with] the Exodus movement, the ex-gay movement, had private calls with, you know, bishops and pastors, you know, "I want to be delivered from this homo-

sexual spirit" because that's the language they gave me. And I went through torment: at my largest, I was 330 pounds.

EL: Oh my goodness! So you sublimated it into eating.

PS: Absolutely. Total depression and all of this time I spent, I started preaching at fifteen, and I spent the last two years of high school and all four years of my undergrad traveling full-time.

EL: As a preacher?

PS: As a preacher. So I averaged about thirty to thirty-five revivals a year. Thirty to thirty-five weeks out of the year.

EL: Around a region or where?

PS: Around the country and internationally. And all along I was killing myself softly inside.

Pastor Sanders even made himself deliver anti-gay sermons, part of his effort to make himself fit into his role as a preacher. "I was trained to do that. . . . [I]f you didn't, you were automatically questioned. If you did not have a sermon or two in your belt about the adulterous fornication, then you were questioned." But following the death of his grandmother, he began to question the path he was taking, realizing that the various therapeutic models he had pursued had not changed his orientation. He went into therapy to deal with his grief about his grandmother's death and began to accept himself as he was. But the key factor that helped him change was a spiritual encounter that took place when he was about twenty, when he had a close encounter with God, described in the opening of this chapter, in which God told him he had never wanted him to change.

After this transformation, Pastor Sanders realized that he could no longer attend a church he felt was abusive toward him, and so he left the church where he had worshipped for most of his life. He located an affirming church in Atlanta and began the process of reconnecting with religion in a location where he was accepted.

So I went to this affirming church and it was a culture shock for me. This was the first time I had seen another culture, another community of affirming people and believers. And during this time, I went from thirty revivals to literally none. So when I came out, it caused the implications in the Christian communities that I was a part of, [and] I got ostracized. Totally got alienated.

The church had invited Bishop Flunder's mother, Mother Langston, to lead a revival, and Pastor Sanders picked her up at the airport. After talking for a while, Mother Langston told him:

CHAPTER THREE

"Oh, you got to meet my daughter. As a matter of fact, she'll be at Emory doing a class in two weeks and I'll make sure of that." And sure enough, she did. I got a call from Bishop Flunder when she got to Atlanta and [she] said, "My mother says we should meet." And Bishop Flunder and Mother Shirley sat down, and I have been a part of Bishop Flunder's life ever since. It just . . . It spoke to a deep place in me. Seeing the Fellowship, hearing her words. And I'll never forget that first conversation. I felt like my life was pretty much ending. And I had suffered a lot in ministry financial[ly], both financially and socially. . . . I remember sitting across the table from them and I was crying and she said, "Baby, accept [that] you will allow your ministry to die. God can never bring it back in resurrection power. It'll never live again until it dies. It has to die from what it was to become what it will be." And I never forgot those words. Never forgot those words.

Refusing Hypocrisy

We met George Howard in chapter 1. His story of navigating the Chicago area in an effort to find a church where he would feel at home as a gay person is typical of many TFAM members' experiences. George grew up in a Pentecostal church in the Deep South. He explains that sexuality, let alone homosexuality, was rarely discussed there. George describes the church:

They call us Fundamental Pentecostal because there are quite a few rules. No makeup, no jewelry, no drop neck fronts for the women, nothing that exposes your breasts. . . . Skirts below the knee, just very fundamental in Pentecostal beliefs. And sexuality was rarely discussed in that church. They didn't really harp on homosexuality, but they would mention that a woman should not be with a woman and a man should not be with a man. They said man was made for a woman, woman made for man. . . . So there wasn't so much the badgering from the pulpit, but it was definitely not accepted there.

George touches on several themes later in the conversation, including the issue of hypocrisy: even as pastors are inveighing against homosexuality, their congregations, and especially their choirs, include numerous gay people. Music has long been the ministry to which LGBT people, especially gay men, are drawn and where they often serve even as they are disparaged from the pulpit. Later in the interview, George tells me about his many attempts to "cure" himself of his sexuality, in his case by means of fasting and prayer. He also came to the realization that God had made him just as he is; attempting to change his authentic identity would constitute an accusation that God had made a mistake, a claim that is unacceptable in its essence.

But not going to church made him feel incomplete, so he made a number of efforts to find a church that would meet his needs.

It was because having grown up in the church, there was a huge void. I'm not a fan of the electric church, you know the television or the radio. It's not like being in fellowship with other people. And so it was, it was a huge void for quite some time. But I just preferred not being in the atmosphere where I felt I was not being true to myself.

In other words, George was looking for a collective location where he could worship God with a like-minded and supportive congregation, where he would no longer have to endure the hypocrisy and hostility of a homophobic church environment. He tried an Apostolic church for a while that a friend had recommended. But he didn't find a comfortable situation there.

When we got there, the minister was doing a fiery sermon and as he backed toward the end, he came down on homosexuals. He said something to the effect that he couldn't see how people could be homosexuals. He couldn't imagine how a man could be laying up in the bed with another man, his big crusty feet up against my crusty feet. And you know when the offering came around—pretty much before I go to a church, I pretty much know what I am able to give and willing to give—and when offering time came around, almost like clockwork, [I] opened my wallet, took out what I was going to give and had a flashback to what he said in the pulpit, and I said to myself, "Why would I support any of that?" and I put my money back in my pocket, and the person who was taking up the collection happened to be right there and seen me do it. And they looked at me with this look of bewilderment as if to say, "What are you doing?" And I reached for the pan, held my money in my hand, and passed the pan right along. And that was one of the points. Another point of my life when I said no more am I going to support something that is against me, I just knew that that is a part of being the hypocrite that was supporting what I heard from the pulpit. And looking around the congregation and seeing the number of homosexuals I've been seeing all over the city and at different functions, you know cheering this man on while he bashed them from the pulpit.

His next effort to find a comfortable congregation involved Trinity United Church of Christ, well known as the Chicago church then headed by Rev. Dr. Jeremiah Wright that President Barack Obama had attended

CHAPTER THREE

with his family. George describes it as claiming to be affirming, though he didn't see this put in action. Around this time, his cousin "Wendell Barrett" arrived in Chicago. Wendell had also grown up in a conservative black church, though the Baptist church where he was raised had a more restrained worship style than George's home church. He was a musician and made the rounds of lots of different churches to play gospel music, but he was still having a hard time finding a church where he could feel comfortable as a gay man. His experience in southern black churches was similar to George's.

All of these churches, all of the better musicians—I may be a little biased—but all the better musicians, the more commonly sought-after musicians, all of them are gay. All of them, even the ones that are married. In small towns that I find, there is a lot of that in churches. Especially black churches, you have a lot of homosexual men married with children carrying on relationships and people look the other way. Everyone kinda knows and as long as there's not a big scandal, you know someone finding out in a big way. No one says anything and it goes on for years.

Wendell continues:

In the South, charismatic church—this is just my opinion, belief, there's no fact in this—I think a lot of closeted gay men are attracted to religion and particularly charismatic, Pentecostal, that kind of [church], in the South because for them, it's a good place to hide. As long as they're there standing up, they're bashing from the pulpit. No one would ever expect that in actuality those are the ones that are out there sneaking around doing things. The assumption is in the South when you're a musician, saying you're a musician, a church musician especially, is the same as saying I'm gay. . . . So, it's not uncommon for ministers, deacons, men who feel like when there's no one around, to be overt and forward and make passes at you. These could be married men, and it's supposed to be like, "Well, you're a musician aren't you?" Because somehow, there's this supposedly unspoken. . . . Because they feel like, "I'm a deacon or a pastor, [so] I can't go to gay clubs or hang around with gay people. Because you know, then my reputation. But you're a musician and that means you're gay and you're in the church, people see us talking and that's okay, because we work in the church together." It's like, that always bothered me. In fact, that's one of the main reasons why for a long period of time. . . . I stopped working in black churches. I only worked in predominately white churches, then unfortunately I got another kind of backlash because people would say, "Oh, he has [an] identity crisis. He's confused." And I know who I am. You know what I found in predominately white churches [was] that they never approached me like that. In the South, unless I told them, they never made the assumption.

Wendell found Pillar of Love through a man he was dating and soon introduced George to it. At that time, it was meeting at the [Gay Community] Center on Halsted, and so was easily accessible to other nearby gay venues.

The two men describe their reactions to their first visit to Pillar of Love. Wendell explains, "I was enamored at the fact that it was an open and affirming church with an African American worship style." He was particularly amazed to see a substantial number of transgender worshippers, including female to male.

> WENDELL: I just couldn't believe that these were black people worshipping openly. . . . And really, the transgender that was way beyond anything. . . .
> GEORGE: Down South, oh my goodness, they crucify transfolk. . . .
> WENDELL: You know I'd seen female impersonation but it was always, transgender for me was always male to female, so the other way. . . . And to me it represented theater and show. And I had been coming to Chicago for like twenty years, so at least once a year I go into the Baton [Show Lounge] and see shows, drag shows.

Their discovery of Pillar of Love, then, made it possible for them to worship in a comfortable setting, but also to expand their notions of what kinds of people might share their religious background and spiritual needs.

Disfellowshipping

Many TFAM members had stories of being actively rejected by their churches after coming out, even to the point of being "disfellowshipped," or removed from the membership rolls. "Damon Morris's" story revolved around a particularly dramatic version of this scenario. As a teenager, he had received the call to preach and was licensed through the church he attended with his family, the Church of God of Prophecy, a Pentecostal church similar to COGIC.[3] Although he had felt a call to preach when he was as young as twelve, he finally accepted the call when he was eighteen.

> I was eighteen and I remember it like it was yesterday. I was doing, I was singing a song, doing altar call, and people were praying at the altar and the altar singers were singing behind me and in the midst of the song, what we referenced as the Holy Ghost took over my entire being, and I immediately stopped singing and I jumped over the altar and immediately began preaching up and down the church.

CHAPTER THREE

When I came to myself, I was on the floor and I was crying. I remember my pastor walked up to me, and she helped me get up off the floor and she said, "What is your answer?" And I replied, in tears, I could not even answer, I could just shake my head "yes." And that was what, that's how I accepted my call to preach. I remember when I was down on the floor, I remember the spirit of the Lord telling me that if I were to preach His word, that He would cleanse me from every stain and every issue that I had in my life thus far.

Despite receiving the call to preach, Damon went off to college to study business administration. And that was where he first became aware of his attraction to men and feared that this would alienate him from his church. His partner had been attending church with him, but fellow parishoners assumed that they were just roommates. "I never talked to him about it. It was never a conversation that we had, and I didn't come out the closet for him, but I felt like, if I loved him, then I needed to come out of the closet for me." After some time of managing his divided identity, Damon realized that he could no longer sustain the pretense.

DM: In the middle of Praise and Worship at the church where I was licensed at, the Spirit of the Lord spoke to me and he told me that "Today, I deliver you from lying. Worship me in spirit and truth." At the end of Praise and Worship service, they were going in to the offerings, and the Spirit of the Lord spoke to me and told me to leave. And I left and I drove home and I wrote this detailed letter to my mom, and that's how I came out of the closet. I was disassociated from my church. That was . . . the worst feeling I've ever experienced in my life.
EL: Did you know that was going to happen?
DM: I knew that was going to happen because that was our church's teachings. If you were found, if anyone brought charges against you within the church, then you were, you were disfellowshipped. The charges would be brought to you before the church, and then a vote would be cast to have you disfellowshipped.

This is a step taken when a member of the congregation has been found to be sinful in some way—"any kind of sin that could be proven"—and effectively declares the person to be outside the boundaries that define virtuous Christian living.

Once Damon told his mother, the cat was out of the bag.

DM: I told my mom and she . . . told my pastor and it spreaded [sic] through the family like wildfire. My phone rung. I told my mom, "I know you all are going to disfellowship me, and when you all disfellowship me, I want to be there. I want to be at the church. I want to stand there in front of the church, and I want to be disfellowshipped while I'm standing there. That's my only request."

EL: What was important to you about that?

DM: Well, what was important to me about that is I never watched a believer who was gay continue being a believer. I didn't know what that looked like, but I was always taught by my leaders that you stand for something, or you'll fall for anything. . . . Doesn't matter how hard it is, and so I needed the church to understand that I was not running from them. I was not running from the situation. And I was not running from God. But I will stand here, in a humble state, to let you know that I will stand on who I am.

As the situation progressed, however, Damon was never notified about when the congregational meeting about disfellowshipping him would occur.

So they never told me when I was being disfellowshipped, when the charges were going to be brought before the church for me. At that point, that hurt me more than anything else because this is the church I paid tithes into. This is the church that I advocated for many people who had their own issues, and I don't believe in disfellowshipping, never have. But that was the teachings of the church. But I always showed unconditional love to everyone and anyone regardless of what the issue was. So I felt like it was a slap in my face in that I no longer mattered.

Following his being disfellowshipped, Damon and his partner did some research on "gay churches" and found a listing for an MCC quite a distance from their North Carolina home. Once they started attending services there, people told them of an MCC much closer to where they lived. Attending the MCC church provided them with a safe space to worship, but it was a majority-white congregation, with a style of worship Damon described as "Catholic." His style, by contrast, was quite different.

When I feel the presence of God, I'm one of those people, I lift my hands. I may cry. I may say "Hallelujah" [or] something, and they were very quiet. So when I would do it, when I was done, I would look around and it'd be almost, "I can't believe you're speaking out during church! What's wrong with him?"

And he continued to feel a deep call to preach. After hearing about a young gay man who had committed suicide after telling his family about his sexuality, he remembers:

CHAPTER THREE

And when he, when my good friend told me that, immediately in my spirit, I heard God tell me, "How many have to die before you do what I tell you to do?" And it was at that time, I knew there was no church here . . . and even though that young man was nowhere near us, there was no church here. There was no safe haven for same-gender-loving people. There was no safe haven for people who were struggling and felt rejected by their mainstream or what I call the mainstream churches. So at that time, what happened was, we were going to Winston-Salem and I just believed in God. If it was God's will and God really told me this, then it's going to happen. All I need to do is make preparations. So I began to make preparations. We started going up there, I think in July of 2009; when we got there to Winston-Salem to Reverend Hayes's church, there was some people that had moved from Oklahoma who was attending his church who have a set of friends who also moved from Oklahoma. They moved to Fayetteville, and they were a lesbian couple who had four children. And there was a couple that we had met in Raleigh who had two children, and they told me, "Well, this is what God called you to do. We'll help you get the church started."

The experiences Pastor Damon recounts reveal the centrality of communication with the Holy Spirit as the force that guides many gay and lesbian church members to reveal their identities. Their decision to come out is driven not by adherence to something purely political, but to an understanding of themselves as having been instructed by God to stop lying and to take up the cause of other gay people.

Cleaning Out Closets

A great deal of anticipation greeted Carl Madgett when he came up to the rostrum to preach in July 2009. He was to be the first transgender person to preach at the national convocation of the Fellowship, held at an Atlanta hotel. Carl was introduced at some length by his pastor, who described his spiritual development, how he had achieved the rank of minister in their Chicago congregation, and told us that he had become "like a son" to her as he worked to overcome obstacles to gaining recognition as a transman, including a disappointing experience in another LGBT-oriented church where the pastors insisted on calling him by the name he had as a woman. She also pointed to Carl's wife and their four-year-old twin daughters as the source of immeasurable support during his transition, particularly his insistence that he be recognized as having the gender identity he sees as constituting his authentic self. So when Carl approached the rostrum, carrying a large cloth sack which he placed behind him, the room exploded in applause. He began his comments with an account of his long struggle to come to peace with the difficulties he had faced in the process of changing his gender, as well as over the death of his mother and a history of sexual abuse. As he prepared to speak, his eyes filled with tears. People in the audience called out words of encouragement: "Take your time."

He then began to tell the story of Lazarus, reading from John 11. Jesus had heard that Lazarus, the brother of Mary and Martha, had died, but he exhorted his disciples to go with him to Lazarus's house in Bethany "to wake him up." When he arrived, he learned that Lazarus had been in his tomb for four days, but he still asked to be taken to the tomb and ordered the people to remove the stone that covered the grave. Carl continued reading from the text:

"But, Lord," said Martha, the sister of the dead man, "by this time there is a bad odor, for he has been there four days." Then Jesus said, "Did I not tell you that if you believed, you would see the glory of God?" So they took away the stone. Then Jesus looked up and said, "Father, I thank you that you have heard me. I knew that you always hear me, but I said this for the benefit of the people standing here, that they may believe that you sent me." When he had said this, Jesus called in a loud voice, *"Lazarus, come out!"* The dead man came out, his hands and feet wrapped with strips of linen, and a cloth around his face. Jesus said to them, *"Take off the grave clothes and let him go."*

Carl explained that we can make sense of this text by viewing it literally as a coming-out story. Jesus's insistence on Lazarus emerging from his grave and shedding his grave clothes demonstrates the centrality of coming out as an essential part of giving oneself over to the Holy Spirit. The grave clothes in the biblical text may be understood to be anything we carry around with us and are unable to get beyond. They could consist in a secret, a memory, a trauma, guilt, or anything else that prevents us from being open and honest with one another or with God. The grave clothes are things that we hang on to because they are familiar, even as they are obstacles to spiritual fulfillment. "Do you have enough faith to live without your grave clothes?" he asked. The grave clothes mark places where each of us died, but to live we need to take them off. He then shifted to a more domestic metaphor, explaining that we all need to do some "housecleaning" to make room for God, and that this will require us to hold a "memorial service" for our grave clothes, now "going to a better place."

Burying the grave clothes, he continued, would provide an opportunity to stand naked before God, to tell Jesus where the hurt began, to begin to tear down emotional walls that had impeded access to a spiritually rewarding life. Becoming more and more passionate with each line, Carl reached into the sack and pulled out an array of old clothes. "We're going to clean out your closet," he said, "You're going to put your grave clothes in the grave you just climbed out of." With the congregation now joining in with calls of "amen" and "that's right"—many standing, clapping, and raising their hands toward heaven—he stuffed the clothes back in the sack, telling the congregation that this is appropriate treatment for our lives in the closet. "We're going to clean out your closet," he repeated as a refrain. The crowd continued to roar with approval, stamping their feet and calling out their support for burying the "grave clothes."

Carl's story was one that illustrated the spatial model that lies at the heart of the approach to coming out espoused in the Fellowship. In this logic, one needs to create an opening through which the Spirit can enter, a space in which it can take up residence. When I presented this interpretation to a congregant in the Chicago congregation, she agreed and said, "It's like casting out demons." Honesty is not simply a matter of truthfulness; it organizes the spiritual space in the body and soul, reflecting an underlying notion that divine communion can only be achieved if a person has paved the way, cleared a space that is free of moral impediments, in order to be further cleansed by the coming of the Holy Spirit.

Coming Out in the Fellowship

TFAM teaching on coming out emphasizes the moral peril that comes from not being honest, open, and authentic. This kind of concealment will lead to losing one's moral compass, to falling into destructive personal behavior—Fellowship preachers frequently invoke crime, bad relationships, and drug and alcohol abuse as the price of denying one's whole identity. In other words, the path to leading a fulfilling and virtuous life is grounded in being truthful about one's identity because such honesty— coming out—allows one access to the cleansing presence of the Holy Spirit. This mandate means that dueling identities are merged into one, facilitating spiritual transformation. In this way, concealing one's true identity is akin to indulging in sinful behavior in that it distances the individual from meaningful communion with God. That this source of spiritual transformation can be achieved in a black Pentecostal church makes it even more powerful, as it enables a claim to historically African American worship at the same time that truth about one's identity is spoken.

As I emphasized earlier, access to this sort of spiritual journey is not facilitated by simply finding a gay-friendly—open and affirming—

congregation in which to worship. A social solution to the problem of LGBT exclusion is just that, a social solution. For black lesbians, gays, and transgendered persons steeped in the traditions of the black church, a social solution can't provide a satisfying resolution of spiritual problems any more than it can provide a straightforward way to reconcile seemingly contradictory black and queer identities. And while on one level, worship in an expressive Pentecostal congregation allows one to recall the worship practices of one's home community—forms of worship that in many ways stand for black identity in the United States—the need for this kind of ecstatic religious experience does more than speak to nostalgia. It offers a fundamentally different way to think about the expression and revelation of LGBT identity, one that demands that space be left open for the ingress of the Holy Spirit.

This approach is not only personal. Over and over in sermons and personal testimony, Fellowship congregants spoke of the fundamental hypocrisy they had encountered in the black church. One member described her visit to the annual convocation of the Church of God in Christ (COGIC), the largest black Pentecostal denomination in the United States, which she attended as a commercial vendor. Over and over, she told me, blatantly gay men approached her display table, some wearing makeup, others using body language that proclaimed their queerness to anyone who could see. The usual role these men played in their churches was in music ministries—directing choirs, playing the organ or piano, overseeing other performance aspects of services, in dance ministries, or directing children's musical participation. Although she suspected that these men approached her table because of her obvious presentation as a butch lesbian, no words about this were spoken. Many of the men took pains to refer to their wives and families, carefully contradicting the evidence of their appearance. None took issue with COGIC's unrelenting rejection of homosexual and transgender members, its official refusal to confront not only HIV/AIDS, but other issues that affect sexual minorities, particularly the recognition of same-sex unions.

The stories that TFAM members tell about the importance of coming out in their spiritual lives indicate that the iconic LGBT-rights quest for visibility and recognition, based on an underlying struggle to conquer shame, takes on expanded meanings in the context of Fellowship worship. While the coming-out experiences of church members may also do some of the political work most observers have long seen as the foundation of coming out, Pentecostal understandings of how spiritual fulfillment comes about lead to coming out as having a very different valence in the TFAM context. Authenticity facilitates the ability of the Holy Spirit to inhabit a person; that is, concealment and shame thwart the possibility of welcoming the Spirit and benefiting from its presence. In the course of this process, coming out achieves a new meaning that eclipses the limitations that inhere in it as an act solely concerned with mental health or political agendas. This process oscillates back and forth between the LGBT movement's mandated resistance to heteronormativity and the embrace of tradition, as TFAM members use their understanding of inhabitation by the Holy Spirit as a way to make sense of the politically obligatory process of coming out. That these two seemingly contradictory routes to achieving a sense of dignified personhood can proceed simultaneously is the unique accomplishment of TFAM.

Certainly, TFAM members who come out as gay, lesbian, bisexual, or transgender experience many of the struggles and achieve many of the benefits that have been documented elsewhere. But the pressure to come out only partly draws on the ways in which such revelation will advance political agendas. TFAM members may face discrimination on their jobs or may have to contend with rejection by their families after they reveal what they consider to be their authentic identities, but they will do so with the knowledge that a force more important than those worldly matters supports them. They will also have the support of their church and their fellow congregants, and the knowledge that they are embraced and validated in their church family.

FOUR

"Old-Time Religion": Invoking Memory

I was in a church in North Carolina in 2010 during the main ritual event of the East Coast Regional Conference of the Fellowship. "Pastor Williams," an elderly man who had been preaching since his teens, was delivering the sermon. He had come out just a few years earlier, when he was in his early seventies, and the people sitting near me told me that this had compromised his position in the traditional black church he pastored. Not long after that, he found his way to the Fellowship. The sermon was rousing, with the pastor using the story of David and Jonathan and a rather original interpretation of Genesis to argue that same-sex love was authorized in the Bible.

    As he preached and became more and more passionate about his message, Pastor Williams moved away from the lectern, trailed by his nephew, who carried a bottle of water and a white towel with which he frequently mopped the pastor's brow. Pastor Williams spoke in the repetitive fashion of black sermonizing, moving through the aisles and reaching out to touch the worshippers (Davis 1985; Mitchell 1990). Congregants began to leave their seats, and as they approached him, he extended his arm, placing his hand firmly on their foreheads. Most who were touched "fell out," that is, collapsed backward into the arms of others, but some others danced, shouted, spoke in tongues, or otherwise showed that his sermon had put them into direct contact with the Holy Ghost. I was sitting beside two young men, clearly a couple, both sporting long dreadlocks. One of them jumped up from his seat to join the throng of worshippers in the aisle. As he moved past me, he said approvingly, "This is *old-time*. This is *old-time*."

This wasn't an isolated occurrence. Worship experiences in the Fellowship often drew on themes associated with a past that congregants appeared to share. Invocations of "old-time" and reminders of shared African American history emerged as central themes both in worship services and in the stories members told me about their own spiritual journeys. Fellowship congregants call these reminders of what they define as their religious past "traditional" and "old-time." "Old-time" is a complex descriptor of worship practices. On one level, "old-time" refers to devotional practices that recall "traditional" black churches, and engender nostalgia even in a setting that differs in important ways from what would be found in such churches—particularly in the welcome extended to LGBT worshippers. The recalled churches either were located in the South or established outside the South by migrants to northern and western cities. The "old-time" practices I will describe all draw power from worshippers' memories of the past or stories they learned about the past that they have internalized. Regardless of their source, these stories seem to have been cleansed of the exclusion and bigotry that congregants may have suffered in the past. Members of the Fellowship can thus reclaim a version of the past that triggers nostalgia without requiring them to confront the rejection they may also recall from their past church experiences.

A number of issues circulate in any discussion of how people use history and/or memory to construct accounts of the worlds they have inhabited or that shape their present. There is a decided consistency to what different worshippers identified as "old-time" or "traditional"; stories resonated with one another, generating agreement, it seemed, on what counted as "old-time" or "traditional." I don't take this to indicate greater accuracy, but as a mark of cultural expectations for what makes a good story and as part of how cultural continuity is crafted by black people, or indeed by anyone representing themselves in any particular way.

For worshippers in TFAM, "old-time" expressions of spirituality mark the authenticity of their practices, an issue of some importance as TFAM might be accurately considered to have departed from many of the traditions associated with the black churches in which congregants were raised. Certainly, TFAM differs in significant ways from that heritage, principally in the expansive welcome it extends to persons who would likely not have been made to feel comfortable in a traditional AME, Baptist, or Pentecostal church, and in the accommodations it makes so that those worshippers can express what are referred to as their "authentic identities." This means that at least two kinds of authenticity come into conversation at these ritual occasions—that of the spiritual practices in the worship service and that associated with the worshippers themselves in all their diversity. TFAM is saying that individuals whose authentic identities depart from heteronormative gender and sexual standards are entitled to a worship experience that convincingly reflects their memories and that can therefore stir their emotions. In essence, these worshippers are insisting on unrestricted access to practices embedded in memory, even if these are transformed in the process of being enacted in TFAM.

What Are Memories For?

In *The Past Is a Foreign Country*, historian-geographer David Lowenthal considers the ways in which memories of the past may be used in the present to achieve particular ends. "The surviving past's most essential and pervasive benefit is to render the present familiar" (1985: 39), he explains, arguing that without memories, our present experience would be incomprehensible. The past is so essential in rendering experience comfortable that it is reproduced in whatever we create. It also "validates present attitudes and actions by affirming their resemblance to former ones . . . [while the] ability to recall and identify with our own past gives existence meaning, purpose, and value. . . . The past is integral to our sense of identity" (40–41). How the past is imagined and reconstructed thus becomes the central question for scholars of social/collective memory and its uses.

The past may be maintained in the present spatially, by remaining in places with which we have long histories, or by taking place-names or various kinds of keepsakes along with us when we are compelled to move, what Lowenthal calls "portable emblems of the past" (42). For many of the black congregants who belong to the Fellowship, the Great Migration (approximately 1910–70) is recent history—parents or grandparents of adult members outside the Deep South probably participated in it or know others who did—so roots and connections with the South are common in their personal histories. Continued communication with people in their former homes, through letters and visits, and more recently computer-mediated technologies, may make possible regular travel, family reunions (Harrison 1995), and other forms of continuity, assuming that such continued contact doesn't present physical risks (Wilkerson 2010). In recent years, blacks from the North have even begun a return migration back to the rural South, which now seems safer and more benign than when migrants departed—and possibly safer than the northern cities where they settled—and is after all, the site of powerful remembrances. But as Carol

Stack recounts, the elements of a remembered home can become a touchstone for painful memories as well.

> Embittered and proud men and women remembered fields and pecan groves, funerals, red bugs and thunderstorms, dark creek water, foul-mouthed white bullies, broken bottles in the ditch, and the sound of car tires spitting gravel on a summer night. (Stack 1996: 17)

For some of the return migrants Stack interviewed, people who had come north in the years of the Great Migration, hearing the sounds of the old hymns and sermons in church evoked such intense nostalgia that the desire to return "home" became irresistible. The South was remembered as "home of my ancestors, site of my blood and shame, focus of my birthright, still to be redeemed" and as "garden of my childhood, home of love's embrace, clear skies, lost sanctuary" (Stack 1996: 18). While some try to elaborate Afrocentric cultural elements as a source of pride or as a way to confront the hegemony of white America (Abrams 2014), Africa is too remote to serve as the affective heart of memory for most. For most worshippers in TFAM, the South is the place triggered by memory, and much of that memory centers on religious and worship practices.

Physical mementos, like photographs and other relics, can evoke collective or individual pasts, as can language, music, and, in a particularly powerful way, food (Kalčik 1984; Sutton 2001). What anthropologist Jon D. Holtzman (2006) calls "gustatory nostalgia" has long offered a pathway for diasporic or expatriate populations to connect to their histories in a particularly embodied or sensual way. The definition of a "national cuisine" is also a key mechanism by which national and ethnic identities are (re)invented and solidified (Ray 2004; Wilk 1999).

Worship fits into this story as well. Memories of church services in the South draw on many sources: the music; fans waving in the warm air; the intense feelings generated by prayer and spiritual fulfillment; the sounds of the sermons, with worshippers calling out their encouragement to the pastor; and of being overcome with the Spirit, speaking in tongues, and falling out. As I will discuss later, a frequent theme at Fellowship events, often used as a metaphor in sermons, for example, draws on mention of black American cuisine. Such references arouse memories of meals eaten with older family members—grandmothers figure prominently in these accounts—and stimulate powerful memories of taste and smell. Gospel music also draws worshippers into remembrances of the churches where they grew up, tying their experience to all kinds of black churches, but especially the Church of God in Christ or other Pentecostal churches, in which many were raised (Darden 2004; Harris 1992; Jackson 2004; Southern 1983).

Nostalgia for an idealized rural alternative to the urban realities of most TFAM members draws on the kind of romanticism discussed by Raymond Williams (1973), in which the pastoral retains an aura of perfection and simplicity. Madhu Dubey has challenged the dominance of the southern folk aesthetic in the work of such authors as Toni Morrison and Gloria Naylor, among many other African American literary figures, and further cites the reliance that anthropologist Carol Stack places on such images in her work on return migration to the South (Dubey 2003; Stack 1996). Dubey argues that the "South" offers an idealized vision of community that seems difficult to achieve in the urban North, with "community" merging into "village" as a source of authentic values, effectively pathologizing black urban life (Dubey 2003: 238). Certainly, this focus on "community" is one that animates literatures not only in minority racial and ethnic populations in the United States, but is notably a driving force in the shape of LGBT studies (Kennedy 2002; Murray 1979; Weston 1995).[1]

Tradition in TFAM Churches

Services in TFAM churches are organized in a way that replicates customs followed at the kinds of churches that worshippers would probably have attended in the past. But at the same time, some elements tend to be inserted into the order of worship that intensify claims that the congregation is making to specialness or difference. Most typically, there may be a declaration or proclamation of the mission of the congregation that highlights its adherence to the doctrine of radical inclusivity and the ways in which it departs from church "as usual." The service conducted at Chicago's Pillar of Love on February 26, 2012, offers a typical example. After an opening hymn, there was an invocation, a short prayer, scriptural excerpts read by congregation members, and Praise and Worship featuring a pianist, a drummer, and the praise team. This was followed by what the program designated as "T Time,"[2] when worshippers were invited to come forward to share "truths and testimonies." The Prayer of Affirmation, which had been composed by the pastor and was recited at every service, was the next item.

I am God's child. Whether I am lesbian, gay, bisexual, transgender, queer, or heterosexual, I was wonderfully and beautifully created by God. God loves all of me, just as I am. To honor God, I desire and strive to be the best that I can be and to be all

CHAPTER FOUR

that God created me to be. It is my duty to love my brothers and sisters, and I will try to love at all times and to speak words that give life and do not injure. I ask for God to lead me and guide me and to help me to surrender to the will of God for my life. I am strong and capable and able to succeed in all things with the help of God. For through Christ Jesus, I am Abraham's seed. And by faith, I claim and receive the Promise and Blessings of Abraham. Amen.

The Prayer of Affirmation was followed by the Welcome, which involved almost everyone in the congregation circulating to greet and embrace the other worshippers. People got out of their seats and moved up and down the aisle, hugging each person encountered and murmuring such phrases as "bless you," "welcome," "so glad you're here," and other expressions of warmth and fellowship. For some, these embraces were comfortable, appeared to be a matter of habit, and involved extensive exchanges with other members; some worshippers, however, were a bit more reticent, seeming unsure of how effusive their greetings needed to be or shy in greeting strangers. This portion of the service concluded with worshippers returning to their seats, hearing announcements, and then preparing for the "service by giving," or the offering. Two ushers holding baskets stood at the front of the sanctuary, and congregation members filed row by row to the front to deposit their offerings in the baskets. The program noted after the listing of the "service by giving" that congregants should let their "giving reflect the gifts that [they] have been given."

Following the collection of the offerings, a group of children trooped up to the front for a "youth moment," led by an adult member who works with the congregation's children. The children had clearly practiced a short presentation that was punctuated by exclamations from the congregation about how cute they were. More music and hymns were offered by the praise team, after which the homily was preached. The homilies or sermons vary considerably in length at TFAM churches, lasting anywhere from about fifteen minutes to well over an hour; the sermon at this service was a short one, about fifteen minutes in duration. The homily was followed by a blessing for a congregant's new baby, an invitation to those who want to join the church, the benediction, and a closing hymn.

The printed program included a list of principles that the leadership has constituted as fundamental to Pillar of Love's existence. This appears on the last page of every weekly program and isn't read aloud. First, a Mission Statement:

Pillar of Love Fellowship United Church of Christ is committed to the radically inclusive justice-minded ministry of Jesus Christ. With constant leading from God, we seek to be extensions of the grace of God that requires us to work to obtain justice and liberation for all God's people with particular attention to concern for the marginalized segments of our world community while being living manifestations of the transforming power of the Holy Spirit.

Next, a Statement of Purpose:

The purpose of Pillar of Love Fellowship United Church of Christ is to increase personal awareness of and receptivity to the grace of God so that it will be internalized. To that end, the purpose for which Pillar of Love Fellowship UCC was established is to help each individual develop a personal love relationship with God so that God's love for us will be internalized. Pillar of Love Fellowship UCC seeks to motivate each individual to receive and then to reciprocate God's love, thereby yielding each individual with a desire to love self and to love all [of] God's created humanity as one loves themselves.

This was followed by a statement of the Practice of Inclusion:

Pillar of Love Fellowship UCC is a faith community that welcomes the diversity that is reflected in all people. Whosoever comes is welcome, irrespective of race, ethnicity, gender, age, HIV/AIDS status, class, religion, physical ability, and sexual or affectional orientation. We also welcome those who know nothing or very little about the Bible or about being part of a church family. There is no dress code.

Then, the church lists its motto:

We live the LOVE in our name and are courageous enough to be all God created.

Finally, the back page provides two biblical quotations listed as Foundational Scriptures:

Exodus 12:21, 22
(21) The Lord went in front of them in a pillar of cloud by day, to lead them along the way, and in a pillar of fire by night, to give them light, so that they might travel by day and by night. (22) Neither the pillar of cloud by day nor the pillar of fire by night left its place in front of the people.

1 John 4:7, 8
(7) Beloved, let us love one another, because love is from God; everyone who loves is born of God and knows God. (8) Whoever does not love does not know God, for God is love.

CHAPTER FOUR

The program, then, clearly enunciates what Pillar of Love is all about. It calls for a standard set of worship practices and also presents those features that constitute the special objectives of this particular church. It stresses, for anyone who might have been unsure, that this is a congregation that welcomes those whose gender/sexual identities might diverge from heteronormative standards, and reiterates the principles of radical inclusivity central to TFAM. Some elements of the order of service were improvisational: a different person might undertake a particular role rather than the person listed in the program, the order might vary, or the pastor might decide to call on a particular person to undertake a part of the worship she or he had not earlier been asked to perform. For example, on one occasion when I attended a service with my partner, she was asked, without warning, to come forward and give the benediction. On another occasion, we were introduced to the congregation, identified as Jewish, with Bishop informing the congregation that she and her partner had come to Iowa City a couple of years prior to spend Yom Kippur with us and our *chavurah*.[3] She then asked us to come forward to address the worshippers. We quickly decided to say something about how happy we were to be back with our good friends at Pillar and then recited the Hebrew *Shehecheyanu*, a blessing that offers thanks for reaching a particular time and sharing it with others.[4] The congregation seemed to appreciate our choice.

The order of the service I have described is fairly standard for black (and white) Protestant churches, though each congregation may insert its own special elements, especially if the church has created its own statement of welcome, mission, or inclusion. Some responsive reading is often included, along with readings from both the Old Testament (Hebrew Bible) and the New Testament. Printed programs vary in elaboration, reflecting the number of people involved in assembling the ritual and the resources of the church. The welcome to visitors is a standard part of the service, though it may take place early or late in the service, or occasionally be omitted. The offering section of the service may vary considerably, with some churches having worshippers bring their offerings to the front and others passing the plate or basket through each pew. Many churches now provide accommodations for making donations electronically, with a person stationed in a particular spot equipped to swipe credit cards. There may be more than one offering, as well; particularly when the person giving the sermon is a guest from another congregation, the members may be given the opportunity to make a special "love offering" after the regular offerings have been collected. Collections are typically preceded by exhortations from the pastor or a congregation member to consider the importance of supporting the church, reflect on the benefits she/he receives when deciding how much to give, and enumerating some of the many expenses the church must cover from collections.

Particularly in churches with more resources for musical performance, services begin with a more elaborate Praise and Worship, a section of the service that may extend from as short a time as ten or fifteen minutes to an hour or more. During this time, congregants arrive, greet their friends, find a place to sit, and begin to get in the mood for the worship service that will follow. The musical elements for this part of the service also vary depending on the number of musicians and singers who are part of the praise team. Some churches are known for the excellence of their music ministries: City of Refuge in Oakland, for example, is led by a woman who has extensive professional experience as a musician. The church has a membership large enough to support two gospel choirs, one of which, called Transcendence, is made up of fifteen transgender men and women (Miller and Burkhart 2006). At some services I attended, worshippers began to move into trance states even during this preliminary part of the service, a sure sign that speaking in tongues or falling out is what they had hoped to achieve. In other words, they didn't need a lot of inspiration to begin to be filled with the Spirit; the mere fact of being in the church and hearing devotional music was sufficient to start the process.

Not only those who perform as part of the choir or praise team, but the entire congregation takes an active part in singing the familiar songs, harmonizing, and creating a mood that can transport worshippers into states of ecstasy. Some worshippers just sway to the music; others may join in with a tambourine or with rhythmic clapping. The level of musical skill in the congregation is substantial; though only some of those singing, including the music ministers and choir directors, have formal musical training or can read music, they have a large repertoire of hymns, anthems, and gospel songs and have mastered skills of harmony. Some worshippers, though, are hardly amateurs; many have worked as gospel singers, as performers of popular music, and as backup singers, and they bring the full range of their talent and experience to church.[5]

The familiar order of worship is a clear part of what makes it possible for worshippers to experience inhabitation by the Holy Spirit. The music is well-known—almost no one (except for this anthropologist) refers to the hymnal to refresh their memory of the words or the music being sung—and this familiarity summons up recollections of spiritual experiences they have had in the past. This is a particularly evocative form of nostalgia and, like other forms nostalgia can take, may not draw on factual accuracy as much as it works with the kinds of feelings that memories make accessible. Although the anthropologist had to consult the pro-

CHAPTER FOUR

2 Ecstatic worship at a TFAM service (photo by Veronica Jordan).

gram to know what was coming next, the worshippers rarely needed to check on how worship would unfold. It was clear from the demeanor of the worshippers that the order of service, the music, and the form of worship appeared to be deeply familiar and comforting. What is omitted as congregants enjoy the familiar cadences of past worship is the rejection and hostility that might have characterized their earlier experiences in churches where they were marginalized because of their performance of gender or sexual identity.

But as David Lowenthal (1989) has titled an essay, "Nostalgia tells it like it wasn't," some of these "memories" may stray from absolute accuracy. He observes that recent use of the term "nostalgia" is often dismissive, rejecting the commercialization of memory and paying more attention to the iniquities that may have been characteristic of past times. The ways in which nostalgia may also be reactionary are central to this at least partial rejection; the privileged are seen to be those who benefit from recalling the past. Literary theorist Svetlana Boym has defined nostalgia as "a longing for a home that no longer exists or never existed. Nostalgia is a sentiment of loss and displacement, but it is also a romance with one's own fantasy" (2001: xii). And, indeed, TFAM's use of nostalgia embodies these ambivalences and ambiguities. Members tend to focus on the elements of worship that are meaningful to them, and to distance themselves from the hypocrisy and homophobia that may have been equally central to their past experience. Taking possession of the remembered forms of observance in TFAM congregations helps worshippers to erase the message that they are unworthy of remaining in the faith environment in which they were raised and to instead affirm their right to experience the worship traditions that have made them who they are.

Authenticity

In *Culture and Authenticity*, Charles Lindholm (2008) reviews the complicated ways that authenticity is called upon in a variety of cultural contexts, particularly emphasizing the high value that persons in modern societies place on such displays. As he points out, authenticity can be sought in many different ways, both internally and externally, and thereby performed in order to solidify specific kinds of personal and collective claims.

First, there is the individual presentation of self, opportunities to "be oneself," but which have been occasions for discomfort or even danger in the past. Lindholm has remarked that in American culture, emotion or "the notion that feeling is the most potent and real aspect of the self" marks particular expressions as authentic or as the revelation of our "essential selves" (2008: 65). Congregants must tear away masks and reveal who they really are, what Bishop Flunder often refers to as their "authentic identities" (see chapter 3 for more on how this shapes the process of coming out). That "authentic" also means "God-given" is basic to the value the entire congregation places on such revelations. The congregation wants to embrace each worshipper for who she/he is, understood to be how God made him/her, repudiating judgments and hierarchy. In particular, revealing something about the self that is (or was) unlikely to be socially advantageous is seen as especially authentic. The fact that one would risk social approbation, discrimination, or other forms of mistreatment at the hands of those who don't sympathize with the particular identity being revealed means that one must feel very strongly and is likely to be motivated by the deep inner resolve that comes from the intercession of the Holy Spirit.[6]

As we have seen, worship in congregations affiliated with TFAM follows the conventions that resonate with what congregants remember from their old churches. As has been described for black churches in general, this is characterized by expressive prayer and a call-and-response style of preaching that makes congregants active participants in the creation of spiritual intensity (Davis 1985; Hinson 2000; Mitchell 1990;

Wharry 2003). Along the same lines, sermons in Fellowship churches resemble those that typify the black churches in which most congregants and clergy were raised: they rely on the participation of the congregation to convey their message. While most sermons have clearly been carefully prepared in advance—as evidenced by the paper text or sometimes the electronic device that sits on the lectern—members of the congregation signal their involvement by calling out responses as the sermon progresses; "Hallelujah," "Amen," "Yes, yes, yes," "My, my, my," and "Thank you, Jesus" are frequent expressions of approval. Enthusiasm may also lead congregants to call out, "Preach" or "Take your time," as the preacher eases into her/his message. These discourse markers, or "sermonphones," contribute to the rhythm of the sermon (as do chords from the piano or organ and drumrolls), but also indicate that the worshippers are engaged and expect the sermon to engender intense spiritual feelings (Darden 2004; Spencer 1987). They also may lead to changes in direction by the preacher, as she/he responds to the congregation's responses.

Some worshippers are overcome with the communion they achieve with the Holy Spirit, dancing, shouting, and sometimes collapsing in a state of trance some call "slain in the Spirit" or "falling out"—practices known as gifts of charisma and historically linked to African and African diaspora traditions (Alexander 2011; Hurston 1981; Raboteau 1978); and glossolalia, which many regard as indicating complete inhabitation by the Holy Ghost (Alexander 2011; Goodman et al. 1974; Samarin 1972). But, as is the case in most traditional Pentecostal churches, not everyone has these experiences or has them at every service; at the same time, some worshippers appear to be so predisposed to achieve spiritual fulfillment that they begin to show these particular markers of trance even before the service has gotten under way, for example, during the Praise and Worship musical prelude that usually precedes each service. There is considerable variation among churches or between services at the same church in the degree to which these gifts of charisma, such as glossolalia, are displayed. Some services are rather reserved, while others may call forth exuberant displays of dancing, shouting, and speaking in tongues. A lot depends on the sermon, but other variations seem to have to do with the expectations and needs of worshippers on particular days, with the makeup of the congregation, and the individual style of the preacher.

All of these variations mean that the order of service may change to accommodate the display of charismatic gifts on the part of congregants or the officiant. Depending on the responses of the congregation or feelings that may come up for the person presenting the homily, the direction of the service may change, sometimes involving the rearrangement of items listed in the program. This sort of spontaneity brings with it the imprimatur of authenticity; displays of emotion or spiritual elevation that are unplanned are, by definition, more deeply rooted in the authentic spiritual experience of the individual and thus contribute to the depth of the experience of the entire congregation. The improvisational element thus underscores the importance of worship being contingent on how the Spirit decides to move. Flexibility makes way for the Spirit to direct worshippers toward particular forms of worship whether that be a spirit of rejoicing, healing, chastening, or renewed commitment. In Victor Turner's terms (1967), such ritual practices open up liminal spaces—"moment[s] in and out of time" (1969: 96)—in which uncertainty makes the formation of new understandings more possible.

Hymns are particularly powerful instruments in evoking memories of past spiritual experiences, but sermons—both in terms of content and style—explicitly remind congregants of their linkage to "old-time" churches they may have attended in the past. One of my graduate students, an African American lesbian from the Deep South, accompanied me to Chicago for a service celebrating Pillar of Love's anniversary. This was her first exposure to TFAM, and she remarked to me that the hymns were more "traditional" than she had expected. She told me that the opening hymn, "What a Friend We Have in Jesus" (African American Heritage Hymnal 2011: 431), was sung regularly at the Baptist church she attended as a child. Singing this hymn made her feel at home, though she went on to explain, "This is so traditional. But it's different because of who is doing it." Other references reinforce these associations, including mention of southern black cultural practices, food, and folk wisdom, which regularly appear in sermons. This strategic use of shared memory enables congregants to focus on achieving communion with the Holy Spirit without having to attend to conventional gender identities or figuring out how to worship in a church that, while welcoming to LGBT members, might lack some of the familiar and comfortable attributes that signal the proximity of God to black worshippers.

As I've already suggested, some aspects of "old-time" simply seem to draw on familiarity to enhance comfort, engendering nostalgia, but sometimes also resentment and the recitation of past abuses. So the mention of grandmothers, for example, which is often linked to reminiscing about food, but also to memories of particular words of wisdom they may have imparted, leads congregants to feel at ease in the milieu of a TFAM church, sharing the spiritual experience with others whose grandmothers they believe to resemble their own. But this may be a double-edged memory, as grandmothers might have been the individuals who enforced moral regulations, monitored one's movements, and perhaps erected obstacles to sexual and social exploration.

Gospel Music

Music provides a vital route to reenacting the past, particularly in church settings. Whether TFAM churches have substantial resources—large choirs, organs, elaborate sound systems—or have just a few congregants who serve as a praise team with the accompaniment of a piano and perhaps drums, the singing of hymns is a vital part of worship. The music clearly elevates most worshippers to a level where they can more readily be prepared to accept the Holy Spirit, and it also reminds them of the churches where they were affiliated in earlier days, probably with their families.

Sermons are often accompanied, as well, by congregants standing up at dramatic moments, applauding, and/or raising their hands to receive the spirit and to give praise (Hinson 2000). The hymns sung are known by most of the congregants, and the form of performance adheres to gospel style. Indeed, some church leaders, including Bishop Flunder, have backgrounds as professional gospel performers. But even most of those members of the congregation without professional musical backgrounds sing well and are adept at harmonizing.[7] Historian Jerma Jackson has shown that the close linkage between music and worship is particularly characteristic of the Pentecostal Church of God in Christ (COGIC), where it expresses an understanding of "religion as a corporeal experience in which the physical and emotional reinforced each other" (2004: 21). Music also was an arena where women could take a leadership role, even though they were barred from the pulpit in COGIC churches. Because musical ability was regarded as "the power of God working through an individual" (22) or as "the manifestation of a divine gift" (38), women were encouraged to display their musical skills in church and took a central role in the development of gospel as a musical genre. This music sometimes moved into the secular domain, and artists like Sister Rosetta Tharpe, who started in COGIC, were able to achieve great success performing in nightclubs and on the radio, though this sort of commercialization was not without controversy. Based on the success of gospel artists, the rhythmic aspects of the music came to represent black culture and history and to provide the foundation for feelings of community. The radio performances also contributed to the growth of black radio stations, and because of their accessibility to all audiences, at least partially challenged the segregation that characterized church attendance (Jackson 2004).

As folklorist Glenn Hinson has shown, gospel music stands as a particularly important element of worship. Song, he explains, originates in God's will and is understood by congregants to constitute a form of praise that is particularly pleasing to God, who after all, brought song to the mouths of angels (2000: 110). The word "gospel," derived from "God-spell," refers to the "good tidings" brought by the divine acts of Jesus's birth, baptism, ministry, healing, death, and resurrection as detailed in the New Testament (Jackson 2004: 64). Music historian Eileen Southern (1983) traces its emergence to Baptist and Pentecostal churches early in the twentieth century. She points out that the characteristics of this genre, in contrast with spirituals, centered on instrumental music—keyboard plus percussion and possibly guitar, saxophone, trombone, or violin—with an early collection, *Gospel Pearls*, appearing in 1921 (1983: 450). The keyboard provided a vigorous rhythm, with improvisation, by the performers or the congregation, also being central to the music. A young composer named Thomas Dorsey (born 1899), who formed a gospel chorus at Pilgrim Baptist Church in Chicago in 1932, is credited with launching the genre we are familiar with today.

"In contrast to the restrained music that had dominated mainline Baptist services, Dorsey's chorus swayed to upbeat rhythms with an exuberance that echoed the emotions of sanctified worship" (Jackson 2004: 50–51). These rhythms were derived from the blues, which blossomed in the race music industry and in vaudeville; Dorsey, who grew up in Atlanta, achieved considerable success as a blues composer and arranger, touring with Ma Rainey and leading her backup band. But a spiritual crisis brought on by a serious illness led Dorsey back to the faith of his youth and convinced him to give up commercial music for sacred music, using his skills to endow his songs with the same emotional power that had characterized his work in the blues. The blues were based in the hard lives of black people, and the hymns that Dorsey and those who followed him composed similarly called upon the deep feelings of pain and sadness that black people experienced, calling upon God to lift them up and redeem them (Jackson 2004). While spirituals originated in the songs created by slaves to overcome their abject circumstances, "forging a spiritual universe distinct from the material world . . . [in which] they cast themselves as God's chosen people" (Jackson 2004: 1), spirituals later came to be seen as constituting their own genre, favored by the emergent black middle class, and performed with restraint. Dorsey's story was not unusual: as anthropologist Charles Keil reports (1966), many blues artists either started their musical careers in church singing gospel or moved into religious performance after having sung secular blues, perhaps becoming disillusioned by their experiences in the world of commercial music.

Gospel was distinctly urban, engendered by the Great Migration and inflected by the secular music of the blues, though framing itself as distinct from the "Devil's music," even as some practitioners asserted that "the devil should not be allowed to keep all the good rhythms" (Darden 2004: 141; Levine 1977). It emerged from the Pentecostal churches that grew out of earlier Holiness movements, spreading in the years following the Azusa Street Revival in urban areas where black migrants had settled — especially Chicago, Philadelphia, New York, and Detroit — and flourished in the worship experience of working-class blacks, who toiled long hours for little money and continued to suffer discrimination after migrating to the North. Pentecostal churches also encouraged the use of musical instruments, including "worldly" instruments like guitars (Sister Rosetta Tharpe's instrument), made room for holy dances, and readily incorporated ragtime, blues, and jazz motifs into worship (Darden 2004). This was considered to be liturgical music, intended for worship services, and was performed in two kinds of gospel groups: the all-male gospel quartet (which usually sang a cappella) and the gospel chorus, typically made up of women accompanied by keyboard and other instruments. In both kinds of performance, call-and-response is characteristic, as is improvisation and the active participation of the congregation (Best 2005; Southern 1983).

Despite their musical similarities, however, gospel and blues have sometimes been characterized as drawing on different needs and impulses. Famed gospel singer Mahalia Jackson put it this way, "Blues are the songs of despair, but gospel songs are the songs of hope. When you sing them you are delivered of your burden" (Jackson and Wylie 1966: 72). Other commentators, however, have argued that gospel and the blues might be better thought of as different points on a spectrum that captures the African American experience. James Cone (2011) has noted that there is also "deliverance" in the blues, which has prompted a new interrogation among black theologians who see the blues as an extension of black gospel or vice versa, that is, understanding the two forms as inextricably embedded in one another.[8] Unlike the more restrained worship that predominated in churches catering to middle-class and upwardly mobile blacks, Pentecostals embraced spiritual forms that had distinctly African elements, that is, worship that was exuberant and rhythmic. This is the music that resonates in the memories of TFAM members and that makes worship services powerful and uplifting experiences.

Besides providing a way for women to achieve prominence in their congregations, gospel also sometimes elevated gay people to central performing roles. Historian Wallace D. Best (2005) describes the music that emerged at Chicago's First Church of Deliverance, a spiritualist congregation on South Wabash Avenue, which also featured the first Hammond organ in Chicago (in 1939), an innovation that eventually revolutionized gospel performance around the country. "The church welcomed gay people and Reverend Clarence Cobbs [the presiding pastor], along with many of his staff, was rumored to be gay. . . . After attending the live broadcast at the church, which ran from 11:00 pm to midnight, club goers would simply walk from First Church of Deliverance to one of the area nightspots, usually the Kitty Kat Club, the Parkside or the 430" (Best 2005: 188). One of my Chicago narrators, in fact, told me that the church was widely described as "the sissy church" back in the period when Pastor Cobbs was its leader and continuing into later years. As performance scholar E. Patrick Johnson (2000) has compellingly described, African American gays have sometimes used the sacred space of the black church in conjunction with the secular space of the gay nightclub to achieve a state of spiritual wholeness.

Soul Food

Scholars of ethnicity have written extensively about how foodways provide an arena where identity claims (among others) are made and literally embodied (Caplan 1997; Douglas 1984). As sociologist Richard Alba (1990) explains in his examination of ethnic identity among white Americans, the authenticity of food preparation may wane as groups intermarry and move further from their immigrant forebears. His research shows, however, that the cooking of ethnic food (or food reputed to be ethnic) remained popular for holidays and other special occasions, while his informants tended to agree that mothers or grandmothers were the most skillful at preparing ethnic cuisine. He also found that those for whom ethnic heritage constituted a large component of personal identity, the consumption of ethnic dishes appeared to be more frequent.

Along similar lines, folklorist Susan Kalčik (1984) has shown how patterns of food consumption are closely tied to both ordinary and celebratory expressions of identity and belonging. Following Frederik Barth's

(1969) approach to ethnic groups as optative and performative, she argues that shared consumption of ethnic food can help self-ascribed members of groups to perform their identities and to constitute the boundaries that separate them from members of other groups. The repeated choice of specific foods from generation to generation signifies the continuing relevance of ethnic identity to those sharing meals (as well as using "in-group" language, telling jokes, and in other ways of performing their claims to belonging). As anthropologist Mary Douglas has explained, "If food is treated as a code, the messages it encodes will be found in the pattern of social relations being expressed. The message is about different degrees of hierarchy, inclusion and exclusion, boundaries, and transactions across the boundaries. Like sex, the taking of food has a social component, as well as a biological one" (Douglas 1971: 61). Meals are social and ritual events that involve particular participants, occur in a specified order, and include expected elements—that is, they repeat or purport to repeat past events. They consist of foods that are considered appropriate for the occasion and exclude items that would violate the boundaries established by the meal and its setting. Such patterns of eating "traditional" foods may be especially compelling for members of minority groups who find themselves surrounded by outsiders. As American studies scholar Richard Raspa (1985) argues, the preparation and consumption of foods linked to ethnic identity can assist in the continuing importance of maintaining separation from mainstream culture and cementing the closeness of family life, a function that is especially vital for the Italians he studied who live in Utah, surrounded by the majority Mormons who view them as exotic and somewhat dangerous.

This analysis has particular resonance for examining African American culinary habits. The shared consumption of what has come to be called "soul food" offers an opportunity for reaffirming mutual experience and thereby making clear how those eating the meal are connected to one another (Miller 2013). Soul food, while containing many items that are also part of southern cuisine as a broader category, reinscribes its history with each meal. Its origins lie in West Africa, though the style of cooking that developed in the region had already been influenced by the introduction of ingredients from the New World (such as cassava, maize, and plantains) largely as a result of the Atlantic slave trade. These elements continued to be consumed by slaves who survived the Middle Passage, though their options were limited and their ability to maintain familiar styles of preparation were hindered by availability and resources (Miller 2013).

As slaves came to be distributed across the Atlantic seaboard and the Deep South, various foods entered their diets, though the particular options available to them were regulated by the preferences and budgets of their masters. Nonetheless, the southern diet that coalesced was based on "'the 3-M's': meat (pork), meal (cornmeal), and molasses" (Miller 2013: 19). Regional differences took hold as well, as did variations depending on whether slaves were in rural or urban settings. The distinctive dishes that have come to be identified as "soul food" consisted of the cheaper foodstuffs available: greens and pork fat back, black-eyed peas, chitterlings, ham hocks, pigs' feet, and other items the more privileged whites disdained, sometimes just because black people ate them. Because of the privations of the Civil War, however, many of these foods later entered the cuisines of white people as well and came to be labeled southern cooking (Miller 2013: 29).

When I attended the Midwest Regional meeting of TFAM in 2014, held in St. Louis, conversations about food and its eventual consumption emerged as an evocative expression of connection with the past. On the way to a renowned local soul food restaurant, where a large group of TFAM people would be meeting for dinner, Bishop Pennese spoke at length about the various kinds of food we might have when we got there and about where the best examples of authentic dishes could be obtained. As we passed a fried chicken chain restaurant, she talked about how good their chicken was and how she might go out and have some later in the week. She then shared with us that as a child she used to come to St. Louis, Missouri, with her family to visit her mother's relatives. One of the special dishes they would have was called "snoots" and was made from pig snouts. She explained that this is a St. Louis specialty and lamented the fact that it is unobtainable in Chicago.

As we got closer to the restaurant, she and the others in the car began an animated discussion of what might be on the menu tonight, a conversation that veered into reminiscences about the way that mothers and grandmothers prepared particular dishes. We then arrived at the restaurant and were confronted with a long line that snaked out the door and onto the sidewalk. The line slowly moved into the building and toward the cafeteria-style counter, where the menu could finally be discerned, written on a blackboard above the serving area. Some dishes were regular offerings, while others were specials for particular days. The discovery of which foods would be available provoked another discussion, mainly about the best way to prepare specific foods, whether the style of cooking here would equal what each person remembered from home, and which of the many options she should choose. In the end, several of those in line with me decided to get two entrées, along with the side dishes of vegetables that were included in the dinner menu. Smothered pork chops were thus paired, for example, with fried chicken, while the side dishes—green beans, black-eyed peas, mashed potatoes, rice, macaroni and cheese, okra, or cornbread—not to mention desserts, were piled up beside them.

During dinner, discussion about the food continued. One of the other TFAM attendees at the dinner was the woman who had prepared a soul food meal at the last Midwestern Regional meeting in Cincinnati, and after she was pointed out to us, everyone who had been there compared the offerings at the St. Louis restaurant to her versions of these dishes. The conversation allowed each person at the table (except for the anthropologist, who quietly enjoyed her smothered pork chops) to expand on her experience with the food, the excellence of her mother's or grandmother's culinary skills, and her nostalgia for particular foods that either were or were not on the menu here. It wasn't difficult to see that the subtext for this discourse was the authenticity and intensity of each person's memories, transformed in a particularly embodied way as we literally consumed exemplars of these remembrances (Douglas 1971, 1984). Indeed, the expression of these memories was almost competitive, as each participant in the conversation made sure to assert her racial identity and gain the implicit approval of the group. These were moments when I was starkly aware of my outsider status; though I enjoyed the food on offer, my own family memories center on very different menus.

Bishop Flunder sometimes uses memories of food to enhance the hominess of the congregational setting, as all share what are presumed to be the same memories of iconic food. Nowhere is this more compelling than in invocations of fried chicken, the classic after-church dinner, and a dish that is a key part of stereotypes of African Americans (along with watermelon) (Miller 2013). Bishop's discourses on the pleasures of fried chicken can go on in some detail as she draws her audience into recollections of eating fried chicken, with all the other memories that savoring that dish calls forth.

Bishop Flunder has also expanded on discussions about food to emphasize the importance of expressing one's authentic self with respect to the preparation of food, regardless of the limitations dictated by conventional gender expectations. Here she often refers to the stereotypes of women, and not men, finding creative pleasure in cooking. But some (gay) men find culinary activities to be an arena where they can delight in their creativity, while some women may find cooking unappealing, an activity from which they wish to be liberated. Culinary pursuits ought not to be automatically linked to sex or gender, and, in Bishop Flunder's words, "If a man is the one who bakes the best pound cake, then for goodness' sake, let him bake the pound cake!"

Her use of fried chicken imagery draws the whole congregation into a space of warm nostalgia and reminds them that she is like them, also a lover of fried chicken. The space in which the service is taking place, then, becomes redolent with aromas of dinners prepared by grandmothers and is validated as a place that is authentically African American. Fried chicken is so intimately related to church events—both as what is eaten at church dinners and food that can be sold to raise funds for the church—that it would be difficult to exaggerate the importance of this particular food in the memories of the TFAM congregations. Indeed, black religious scholars Jualynne Dodson and Cheryl Gilkes have noted that the chicken is often called the "gospel bird" (1995: 523), calling attention to its combined nutritional and symbolic importance. American studies scholar Psyche A. Williams-Forson says that chicken is "not just for eating but is also a useful tool in social action, self-help, and social uplift" (2006: 136), going on to explain that cooking chicken has a significant place in the construction of cultural identity for both women and men (137)—although in my conversations, women were usually more involved in discussions of food.

Bishop Flunder made use of a series of lighthearted comments about food when she addressed an audience of outsiders to the Fellowship at a conference that TFAM co-sponsored with the MCC in 2010. Held in Acapulco, Mexico, the conference attendees were predominantly Euro-American members of the MCC. A small contingent of TFAM members was present, and several of them told me that they sensed some nervousness about them among the MCC participants. TFAM people started joking that the MCC folks were afraid the "Pentecostals" would begin to speak in tongues or fall out without warning. So when Bishop Flunder took the podium at one of the large services, she delivered a sermon that was intended to put those unfamiliar with TFAM at ease. She used humor, talking about chitlins (chitterlings) as an iconic food among African Americans, conceding that members of other ethnic groups find them intensely unappealing, but that they might be an acquired taste. After getting most of the audience to laugh about this food that makes them so anxious, she made clear that relishing chitlins is not a precondition for being able to work together in allied churches in pursuit of the same goals.

Hair

Nostalgia also extended to other recollections of congregants' experiences of being black. It wasn't difficult to capture the worshippers' attention if one started talking about hair, particularly in connection with the

CHAPTER FOUR

struggle African American women in particular have long had with taming what they were told was their "bad hair." As a number of researchers have documented, the difference between African American hair and the (ideal) qualities of Caucasian hair have long been a source of concern for black people, especially women (Banks 2000; Byrd and Tharps 2014; Jefferson 2015; Rooks 1996). Noliwe Rooks, for example, reports that in the period when she conducted her research, black women purchased 34 percent of all hair care products sold, far outstripping the per capita consumption of the general population (1996: 117).

A number of issues surface when the issue of hair is raised: the systematic disparagement of black physical characteristics—including hair, facial features, and skin color—that characterized the time of chattel slavery and that has carried over to the present, as well as the enormous economic investment that black women, in particular, make in products and treatments intended to make their hair conform to white standards of beauty. Over the period of both the civil rights and the Black Power movements, with their commitment to enhance black empowerment and self-esteem, hair loomed large as a physical expression of racial pride (or lack thereof). The emergence of various types of natural hairstyles—including braiding derived from African prototypes and the extravagant Afros sported by such iconic cultural figures as Angela Davis—speaks to the emphasis placed in recent years on expressing pride in African traits and elaborating their expression.[9] Yet some authors also describe their fond childhood memories of sharing the ritual of having their hair straightened with their sisters (hooks 1989, cited in Rooks 1996: 9), nostalgic feelings that outweigh the fraught politics of hair straightening. Rooks cites several instances in African American literature where hair—whether straightened, braided, or left natural—comes to stand for identity, community, politics, class, and much else (1996: 5-6).

In her opening remarks at the 2014 Midwestern Regional Conference in St. Louis, Bishop Flunder spoke about self-esteem, arguing that black people often take to heart negative things that have been told to them about their value. She used the shared experience of hair care in couching her argument.

There was a time, in the time of chattel slavery in particular in this country, where people convinced us entirely that we have bad hair. Anyone walking with me? Let me use my hair as an example.[10] This is bad hair. This is what I was told. And when people were cute, people would say, "Oh, she's so cute, and she has good hair." It was the prerequisite for cuteness to happen. And the consequence was that we tried to figure out in any conceivable way that we could how to get that hair not to be bad. And in the history of African Americans, we have done some dreadful things to ourselves trying to get that thing worked out. We pretty much got it down. But some of us remember, go far enough back to remember conks in the kitchen.[11] [This brought laughter from the congregation.]

And it didn't work out too good. Some people's hair never grew back. They burned their scalp so that that was it for them; they had to wear wigs for the rest of their lives. And if anybody remembers the Jheri curl, for those of you who are too young to remember the Jheri curl and its origin.[12] It was from the pit of hell. The problem with the Jheri curl was the Jheri curl juice. And because I like to hug people, and one whole side of my face and my clothes and everything was just covered with Jheri curl juice [*laughter*]. Anybody remember that? And you'd dress yourself up and that collar or whatever you had on was just full of Jheri curl juice. And if you'd sweat, you'd swing Jheri curl juice on everyone. It was rough. It was hard.

And finally we reached the point where we did start to believe that all of us make our choices. . . . I'm not suggesting that one way is better than the other. But there is a key point here. And that is that we reached a point where we started wearing natural hair for beauty. And that was huge for black people. Because we didn't believe for a long time that our natural hair had beauty. For Sunday, our preparation was on Saturday, and it was horrible. I want to say to our European American brothers and sisters, you have no idea what we went through. [She makes a sizzling sound that elicits a round of laughter.] Somebody knows that sound. If you don't understand it, this is not for you. [She repeats the sizzling sound, to more laughter.] And the steam went up. And they said, hold your head still. Hold your ear. And almost all of us have some little track lines from where we got burned. [Another repeat of the sizzling sound.] That's what happens when you don't hold still. And they'd fry your hair, but you'd have a pain in your leg. I never could understand how you get burned on your head and you could feel it in your knee. Some kind of way your nerves was connected. It was terrible. And then you couldn't do anything. You couldn't go swimming. You couldn't do PE because you'd sweat that hair back. And after all that work they did, and go to the sundry store and get ribbons to put in your hair, and fix you up and turn you into something, you could go to church, and do something about that bad hair.

By the time Bishop finished this account, most of the congregation was laughing, with many exchanging meaningful looks with people sitting near them. She managed to convey a number of messages with her depiction of the misery of having one's hair straightened to make it "good" by white people's reckoning. First, of course, is the futility of trying to look like—and be—something or someone you are not. Straight hair is not authentic for most black people, and the measures they had to take in order to temporarily attain a beauty ideal that had nothing to do with the natural condition of their hair are, in retrospect, laughable. Her story, complete with the sound effects of the hot comb going through one's hair, summoned up memories to the congregation, particularly the majority of the women who are old enough to have commonly used these techniques; they have a visceral understanding of Bishop's contention. They all remembered how controversial the move to various kinds of natural hairstyles was and what a relief it was to give up a losing battle against kinky hair (Byrd and Tharps 2014).

But Bishop also said, "I'm not suggesting that one way is better than the other," in describing decisions black people make to use various techniques to straighten their hair. In other words, she acknowledged the enormous social pressure exerted on black people, especially women, to enact standards of appearance that required herculean efforts and that left scars and painful memories in their wake. Being able to present oneself with straight hair, or some reasonable facsimile thereof, has had ramifications for success in school and being hired for jobs and keeping them. Resisting such pressures demands courage but perhaps sometimes a touch of recklessness, and she was clear that no one should judge or condemn those who succumb.

This message reinforces the larger significance of TFAM—the resolve not to try to be someone or something that you are not. Members are urged, as we saw in chapter 3, to reveal their authentic identities, to come out to themselves and to the wider world, and to understand that no matter how much their identities diverge from what they've been told they should aspire to, God loves them and sees them as part of his creation. If you are gay, lesbian, bisexual, or transgender, TFAM urges you to see yourself as a legitimate part of God's work, to accept and indeed embrace yourself as a reflection of his holiness.

But by focusing on black hair or black religion or African American cuisine as a source of nostalgia, Bishop Flunder reinforces the feeling of comfort that penetrates every part of TFAM worship. The order of service is familiar, the hymns are the old beloved ones, and the style of worship is expressive and collaborative. But she also makes a more abstract point that would otherwise require a complicated exegesis: she argues convincingly that cultural hegemony shapes how people—in this case, black people—feel about themselves. She continued to talk about hair:

How did we get to understand that we had bad hair? Someone told us that we had bad hair. And they told us, and they told us, and then one day we believed it such that now the colonizer doesn't have to tell you anymore that you have bad hair.

We tell ourselves. I need you to hear that. We believed it and then we took it as our own mantra. And so out of slavery, we still have some things that are left over that remain in our spirits. Because we were convinced. Once somebody convinces you, they don't have to tell you anymore.

She then shifted the message to how gender and sexual identity play into understandings people have about the limitations they must necessarily face in life.

People told us that women were called to suffer. It's a woman's role, to suffer. And a lot of us took that to heart. And those of you that are more female-identified, even as same-gender-loving, I found that to be true, that we believed that our responsibility in a relationship is to suffer. That's what we were taught. And we believed that same-gender-loving people offended, that we can never expect to have greatness. If we could have mediocrity, we should be satisfied. Because we were taught to believe that we just barely get by anyway. So don't expect a whole lot. Just thank God you've got somewhere to go. That you've got a church to belong to. . . . It's amazing how insufficiency can be written on the table of your heart. And our greatest task in life is to get rid of our low esteem, our own low esteem. Because low self-esteem is what makes it okay for us to not treat our own selves right. Now you will never be able to treat anybody right until you learn how to treat yourself right. You'll never be able to love anybody until you learn how to love yourself. And I need you to hear that. And how much you love yourself is evidenced by how you treat yourself. This is good what I'm saying to you right now. How *you* treat *you*.

Here Bishop Flunder uses the shared memory of "bad hair" to invoke the larger story of how people come to have low self-esteem and low expectations for themselves. Race and enforced servitude may be the foundations for this, but they also can be rooted in physical attributes, gender, or sexual identity. No matter: the process she clarifies is the same. It is the introjection of the values imposed by cultural hegemony that makes it unnecessary to remind people that they don't really matter; once those messages have been absorbed, they have the force of habit behind them (Bourdieu 1977). This might otherwise be a complicated theoretical point, but when conveyed through memory and nostalgia, it is crystal-clear. Making this argument also softens observations that might otherwise seem to judge those who straightened their hair or made other efforts to approximate white standards of attractiveness. No one can be blamed for internalizing a message that has become so deeply integrated into individual consciousness.

CHAPTER FOUR

Other Church Customs

Worshippers speak both with anger and a sense of loss about the churches they attended before finding TFAM, churches that rejected and stigmatized them because of their gender or sexuality. These reminiscences may move into joking about particularly rigid practices they recall—no makeup or jewelry for women, dark suits and white shirts for men, no secular dancing, no popular ("devil's") music, and entire Sundays (not to mention one or two evenings during the week) spent in church—competing with one another to recall the most oppressive requirements imposed on them when they were young and how they evaded or sabotaged these constraints. These were also occasions where my outsider status was a source of great amusement; I often was baffled by jokes, sending those around me into peals of laughter.

On the one hand, as I have shown, Fellowship churches mostly adhere to "old-time," and therefore predictable, church practices: music, the order of service, liturgy, and ways of conducting the offering all echo the traditional customs members recall, whether fondly or disdainfully. Bishop Flunder calls this style "Metho-Bapti-Costal," playfully suggesting a pastiche of practices from the churches most worshippers would recognize. She argues that these choices are mainly sentimental, as "God can move through any culture," but that *"they are ours*, and they should remain" (Flunder 2005: 11; emphasis in original).[13] She thus emphasizes Fellowship members' ownership of their traditions, their right to use them no matter what their personal attributes may be.

On the other hand, Fellowship churches have eased some of the more onerous restrictions that worshippers may recall from their old churches. Services typically last only two to three hours, and requirements for dress are relaxed, to say the least. Congregants often wear jeans and other casual attire; women may wear pants, makeup, and clothing that would not have passed the standards for modesty in the churches of their youth, and of course there's lots of cross-dressing. Though not all congregants indulge, there are no restrictions on consuming alcohol when going out for a postchurch lunch or celebrating an important occasion. Importantly, Fellowship churches encourage members to follow God's plan for them, revealed through inspiration from the Holy Spirit, and to involve themselves in various kinds of church-centered and community service (ministries), not excluding work on progressive political causes. Jettisoning homophobia has also meant that Fellowship churches have eased the requirements on members to separate themselves from the outside world. Members of churches are expected to engage with the outside world, and many sermons indeed call on them to strengthen their political and community commitments.

Practices that can be linked to Africa also count as "old-time." Still, worshippers don't all agree that particular practices or styles of worship have their origins in Africa, and some reject terminology that would suggest these practices are in some way derived from "pagan" religions. This applies especially to trance and possession, revealed in dancing, stomping, and speaking in tongues, which members call "inhabitation" or "visitation" by the Holy Ghost. When I used the word "possession" in a paper I was writing, one of the pastors corrected my language. Yet Fellowship leaders, along with most anthropologists, agree that these religious behaviors reveal continuity with the West African religions that slaves brought with them to the New World. At the same time, however, Fellowship leaders like Bishop Flunder often point out that the style of movement that appears in ecstatic dancing also resembles Native American dance, another influence on contemporary African American cultures. In making this point, Bishop goes beyond the views of scholars who have traced the close association between rhythmic movement, music, and worship to African foundations (Herskovits 1990 [1941]; Matory 2005).

The emphasis on continuity with African and/or Native American traditions provides another foundation for claims to authenticity. Indeed, the TFAM catchphrase "We are family" expands on this interpretation of belonging in the world. Bishop Flunder has spoken extensively about generational continuities, whether these are defined as biological through the passage of DNA from the past into the future, or cultural, with reference to music, food, and the performance of shared heritage.

The attraction of "old-time" easily slides into a veneration of history, particularly in the invocations of the Pentecostal past that are common in sermons. These often center on recollections of the Azusa Street Revival, widely proclaimed to be the event that launched modern Pentecostalism. The hallmark of Azusa Street, according to these accounts, was the radical egalitarianism that characterized worship with whites and blacks, and men and women all taking part in praising God and exhibiting the gifts of charisma regardless of their social status in the secular world.

Fellowship preachers draw on this history to argue that their practices are consonant with what occurred at Azusa Street, and that radical inclusivity in fact offers a more authentic re-creation of Pentecostalism than what became normative in most other churches that trace their origins to Azusa Street. Some use the term "neo-Pentecostal" to describe their movement, explaining that other Pentecostal churches (the black COGIC and the white Assemblies of God are the largest such denominations) have lost their way. Bishop Flunder views the judgmental stance of most African American churches, which leads them to distance themselves from marginalized populations, to be a symptom of what she calls "oppression sickness," whereby they reproduce the exclusionary strategies they absorbed from the white church in the context of slavery and, indeed, may adopt biblical arguments in support of class bias and homophobia that eerily recall the reasoning of pro-slavery Christians in the nineteenth century (Flunder 2005; Griffin 2006: xiii).

I attended the 2011 National Fellowship Convocation in Las Vegas where the young Pastor Troy Sanders was leading a service. Besides being a gifted preacher, Pastor Sanders is a fine singer, and he integrated hymns with his call to prayer. As the music progressed, he exclaimed, "This is old-time church!" and moved on to describe his grandmother's prayer practices back in the rural area of South Carolina where he was raised in an Apostolic church (one of the strictest forms of Pentecostalism). As we saw in chapter 3, Pastor Sanders's promising preaching career was threatened when he realized that he was gay. His encounter with Bishop Flunder and especially with her mother, Mother Langston, provided a key foundation for him to reconceptualize his calling. He explained, "Mother Langston reminded me of my grandmother who had passed. They had the same type of spirit. And so we connected in a very real way. [I] had a real affinity for her. And so, out of that, the rest is just history." The connection with the spirit of his grandmother was central as he was able to identify the Fellowship with his own history in the church, as well as with the collective transmission of religious practices from generation to generation. He became very active in TFAM and is now the founding pastor of a new Fellowship church in a large southern city. He also serves on the TFAM Executive Committee and is Episcopal Assistant to the Bishop for the Southern Region.

As he continued to explain his connection to "old-time" practices, Pastor Sanders suggested that customs with African origins also were "old-time."

I feel like it has been a gift given to me by God that I tend to marry [the] contemporary world and the traditional world. I have an affinity for a number of the traditional hymns of the church and I have awareness of that. And that calls to me. That whole ritualistic, that whole beating of the drums, the Yoruba expressions, and those kind of tribal type things.

In other words, not only the hymns of the old church, but also traditions that he connects to Africa, are significant in making the inclusive world of the Fellowship a meaningful experience for Pastor Sanders. His perception of historical validity in religious practices is central to his ability to receive the message of acceptance that the Fellowship offers; if the deep emotion produced by the black church feels the way it always did, then the worshipper can trust the legitimacy of his inclusion. But Pastor Sanders's story indicates that he had to free himself of the past, a task facilitated by the death of his grandmother and his discovery of a new grandmother figure in Mother Langston, if he was to be able to re-embrace a version of the past that welcomed all of whom he believed himself to be.

While the Fellowship sees itself as directly communicating the true message of Azusa Street, members sometimes struggle to reconcile the embrace of radical inclusivity with their expectations for an encounter with God. As Bishop Flunder sees it, the scars that result from years of oppression in a hostile church environment do not disappear immediately; to overcome the damage done by oppressive religion one must reinterpret history. To heal in the Fellowship, individuals embark on a period of unlearning the belief that they are unworthy, discarding the version of the past that obstructs their quest for spiritual fulfillment along with vilifying biblical interpretations.[14] The metaphor she uses is of a "welcoming table [where] an individual's seat at the table is not given *in spite of* who they are but *because of* who they are" (Flunder 2005: 11; emphasis in original). Having the table be "old-time"—familiar and safe, with one's grandmother providing the comfort foods of one's youth, the choir singing the well-known hymns, and the congregation praying in the expressive, animated fashion that one grew up with—all of these elements signal the promise of spiritual fulfillment in a welcoming community.

Embracing and Unlearning the Familiar

Membership in a TFAM congregation engages worshippers in a process that puts them in touch with both pleasant and troubling memories. Invoking these memories, however, is used by most to engender an atmosphere steeped in comfort and sentimental in its celebration of the past—or the past they either have been told about or wished they had experienced. The processes by which black people long disavowed their bodies and hair are summoned in ritual contexts, reminding congregants that authenticity is far preferable to practices that seek to conceal one's identity. Just as this message speaks to the experience of African Americans, it also reminds worshippers that their sexual or gender identities are as essentially part of them as their race, their skin color, and their curly hair. Various substances are invoked, some more ephemeral, like food, or performed in the moment, like gospel music. This engagement with the past also offers a remedy to whatever in the present is problematic or unacceptable, just as it did in the past. For TFAM this means, for example, repudiating the racial boundaries of most churches in favor of radical inclusivity, which is justified by its proclaimed origins in Azusa Street. Safety and comfort in an atmosphere that reminds one of the actual or imagined past make possible the spiritual journey that brings worshippers to TFAM. But safety—either as an African American or as an LGBT person—is not the only goal here; spiritual wholeness is a far more central objective of TFAM congregants.

FIVE

"What a Fellowship": Radically Inclusive Futures

During a break between workshops, I was chatting with some of those who were attending the 2012 Midwest Regional meeting of the Fellowship, when one woman asked me which congregation I was affiliated with. I explained that there was no TFAM church near where I lived, but that I considered Pillar of Love in Chicago to be my "home" church. "Where do you live?" she asked, and I replied that my home was in Iowa City, Iowa. "And you don't have a TFAM church there?" she continued. I explained that I didn't think Iowa had enough black residents, let alone black people who are LGBT-identified, to provide the foundation for forming a congregation. "What does that have to do with it?" she responded. I looked around the room, which was filled with about fifty people, all LGBT and, except for me, African American and pondered her meaning.

When I attended services at Bethel Christian Church, the TFAM-affiliated church in Washington, DC, that same year, one congregant explained to me how she decided to affiliate with this particular church, after some months of attending the local Metropolitan Community Church (MCC) congregation. "I don't need to be told that it's okay to be gay. I already know that. I'm here to worship God." She went on to explain that, unlike MCC, Bethel is not a gay church.

This chapter considers what I call the *aspirational narratives* put forward by the Fellowship of Affirming Ministries. I will discuss some implications of these aspirational narratives for questioning our understanding of how these churches serve LGBT worshippers and suggest some of the possible paradoxes that may be built into the expanding notion of radical inclusivity. In particular, I will argue that the discourse of radical inclusivity rests on an understanding of community that transcends the quest for "safe space" usually associated with LGBT collectivities. In other words, radical inclusivity generates a kind of imagined community (Anderson 1991; Wolkomir 2006) that is all-embracing and can do this even as not all members share the same definitions of community. Nonetheless, this aspirational narrative serves to set TFAM apart from other predominantly Christian organizations while still offering worshippers entry into a space that is safe and accepting of their identities.

As I discussed in chapter 1, TFAM's theology centers on and elaborates the principle of "radical inclusivity," defined on the organization's website as "the intentional inclusion of all persons; especially people who have traditionally lived at the margins of society, such as people suffering from substance abuse; people living with HIV/AIDS; same-gender loving people; the recently incarcerated; and sex industry workers."[1] At the outset, TFAM's notion of who these marginalized and rejected persons were reflected the immediate crisis presented by the HIV/AIDS epidemic and was evidenced in the failure of most black churches to address issues raised by the epidemic (Cohen 1999). These churches had also systematically excluded or disparaged LGBT congregants in general, no matter how central to church operations they might be—as choir leaders and members, as teachers, and in many other important roles—and offered few if any routes to official leadership for women (Flunder 2005; Johnson 2008). Others whose personal histories had stigmatized them in the black church were also embraced by the call for radical inclusivity: the formerly incarcerated, substance abusers, the homeless, and sex workers, many of whom, of course, overlapped with those who were LGBT or affected by HIV. This is not to suggest that such rejection is found solely in black churches. There is ample documentation of a pattern of discrimination in US churches across the spectrum. However, being banished from one's church, as we saw in chapter 1, has a particular sting for African Americans because of the historic centrality of the church in black community life.

The outreach of TFAM to these rejected and stigmatized populations remains central to the coalition's mission, most recently embracing large numbers of transgendered members with the creation of a ministry called TransSaints, which has a substantial online presence. But while black LGBT individuals who have been distanced from traditional church life remain at the center of TFAM's call, the shape of radical inclusivity has expanded in recent years to include the potential inclusion of *all people*, regardless of race, sexual/gender identity, and religious background. Even when the persons participating in religious events are nearly all black and predominantly LGBT, church members repeatedly, and emphatically, told me that TFAM churches are *not* gay and *not* black.

Literature on gay churches has often cast them as islands of safety and refuge for LGBT people excluded from other religious institutions (Griffin 2006; Tinney 1986; Wilcox 2003), drawing on studies that understand gay and lesbian communities as conceptually, and sometimes spatially, bounded sites that permit their members to opt out of contact with an outside world that is rejecting, unsupportive, or that threatens violence (Bailey 2013; Beemyn 1997; Erzen 2006; Kennedy 2002; Krieger 1983). This form of community building recapitulates the formation of African American churches such as the African Methodist Episcopal (AME) in the eighteenth and early nineteenth century, when black worshippers responded to discrimination by their white co-religionists by forming their own denomination (Lincoln and Mamiya 1990; Newman 2009). One reading of this kind of community appears in Stephen O. Murray's classic article (1979) that likened gay communities to ethnic enclaves; such understandings cannot help but incorporate romanticized notions of community that have proliferated in social science discourse (Creed 2006). These are the images of community that drew the gay people Kath Weston described in her work to migrate to San Francisco in search of personal safety and acceptance, but which, she reported, many failed to find (Weston 1991, 1995).

Community studies have the same central importance in LGBT research that they have long had in research on ethnic minorities and on stigmatized populations: they work to repudiate images of such populations as deviant and dysfunctional and show them, instead, to have the same cultural coherence that obtains in more normative groups.[2] Esther Newton (1979 [1972]), for example, examined the lives of drag queens and street fairies in the 1960s, persons who lived on the margins of gay life, often impoverished and rejected even by other gay men,[3] and found that their lives were organized according to internally consistent cultural rules. This analysis mirrored the anthropological dictum of cultural relativism, of course, though it was innovative to apply such insights to our own culture. Newton's early research, which launched the study of LGBT populations in anthropology, is echoed in much of the work that followed it in the four decades since its publication, where community studies have dominated much of the research, as they do in historical studies of LGBT populations (Boellstorff 2007; Kennedy 2002; Weston 1993).

All of these approaches to LGBT collectivities have tended to empha-

CHAPTER FIVE

size the struggle of LGBT people to locate safe and supportive spaces in which to live, work, and worship. But I will argue here that they underestimate the importance of ties that reach across their presumed boundaries, a limitation that I have highlighted in my research on lesbian mothers (Lewin 1993), same-sex commitment ceremonies (Lewin 1998), and gay fathers (Lewin 2009). In all of these ethnographic works, I have shown that connections with non-gay persons, particularly biological family members or what Kath Weston famously called "straight families" (Weston 1991), indeed loomed larger in the lives of my interlocutors than most would imagine. In this chapter, I will extend this analysis to argue that TFAM congregations, while providing their constituents with a space where they are respected and embraced as LGBT people—a safe space—also seek to enhance their reach beyond community borders and to bring people from beyond those borders into their community, even as this outreach may pose a threat to feelings of safety.

Expanding Radical Inclusivity

Bishop Flunder's widening concept of inclusivity draws on her understanding of the meaning of Pentecost as the formative moment in the spiritual life of the coalition and the responsibility of TFAM to enact the vision that is fundamental to its message. Pentecost represents Christianity's first great ingathering, with the ability of people to suddenly speak in languages they don't know standing as a powerful symbol of the breadth of outreach on which Jesus insists. *All* of the people around the world, including those not present with the disciples on the Day of Pentecost, are to be embraced and welcomed.[4]

Preaching at the TFAM Midwest Regional Conference in 2014, which had the theme "We Are Family," Bishop Flunder used the idea of inclusivity to question notions that particular religious paths are superior to others. To make this point, she drew on an account of how DNA is passed through generations and continues to exist even after particular individuals have died, focusing her comments on the continuities among lifeforms in the world. The knowledge that each of us contains elements of people who have preceded us in life teaches us that we have a connection to *all* other people.

[Jesus] is saying to us that there is a welcome table that needs to happen for the most marginalized. . . . An openness to other faith paths and other sheep. . . . Jesus told his disciples, I have other sheep—that are not Metho-Bapti-Costal and black. [An "amen" from the congregation.] Other sheep who don't clap on the two and the four. Our mission is not to be cloistered in our religiosity. Our mission is to stretch ourselves and understand the depth of what family really means.

At the same time, however, she pointed out that TFAM members have special obligations toward the world, largely because they understand these connections and can put them into action. This perspective generates a messianic message, along with a certainty that what TFAM is doing to further social justice echoes the work of the earliest Christians.

We have a prophetic responsibility. We are Acts 2. The new Book of Acts. We are the ones responsible now to do some of the things that couldn't happen in the first century AD. We are the new Pentecost. We are the fresh revelation. The change is coming through us. We who once were the tail are the head. We who once were the gum on somebody's shoe are now the prophetic voice of God in the earth. And that's why God uses us like God uses us.

Here Bishop Flunder referred to some of the New Testament texts that are understood to authorize the Pentecostal practices of speaking in tongues and other forms of ecstatic worship. She also spoke of the involvement of African American people in artistic pursuits and in prophecy, thus reinforcing the notion that TFAM is, indeed, a church primarily focused on black people and that black people have special gifts that demand recognition. At the same time, this language positions TFAM's mission as deeply connected to the fundamental message of Christianity, particularly in terms of its expansiveness and rejection of sectarianism.

But in taking this position, Bishop Flunder challenges the very foundation of a cohesive church, asking congregants to let go of their understanding of even their most treasured doctrines as incontrovertibly correct. She is joined in this articulation of inclusivity by Bishop Phyllis Pennese from Chicago's Pillar of Love, who explained to me how one can be firm in one's own beliefs while also being able to accept the views of others. She argued that the "unapologetic Christianity" of TFAM did not in any way preclude its members from accepting, indeed opening their arms, to people whose religious beliefs diverge from theirs. In an interview with her, she referred to Bishop Flunder in explaining her position.

Bishop has always said this, that we can mind the same things without having the same mind, that's a quote. And for me it relates to an old lesbian slogan which was "one struggle, many fronts." It's all one struggle in my heart. . . . It's not a requirement for people to have to stop believing what they believe in order for me to feel comfortable in pursuing and living what I believe.

Indeed, some TFAM members identified radical inclusivity as being at the heart of TFAM's refusal to constitute itself as a denomination. "Larry Murdock," a transman who lives on the East Coast, saw this structure as the key to furthering inclusivity. This means that while other churches with specific outreach to either LGBT people (MCC, Unity) or to African Americans (COGIC, AME, etc.) have organized themselves as formal denominations, TFAM has thus far resisted such a move, out of a fear that being a denomination would cause it to congeal theologically, undermining its ability to reach out to diverse populations, perhaps so diverse that they cannot yet be imagined. Larry explained:

I think part of the beauty of the Fellowship is that it has refused to stay in a denominational lane. And it continues to blur denominational lines, and I think that is radical, an extraordinarily radical position to take in terms of kind of a Christian entity that comes together for that purpose—or God-centered entity. I would go so far to say that not everyone that is a part of the Fellowship even identifies as a Christian, which is fine. I think every year, certainly at every gathering, there is a whole new layer of what it really means to step into our ideal of being radically inclusive. I think that's a never-ending growth opportunity.

Bishop Pennese affirmed this interpretation, saying:

As a Christian, I believe that your life experience is enhanced by having a relationship with Jesus Christ. . . . I believe God created us all; we are all saved by Jesus Christ. He's done it for all of us, whether you believe it or not. But when you're engaged in a relationship with Christ, based on my experience, there is this incredible feeling. . . . [But] I'm willing to believe that I could be wrong about all of this, which is why I don't require anybody else to give up or to be what I think that they should be in terms of what I believe. I am fully aware that I could in the afterlife find out that the Yoruba or the Muslims are right and that I've been completely wrong. That doesn't work for other Christians because they say that without a shadow of a doubt they . . . know that they are right. And I just don't believe that.

This account situates inclusivity as the engine of TFAM's growth. Pastor "Daniel Porter," who leads a TFAM congregation on the East Coast, put it this way:

We're looking at other people who may be New Thought and metaphysical, finding another way to be able to align ourselves with even the Jewish community and being able to align ourselves with some of the other communities that are affirming. We won't lose our core [black and Pentecostal] because we can't. It's the base of who we are. But I think that there are some other things that we can share, and we can gain from that. I think we'll become more diverse in our ethnic pieces. I think you're seeing more congregations who won't be—I hate to use this word—but so gay-heavy.... One of the things that's very unique about [our church] is that in our vision and our mission, we don't put that we're here for gay people.

Indeed, recent TFAM convocations and regional meetings have offered a prominent position to leaders of other churches and denominations with which TFAM is forging alliances. These include Religious Science/Spiritual Living/New Thought (as mentioned in chapter 1); representatives of other inclusive religious movements, such as the UCC church led by Bishop Carlton Pearson; and clergy, such as Bishop Jim Swilley, who have come out as gay and then struggled to make their churches LGBT-accepting (Pearson 2006; Swilley 2012). Bishop Pearson, who is African American, is a prominent figure in progressive Christian circles. His positions on a number of issues have earned him the designation of heretic among traditional Bible-believing Christians, with his insistence that there is no such thing as hell being particularly alarming to that population. He calls his doctrine the gospel of inclusion, espousing a variety of Universal Reconciliation that holds that because of the mercy and divine love of God, all people, no matter how sinful, will ultimately be reconciled and gain a place in heaven. He began his career as a Pentecostal pastor but is now ordained by the United Church of Christ and pastors in Tulsa.

Bishop Swilley—who is white and led a Pentecostal megachurch, Church in the Now, in the Atlanta area—came out as gay in 2010, feeling he had to take this action because of his distress over the wave of teenage suicides by young gay men that had recently gotten media attention. He came to believe that the situation of these gay youths would only deteriorate further if people like him continued to conceal their gay identities. After disclosing his sexual orientation, Bishop Swilley experienced an outpouring of hostility and lost his congregation, though his former wife has continued to offer him visible support. He has maintained an affiliation with TFAM and has used his experience as the basis for reexamining scriptural texts and reaching new theological insights.

The relationship between TFAM and the UCC exemplifies the coalitional strategy, which couldn't be achieved if doctrinal, racial, or gender/

sexuality standards defined the breadth of TFAM's powers. The UCC typically sends official representatives to large TFAM gatherings, and a number of congregations have received UCC church buildings free of charge when there were no longer enough longtime (white) parishioners to sustain a congregation. Along similar lines, speakers at conferences and convocations often include representatives of Native American and Yoruba religious traditions. Some TFAM members are also active Yoruba practitioners, for example, and no one suggests that such dual affiliations involve a conflict.

Symbolic representations of traditions that TFAM wishes to embrace and/or recognize as part of members' spiritual heritage include both visual and linguistic elements. Accordingly, the altar at the Oakland "mother church," City of Refuge, incorporates items that include a Yoruba mask, an American Indian totem pole, and a Jewish menorah, in addition to more standard Christian ritual objects. It is also a location where worshippers can place photographs of deceased family members they wish to honor. Both the Yoruba and the American Indian elements receive considerable attention in sermons, where Bishop Flunder, in particular, likes to talk about the complex cultural roots of black religion. In one sermon, for example, she compared the dancing that some worshippers engage in when they are filled with the spirit to dance moves associated with indigenous people in the United States, though the foundations of these movements also clearly resemble the shuffling of the ring shouts, which have been traced to African religion (Callahan 2006; Raboteau 1978, 1999).

Another preacher, Troy Sanders from Atlanta, explained the breadth of radical inclusivity. In an interview, he reminded me of the ultimate foundation for radical inclusivity.

We have to create a place where people can nurse or honor their faith tradition and co-exist with others who may not necessarily share that same tradition. And I think it can be done. It certainly can be modeled. Religious dualism is certainly present in the New Testament. Jesus is the founder of the Christian church but was never a Christian; he was a devout Jew. So I think the paradigm for it is present.

But none of these comments directly address the matter of how much diversity TFAM can absorb before its fundamental character might be transformed in a way that would alienate its core black LGBT constituency. Asking about this proved difficult, however, as many with whom I raised the issue deflected the question rather than answering it. When I asked "Jackson Davis," the pastor of a small congregation in a midwestern city, whether he saw any problems with TFAM's ability to take radical inclusivity as far as it could go, he responded, "Let me turn that question around. When you come here, do you feel at home?" I allowed that indeed, I did. "That's the answer," he said. This interpretation of inclusivity, then, returns to the centrality of comfort and safety writ large as a central mission of TFAM, but still dances around the matter of how much difference TFAM can absorb. The responses I received from others whom I asked about this were similarly oblique; interlocutors didn't seem to want to engage with this issue. No one knows how many people will be drawn to TFAM whose backgrounds do not resemble those of its current constituency, so the question of how racial and religious diversity might be managed remains open to speculation.

Inclusivity, then, is defined in different ways by different TFAM members. On the one hand, it refers to a kind of demographic inclusion, that is, the welcome extended to people who are stigmatized and despised by traditional churches and/or by mainstream cultures—those affected by HIV/AIDS or who are homeless, formerly incarcerated, poor, as well as members of sexual/gender minorities. But on the other hand, this demographic inclusion can stretch to include people who are not black, Christian, Pentecostal, or LGBT. In this sense, inclusivity moves from being about demographic diversity to embracing and welcoming people whose beliefs may not correspond to, and may even diverge dramatically from, the doctrines that lie at the heart of Pentecostal belief and worship practices. It means, in this sense, that the broadest understanding of Christianity as an apostolic practice points to "extravagant hospitality" as what is demanded of TFAM. A larger question of what populations—other than LGBT African Americans—would be most likely to take up this offer of hospitality remains unanswered.

In an interview in 2011, City of Refuge's Pastor Toni Dunbar explained radical inclusivity at some length, focusing on the church's commitment to accept anyone who arrives.

Our philosophy has always been whoever walks through the door is appointed to do that. So whoever comes in, and they reach a critical mass, and we understand their needs, we have to do something for them. . . . Whoever comes through the door is supposed to be there. If they come twice, there's a reason. So the guys who were really dirty and smelly, they get to come to church too. And the people who are recovering but are still a little high, they get to come to church. People who haven't had their meds in six weeks. They get to come to church, because it's a community. You don't kick people out of the community because they're not presentable today.

CHAPTER FIVE

To illustrate the expansiveness of the kind of hospitality that is integral to City of Refuge, and by extension to TFAM, she shared a particularly moving story with me about a man who used to come to the church on a regular basis.

When we first started the church, there was this guy who was alcoholic and he would come to the church, and I felt that it was my role in life to evangelize this guy, to get him clean and sober. So he would come and I'd make conversation. . . . So I asked, "Why do [your friends] call you Wizard?" "It's because I was a physics professor." This guy was a physics professor in Washington State, with a family and seven children, who is now eating out of trash cans. I said, "You don't have to live like this." I gave him a speech, Jesus loves you. And he said, "Yes, I know that Jesus loves me. Do you want me to tell you how I know?" And he says, "Because I am a late-stage alcoholic. I have to have a drink every day or I'll die. And Jesus sends me a drink every day." That was the end of me as an evangelist; that was the end of me as a proselytizer.

This experience taught Pastor Dunbar that her notion of what Christ could do to enhance any individual's life was limited and had failed to consider the deep personal truths a person might use in crafting his own relationship with God. But Wizard's attendance at City of Refuge did more: it also strained the definitions of inclusivity in terms of what a person had to do to be welcome in the church.

Wizard came one day—he was so messed up. He had vermin crawling on him. And he was in church. . . . It was his place to be seen. He wasn't gay, but he couldn't be anywhere else where he was a man and not an object. He was a person. That day he was crawling with bugs, and the ushers took him and they put him in the back. They opened a whole section of the room and put him back there. I came in and I saw that and I just blew up. I made them go get him, bring him and sit him up in the front row next to me. This is his seat, always! That's why he came. Those kinds of experiences. I said to my ushers, "Don't you ever do that again. I don't care if there are scorpions coming out of his ear. Everybody who walks through this door, you put him in the front seat."

Pastor Dunbar explains that everyone who works at the church has had to develop the skills to deal with worshippers who are off their medication, acting out, shouting, even being violent, without making them feel unwelcome.

There a lot of noise, a lot of color, a lot of movement [in church], and people are sometimes overstimulated. And they jump up and start to scream and start to run, and we've got to find a way to corral them without making them leave. What we tend to do is identify someone to say, "Stop it," and they stop. We cultivate that. It's a loving relationship. Come sit with me and I'll put my arm around you. And we find ways. But sometimes we've had to call and have people hospitalized from the service, but as soon as they get out of the hospital, they come right back. What good is the church if these people can't come?

She moves on to telling me the story of another parishioner, an elderly African American woman I've often met at services.

Mother "Ethel" was lying on the sidewalk in front of our church [in its former location in San Francisco] from a suicide attempt. Minister "Frank," who runs the food pantry, found her, brought her into the church. She is now—they call her the Mayor of Sixth Street—she is now a fixture at City Hall. She was an active addict. She had twenty-seven suicide attempts. Frank picked her up and brought her into the church, and now she lives across the street from the church [in San Francisco]. In her own house. She's been reunited with her children. She's doing fabulous work in the community. She's been honored by City Hall and the Board of Supervisors for the advocacy she's doing for SRO [single-room occupancy] residents and for seniors. She is responsible for those beautiful trees and all that stuff. What would have happened [otherwise]?

Those who attend services on a typical Sunday in a TFAM church offer a good illustration of the embrace these congregations offer across lines of class. There are usually people present whose dress and demeanor (and sometimes the cars they are driving) suggest that they are middle or upper-middle class, while other worshippers appear to be down on their luck. People who I guessed were homeless, for example, often bring their pets to church, as they have nowhere to leave them. One Sunday in San Francisco a friend of mine who is a public health nurse at San Quentin accompanied me to services at City of Refuge. Out of about one hundred worshippers present that day, he identified five or six as men he recognized from the prison.

Still, at times calls for inclusivity can profoundly distress some participants. At a regional meeting in North Carolina in 2010, a white transgender woman in one of the workshops proclaimed herself to be an adherent of Wicca,[5] which caused a black woman at the same workshop to question her right to participate in the event. Bishop Flunder heard about the incident and devoted several minutes at the start of the next event to proclaiming the importance of welcoming everyone into TFAM, regardless of race, religion, or other differences. She made a point of singling me out as a European-American Jewish person who was present and was welcome as a participant, as though my association with TFAM confirmed that radical inclusivity was working as intended.

The style of worship, then, is intended to reclaim traditions that most congregants have been excluded from, but to the extent that radical inclusivity can make others comfortable, its embrace is not limited to African American Christians with roots in Pentecostal worship. TFAM's intention to bring together people who want to enhance access to justice for those who have been disregarded and underserved demands, in its leaders' view, a more expansive vision than that of other Christian churches.

But even with its promise to maximize openness, TFAM has not relinquished its commitment to fostering a connection to a Pentecostal black Christian heritage for those who have been distanced from their personal church histories. While stating that black traditions are only one way to worship God, Bishop Flunder still supports following them because "they are ours," even though she believes that "God can move through any culture" (Flunder 2005: 11). What this means for those who are not so identified is not clear, nor is it easy to see how many such congregants can be absorbed before the feeling and practice of worship might change drastically. These two missions may leave participants in rituals having profoundly different experiences—some connecting with their personal history, others having intimate communication with the Holy Spirit, still others appreciating the friendship and warm embrace of the congregation (as is true for me). In this sense, TFAM worship events are multilayered performances that can be experienced differently by actors and audiences, with satisfaction being defined in diverse ways depending on one's position in and identification with the performance (Graham 2005). Performances are multi-vocal, resonating across the audience in ways that may vary with the personal characteristics of individual worshippers and with time (Bauman 1986, 2004; Bauman and Briggs 2003; Borker 1984). The audience plays a vital role in making meaning out of a text, and it is clear that not all audience members do so on the same terms.[6]

Performing Jewishness

At the 2013 national convocation in Las Vegas, I received what at first seemed to be an unusual request. The person who approached me, Jonathan Thunderword, had been a convert to Judaism some years before, not long after he transitioned from female to male. Jonathan was a member of Sha'ar Zahav, a synagogue in San Francisco with a long-standing outreach to LGBT Jews, but he also continued his involvement with City of Refuge, the TFAM congregation in the Bay Area, singing in the transgender gospel choir, Transcendence, and regularly attending national convocations and regional events. He presented himself as a very observant Jew, wearing a *kippah* and *tsitses*,[7] garments associated with the ultra-Orthodox, and I had observed him on one occasion leaving the evening service just before the serving of the Eucharist, which was also my strategy for managing the one part of the liturgy that made me uncomfortable.[8] Jonathan approached me, explaining that he had been invited to light the *Shabbat* candles on Friday evening before the regular service. He asked me to help him carry out this assignment, and I (perhaps too) readily agreed. He then inquired as to whether I had my *siddur* (prayer book) with me, and I had to allow that I did not. (I didn't share with him that I don't actually own a *siddur*.) In any case, we established the basic parameters for the ritual—the lighting of the candles and the consumption of the *challah* (Sabbath braided bread) and wine (or wine substitute), to be accompanied by the appropriate blessings. I went to my room to consult Google to confirm that I had the right blessing in my head for the lighting of the candles, feeling slightly nervous about whether I would be able to perform the blessing correctly.

The small ritual took place with very little fanfare and, indeed, with only a few people present. Jonathan gave a rather learned explanation of Shabbat, emphasizing its central importance to Jewish observance, and played some familiar Jewish music, appropriate for Shabbat, that he had on his iPad. I have to admit I was impressed by the depth of his knowledge (possibly because my own Jewish education is so thin), while also being relieved that I managed to recite the blessing and light the candles without mishap. The promised *challah* and wine never appeared, and so we omitted that part of the ritual.

This nod to the presence of two Jews among the several hundred persons attending the national convocation was repeated, after a fashion, by an altar erected at the front of the same room, purporting to represent key items in Yoruba worship. As far as I know, no ritual observance accompanied this display, but the members of the organizing committee who planned these events definitely wanted to send the message that African spiritual practice was to be included in the convocation and accorded respect. Still, these gestures were not necessarily comprehensive; although

CHAPTER FIVE

Ramadan's start coincided that year with the dates of the convocation, no Muslim observance occurred, most likely because no one had made a specific request.

A number of questions, most as yet unanswerable, can be drawn from an examination of the expansion of radical inclusivity under way in TFAM. Are these claims consistent with its ability to directly embrace the needs of African Americans who have been ill-used by the traditional black church? Can TFAM continue its commitment to Pentecostal (or Metho-Bapti-Costal) worship while also including worshippers from many diverse religious backgrounds? In other words, how elastic can TFAM be while maintaining its founding principles? Does the potential dilemma posed by the expansion of radical inclusivity resemble the issues that arise from the growing comfort LGBT people have in the wider culture of the United States, that is, does radical inclusivity spell the demise of separateness for members of TFAM—a kind of "homonormativity" (Duggan 2003) of religious practice? Regardless of how TFAM manages these potential pitfalls, its commitment to the most expansive form of radical inclusivity allows it to enlarge dramatically the "safe space" model of LGBT institutions. Whether all congregants will define their community in the same way, however, is a question yet to be answered.

Promoting Seminary Education

Accompanying the embrace of radical inclusivity is TFAM's emphasis on education and particularly seminary training for any members who show interest, a direction that departs dramatically from the kinds of Pentecostal churches where most congregants were raised. The stress on direct experience that drives Pentecostal worship also tends to disparage both worship based on texts and the kind of advanced theological training that clergy in many other denominations are expected to complete. Many of the scholars who have written about black Christianity have made clear the ways in which slaves and freedmen embraced forms of Christianity that were grounded in ecstatic experience and not in textual interpretation. Theologian Allen Dwight Callahan speaks of "the premium placed on experience, where the spirit possession of West African religion meets the 'experimental religion' of Evangelical Christianity" as the "spiritual heritage of slave religion." He further notes that "the slaves contrasted 'getting religion' in this way with the Christianity of the master class that they had come to know and despise" (Callahan 2006: 63). The slaves rejected the masters' "Bible Christianity," which they saw as contaminated by hypocrisy and thus not worthy of emulation. At the same time, however, even illiterate slaves engaged in biblical interpretation, embracing the texts themselves even as they rejected the uses of these texts by slave owners. In many ways, the emergence of black liberation theology (Cone 1997 [1975]) can be traced to these early interpretive exercises. It should be noted, for example, that virtually all the spirituals draw on a textual source, most commonly, of course, from Exodus, but also from Psalms, Prophets, and Gospels. So it was the *masters'* use of texts that the slaves shunned, not the biblical texts themselves.

Of course, the masters often drew on Scripture to reinforce their authority over slaves, accentuating texts that spoke of obedience. Callahan cites Cotton Mather's particular use of Ephesians 6:5, "Servants, be obedient to them that are your masters according to the flesh, with fear and trembling, in singleness of your heart, as unto Christ" (Callahan 2006: 32). In this way, slaveholders sought to limit the extent to which exposure to Christianity would promote the idea that slaves were children of God just as their owners were. Along the same lines, theologian James H. Cone speaks of black people's use of Scripture within the context of what he calls "speaking the truth." Quoting from James Weldon Johnson's 1927 *God's Trombones*, he offers the example of a black preacher who affirmed that his relationship to God was much more than *words* about God.

This is the meaning behind the occasion when a black preacher "who after reading a rather cryptic passage took off his spectacles, closed the Bible with a bang and by way of preface said, 'Brothers and sisters, this morning—I intend to explain the unexplainable—find out the undefinable—ponder over the imponderable—and unscrew the inscrutable.'" (Cone 1997 [1975]: 17)

In other words, the book and its words may be seen as obscure, often because of the archaic language employed in the King James Bible, and thus not unlikely to confuse worshippers with ideas that do not honor their experience or "truth." Understanding the passage itself has no utility if its language is not accessible, so the preacher's job is to let go of the specific words, to re-encode it, and thus locate the truth.

Given the historical suspicion of too much book learning among Holiness Christians and the fear that too much education would lead preachers to forfeit their spiritual roots, it is not accidental that the strand of Christianity that was most firmly embraced by slaves was the ecstatic, evangelical worship style of the itinerant preachers associated with the First and Second Great Awakenings. This sort of worship didn't depend on education or even literacy, so it was flexible enough to provide a location where a poor black person could excel and gain a following, sometimes among both black and white worshippers. Of course, before emancipation, teaching slaves to read was prohibited in many states. But by turning texts into songs, evangelical Christianity flourished as an oral tradition that bypassed the need for literacy that characterized the high church denominations. Accordingly, many black churches historically did not require or even encourage clergy to be seminary trained; indeed, such knowledge evoked mistrust. (See chapter 1 for more on Raboteau's account of how "a converted heart and a gifted tongue were more important than the amount of theological training received" [1978: 133–34].)

While inspired spiritual experience is at the heart of worship in TFAM, however, the Fellowship departs from its historical connection to the black church by emphasizing the importance of theological education. The emphasis on education in TFAM seems to have a number of objectives. Importantly, seminary training, particularly at liberal/progressive institutions, provides pastors with the necessary tools to make sense of the parts of the Bible that have been misused to oppress LGBT people. TFAM clergy stress the importance of interpretation of these scriptural texts, pointing out again and again that they were written by human beings who lived in particular historical periods and whose writings reflect the values that prevailed in those times. TFAM thus draws on *contextual theology*, which highlights cultural interpretation, and is most directly concerned with evangelization "aimed at illuminating and transforming men and women as they are" (Bevans 1992: 15). Such approaches insist upon pluralism as the foundation of meaningful evangelical practice (Blount 1995). Other adherents to this type of theology call their work *local theology*, urging ministers to keep the specific circumstances of the communities where they work in mind as they undertake dialogues with various interlocutors (Sedmak 2002) and to focus on the importance of connecting these dialogues to pressing local concerns. These scholars ask the questions: What local concepts can be embraced or adapted to make Christian theology relevant? How can theology be presented so that people recognize themselves in the teachings? Pastor Dunbar's story of her encounter with Wizard, which appeared earlier in this chapter, provides a compelling example of this kind of thinking.

Beyond this, interpretive approaches to biblical texts, what some authors call historical-critical reading (as opposed to literal or fundamentalist interpretations), require readers to employ scrutiny on two levels (Helminiak 2000 [1994]). From one perspective, interpreters of Scripture must deal with authors who composed texts long ago, under remote cultural conditions and in non-modern languages. But as theologians Robert Morgan and John Barton explain, "Modern interpreters have aims and interests of their own.... An enormous range of possibilities emerge when different people with different aims interpret such a diverse collection of ancient texts as the Bible.... Some historians have religious interests, and many biblical scholars are also believers. Some of the latter have integrated their religious faith and their critical reason" (Morgan and Barton 1988: 16). In other words, all readers of the Bible, whether they see themselves as using interpretive methods or not, are operating with conscious or unconscious agendas that inevitably influence how they understand the texts.

For religious bodies like TFAM, then, interpretation is a vital element of trying to establish a foundation for worship that neither demeans nor invalidates the character of the congregation. For example, what do these presupposed proscriptions of homosexuality mean in their original language and cultural context, and what should they be understood to mean to modern believers? Even for fundamentalist Christians who claim not to interpret biblical texts, but to accept them literally, issues of translation loom larger than people in those churches may care to admit (Ammerman 1987).

Sociologist Michelle Wolkomir offers a careful description of how this sort of interpretive exercise is realized in the MCC-sponsored Bible study group in which she participated. In this context, congregants are urged to consider how particular interpretations of the key texts that demonize homosexuality may be judged to be "fraudulent." She explains, "MCC asserts that conservatives have simply misunderstood [each] verse ... [and] that the misinterpretation has resulted from either a mistranslation of key words in biblical passages from the original language or a failure to consider the verse in context with the rest of the Bible and/or the cultural understanding of the time" (Wolkomir 2006: 25). In addition, study groups look at biblical accounts of the same-sex relationships between David and Jonathan (1 and 2 Samuel) and Naomi and Ruth (Ruth) as examples of same-sex commitment, whether or not sexuality was involved. As I have noted, a major element of this approach requires attention to the challenges of translation in interpreting the Hebrew Bible, originally written in Hebrew (with some books in Aramaic), and the New Testament, originally written in Greek (Porter and Hess 2005).

But LGBT Christians face another challenge in understanding and embracing biblical texts. Specific texts (Deut. 23:17-18, Gen. 19:5, Lev. 18:22 and 20:13, Rom. 1:26-27, 1 Cor. 6:9, and 1 Tim. 1:9-10) have been used

CHAPTER FIVE

to justify homophobia and hatred of gender variance, and many TFAM members have been repeatedly subjected to religious messages that vilify them and represent them as sinners who cannot be saved. The most frequently invoked text is from Lev. 18:22, "You shall not lie with a male as those who lie with a female; it is an abomination" (Barton 2012: 239).

So the challenge for gay-friendly theologies is to demonstrate that these texts are not really condemnatory of same-sex love. An enormous corpus of work has appeared since the rise of the gay rights movement that approaches the issues of Christianity and homosexuality, some being personal narratives (cf. Bean 2010; Perry 1972) and others efforts to find support for homosexuality or some sort of validation for homosexual persons in the Bible (cf. Cheng 2012; McNeill 1976; Piazza 1994; Williams 1992). Indeed, some of these interpretations are written by theological conservatives to argue that the Bible doesn't condemn same-sex marriages (Achtemeier 2014; Brownson 2013; Gushee 2015; Lee 2013; Rogers 2009; Vines 2014).[9]

Churches with special outreach to LGBT people have developed targeted methodologies for rethinking the Bible. Some MCC congregations, for example, provide Bible study courses that seek to uncover "what the Bible really says about homosexuality" (Wolkomir 2006: 96), reexamining key biblical passages, especially those mentioned above, that have been used to condemn homosexuality. Those who provide these interpretations emphasize the many areas in which the Bible has endorsed oppression, from the subordination of women to slavery, and that just as one wouldn't legitimate those practices today based on biblical validation, neither should homosexuality be sanctioned solely on apparent biblical grounds. Numerous commentators also note that many practices proscribed in the Bible are of no interest to even the most rigorous Christian (and fundamentalist) followers of the Bible, such as the (kosher) dietary restrictions, the ban on clothing made from "mixed fibers," and so on, so the focus on the (apparent) anti-homosexual verses must be seen as excessive.

Bishop Flunder often emphasizes the difficulties scholars have faced in the translation process, and the many disputes that have arisen among them about the meaning of particular words and phrases. Indeed, the problem of translation has emerged in biblical scholarship as contentious on its own grounds with esoteric issues of how to convey the meanings of Hebrew and Greek words generating an apparently endless literature (Metzger 2001; Nida 1964). The relevance of these difficulties to understanding how the Bible speaks to LGBT people has, of course, generated its own literature, one that overlaps with the larger project of interpreting what exactly the Bible means in a number of frequently cited verses (Helminiak 2000 [1994]).

Both more careful attention to cultural factors that were in place when biblical texts were composed and sufficient linguistic knowledge to make better-informed translations are capacities that depend on the education that one can receive in seminaries or divinity schools. Facility with these approaches is essential if a Christian organization is to effectively repudiate doctrines that condemn homosexuals to perdition. Such knowledge is perhaps more vital for those clergy serving LGBT populations if these worshippers are to overcome their long-standing assumption that being gay and being Christian are antithetical. It also cannot be denied that gaining the imprimatur of a seminary education offers TFAM clergy access to a source of public esteem not accessible without such training. Bishop Flunder's decision to attend seminary in the face of possibly being considered a "para-preacher" is instructive on this point (chapter 2).

Pastor Toni Dunbar, associate pastor at City of Refuge, explains the importance of getting a doctoral degree in establishing one's legitimacy.

It also gives credibility. The same things that I'm saying to you today, I could have said fifteen years ago, but nobody would listen to me because I didn't have a degree. You get a degree, you get credibility. You can go more places. You can talk to more people. You do something that the Scripture describes as speaking in tongues. Speaking in tongues does not necessarily mean glossolalia. It could mean being intelligible to different groups of people at different times and different places.

We Are Family

In the summer of 2014, Bishop Phyllis Pennese delivered a sermon at the regional conference in St. Louis. She began, in classic fashion, quoting Scripture, drawing on texts that emphasize the expanded meanings of "family" that Jesus urged his followers to accept. As Gerald L. Davis explains, the African American preacher demonstrates to the congregation that he has been divinely inspired, that the sermon has scriptural foundations that make it the word of God (Davis 1985: 67–73). "By quoting a Bible verse in support of his announced theme, the preacher is 'proving' to his congregation his continuing ability to respond spontaneously from the depth of his Christian commitment. A function of the Bible quotation is to intensify the nature of the Godly sanction that attends the sermon performance" (73).

Bishop Pennese began her sermon by quoting two biblical passages.

CHAPTER FIVE

Matthew, 12:46–49
While Jesus was still talking to the crowd, his mother and brothers stood outside, wanting to speak to him. Someone told him, "Your mother and brothers are standing outside, wanting to speak to you." He replied to him, "Who is my mother, and who are my brothers?" Pointing to his disciples, he said, "Here are my mother and my brothers."

Ephesians, 2:11–19
You Gentiles by birth—called "the uncircumcised" by the Jews, who call themselves "the circumcised" (which refers to what men do to their bodies)—remember what you were in the past. At that time you were apart from Christ. You were foreigners and did not belong to God's chosen people. You had no part in the covenants, which were based on God's promises to his people, and you lived in this world without hope and without God. But now, in union with Christ Jesus, you who used to be far away have been brought near by the blood of Christ. For Christ himself has brought us peace by making Jews and Gentiles one people. With his own body he broke down the wall that separated them and kept them enemies. He abolished the Jewish Law with its commandments and rules, in order to create out of the two races one new people in union with himself, in this way making peace. By his death on the cross Christ destroyed their enmity; by means of the cross he united both races into one body and brought them back to God. So Christ came and preached the Good News of peace to all—to you Gentiles, who were far away from God, and to the Jews, who were near to him. It is through Christ that all of us, Jews and Gentiles, are able to come in the one Spirit into the presence of the Father. So then, you Gentiles are not foreigners or strangers any longer; you are now fellow-citizens with God's people and members of the family of God.

Bishop Pennese shifts from these biblical quotations to identifying the theme of the sermon; here she diverges from the form Davis describes in that she moves directly to familiar vernacular examples. Thus, the topic of the sermon "I Don't Care What Nobody Say, We Are Family" is first rooted in biblical authority and then more fully elaborated in Bishop's review of her own family history, drawing not on theology, but on personal experience to validate the position she will take in the sermon. This sermon's authority, then, rests both on the divine inspiration provided by the quotations from the New Testament and from the familiarity of the examples she offers from her personal experience.

Some of you know and some of you do not know that I am a biracial child. You may not have known that I'm biracial and that my father was an Italian immigrant because even though I celebrate and embrace my Italian heritage and my family who are Italian, I live my life and have always lived my life as a black woman in this society.

I am doubly blessed by my dual heritage, especially when it comes to family because Italian folks are about loving family and being family. *The Godfather* and *The Sopranos* have, even in stereotypical form, given us a glimpse of the Italian reality which is that family is reverenced [sic] and important to Italians and those of Italian descent. But I get blessed from the other side of myself in that black folks are some family-oriented and family-loving people too. In fact, that's one of the things that I absolutely love about black folks . . . is that we have very non-traditional views about family and the scope of family for black folks ain't never . . . I mean it ain't never, ever . . . been about sameness of biology.

Bishop's shift into vernacular black English makes this more convincing. The audience is with her, laughing, shouting out exhortations to "preach" and comments like "well" and "praise the Lord." She then draws on historical information to ground her argument.

Even before coming to the US, back in Africa, the whole village was considered to be one family. Even slavery and its effects did not and could not eradicate or negatively impact our perspective and configuration of family. Even though many black families were torn asunder during slavery by having members of the same family sold off to different slave owners, often, those who remained were cared for and reared by people who shared no actual blood relationship but they treated one another as if they were family. House Negroes and field Negroes, though different and used as pawns pitted against one another, they managed to stay engaged and true to their heritage and despite their differences . . . they were family. After the Civil War, former slaves would migrate north and find friends to live with who took them in and treated them as if they were family.

And even today, that is one of the things about black folks that is so wonderful and that I love so very much . . . We got Big Aunties who ain't blood, we got Big Mamas that ain't no blood, we got Uncle Willies that ain't no blood, and we got play-cousin Pookies and Sha Nay Nays . . . who may be as different as night is from day and who ain't no blood at all, but who are every bit as much family as if there was some blood relationship that links us together.

Here Bishop Pennese uses black history, as well as vernacular expressions, to make her assertion immediate and persuasive. She draws on her experience in the black community to connect ideas about kinship to her audience in ways that both resonate for them and amuse them. Indeed, there was quite a bit of appreciative laughter in the congregation as she talked about these non-blood relatives.

CHAPTER FIVE

Being a by-product of my black mother and my Italian father developed in me a healthy appreciation for what it really means to be family. I learned some important things from both sides about family.

In my family we stuck together. If one had to fight the bully from down the street, everybody had to fight the bully from down the street. Siblings. Cousins. Everybody. We had better not come home and let our mama or auntie find out that we hadn't all stuck together and fought together. Family sticks together. And I learned from my family that family loves you at all times. They may not like you at particular junctures in your life, but folks who really know about being family love you even when they don't like you.

Family loves you when you're your best self, and they love you when you're your worst self. And family doesn't have to be fancy. I remember days when Vickie [her partner] and I first got together and her family would all show up at her house and there'd be pallets in every conceivable spot on the floor or we would all crawl in the bed . . . six or seven or maybe more of us at a time to watch a movie together. Family doesn't care whether there are dirty dishes in the sink, or if you were able to get your hair did. Family always rolls with the punches, and when you're really family, you don't have to put on airs and pretend to be *anything* that you are not.

The problem is . . . that much of the time we have forgotten what real family looks like and how real family is supposed to be with one another.

And some of you are sitting there right about now beginning to ask what any of this has to do with the text for tonight, and you may be wondering if this is part of the preached message. I'm glad you asked 'cause I'm fitna tell ya what it has to do with the text for tonight.

See, I confess I don't know if black folks are how we are about family because of the Bible, but how we are about family is very much *rooted* in what the Bible teaches us about family.

Here she uses familiar (and idealized) images of families interacting and unconditionally supporting one another to return to the scriptural text that began the sermon. The key strategy here is to embed the biblical story in the ordinary day-to-day realities of her audience.

Jesus, on more than one occasion, flipped the script and redefined for us who family was and what our responsibility is toward one another from the context of that redefinition of family. The Gospel of Matthew points out to us that while Jesus was out ministering to the people, he came upon a situation where he redefined the parameters of family and broadened the meaning of family to include those beyond biological connection. When they told him his mama and brothers wanted a word with him, he pointed to the folks who had become family and said, "Here are my mother and my brothers." Heck . . . even while dying on the cross, the Gospel of

John tells us that Jesus said to his mother and his beloved disciple, *"This man is now your son."* Then he said to the disciple, *"She is now your mother."* And the Bible tells us that from then on, they became family and that the disciple took Jesus's mother into his own home as his mother.

In our text from the Epistle of Ephesians, the Apostle Paul picks up the torch and teaches the Ephesians—and us—about being one family.

And that brings me to this one point for tonight: *Our Differences Do Not Make Us Enemies and Our Differences Can't Stop Us from Being Family.* An old familiar tactic in waging an attack is to divide and conquer. It doesn't take rocket science to know that we are stronger together than we could ever be alone and separate. Hence, the old saying, *"Together we stand, but divided . . . we fall."* The Jews and the Gentiles were very different people with very different ideas and beliefs and very different ways of doing things. Often, these differences pitted them against each other and there was enmity between them and they often saw each other as enemies who threatened each other's ways of being. The Jews thought they were better than the Gentiles and the Gentiles thought the Jews were a bunch of pious hypocrites, stuck on stupid by being stuck *in* tradition. And we're a lot like that, even today, in that we've been pitted against one another in order that we might be divided and it ain't just about being divided as Christians and Jews. [At this point, she nods at me, as the official Jew in attendance.]

Bishop Pennese emphasizes the following set of points using the rhythmic repetition that is characteristic of black preaching (Davis 1985; Hinson 2000).

But we've also become divided and enemies of each other and have forgotten that we're one family when we have light-skinned black folks whose hair ain't as nappy thinking they're better than dark-skinned folks with nappy hair and features that scream their African-ness.

We've become divided and enemies of each other and have forgotten that we're one family when we have clean and sober folk walking around with their nose in the air and their heads up their butts thinking they're better than our brothers and sisters who done got caught up with drugs and alcohol.

We've become divided and enemies of each other and have forgotten that we're one family when we have white LGBTQ folk versus black LGBTQ folk.

We've become divided and enemies of each other and have forgotten that we're one family when we have gay brothers versus lesbian sisters.

We've become divided and enemies and have forgotten that we're one family with each other when six degrees of separation gets flipped into educational degrees that separate us and those with education and degrees look down on their brothers and sisters who may be less educated and who have no degrees.

CHAPTER FIVE

We've become divided and enemies of each other and have forgotten that we're one family when we have Christians despising Muslims and Christians despising Buddhists and Christians despising Hindus and Christians despising anything that isn't exactly Christian like them in the ways they define Christian.

We've become divided and enemies of each other and have forgotten that we're one family when we have straight folk who oppress and impose their heterosexism on to LGBTQ folk, and when we have LGBTQ folk who have no use or love for their heterosexual brothers and sisters.

We've become divided and enemies of each other and have forgotten that we're one family when we have Baptists versus Methodists and Methodists versus Pentecostals and Pentecostals versus Catholics and Catholics versus Protestants, and ain't none of us figured out it's all right to be Bapti-Metho-Penta-Catho-Proto-Jew-Costal!!

This phrase shifts the audience back to TFAM's self-characterization, elaborating and expanding the phrase "Metho-Bapti-Costal" often used by Bishop Flunder to describe the religious roots of TFAM.

We're supposed to know that we are all equally loved by God and that all of us, each and every single last one of us, is created in God's image. We're supposed to know that, and we're supposed to live in accordance with that truth. But I love this quote that reminds us that we have forgotten that we are one family and that we are all created in God's image. Author Anne Lamott's quote says, *"You can safely assume that you've created God in your own image when it turns out that God hates all the same people you do."*

But the Bible teaches us that Jesus died in order that through his death we could become one people, united under one umbrella, one family, and that the barrier of different-ness that kept us from being one family has been destroyed and only exists because *we* re-create it. *We* allow others to resurrect our differences with the purpose of keeping us divided from one another so that we forget what the Bible teaches . . . which is that no matter how different we may be . . . we are all one family.

At this point Bishop returns to another rhythmic, repetitive invocation of the varieties of family.

Top or Bottom . . . one family.

Gay or Straight . . . one family.

Stud or femme . . . one family.

Black or white . . . one family.

Skinny or pleasingly plump and delicious . . . one family.[10]

Educated or less educated . . . one family.

Clean and sober or strung out . . . one family.

Sociopolitically astute or totally clueless . . . one family.

Out and proud or on the down low . . . one family.

Homeless or living in luxury . . . one family.

Believer or atheist . . . one family.

Sweet in spirit or nothing but a hell-raiser . . . one family.

Patiently single or a skank on the prowl . . .

I don't care what nobody say. We are family!!

There are those whose smiles light up a room when they walk through the door, and there are those who need a match to light their crack pipes . . . yet and still . . . we are family.

There are those who have things to list in the column that reports their total assets, and there are those who ain't got two nickels to rub together, yet and still, we are family.

There are those who have locked the gospel away in their hearts from a child, and there are those trying to figure out how to get out of being on lockdown . . . yet and still . . . we are family.

There are those who dress up, and there are those who prefer to dress down . . . yet and still . . . we are family.

One family . . . Not some fictitious and fallacious facade of patriarchal fathering which really serves to hide our faithless fantasies and phenomenal fear of who family really be!!

This phrasing rescues "family" from its usages in other churches and in hostile relationships. For those congregants whose experiences of (biological) family have not been supportive, it reaffirms the moral wrongness of such rejection, reminding the audience that they deserve to receive support from family members, even if they do not. Family is supposed to be about unconditional solidarity and loyalty, and departures from that standard strain the definition of "family."

I know we've been taught and told and we've even been preached into believing that all these things matter and that what makes us different is what necessarily separates us and keeps us from being family. But I came to tell you that that's a bunch of bullshit intended to keep us from loving one another and is specifically designed to keep us from being family!! But I want you to know, TFAM, that we ain't got to stay stuck on stupid. We can resist and reject the lies and take a page out of African black tradition as well as the Bible and deliberately decide to be family irrespective of our different-ness!!

If you're feeling me, then you'll know that you can be Vanna White or Vanna Black but it's absolutely time to buy a vowel and get a clue!!

'Cause I don't care what nobody say, we are family.

Aché[11] and Amen.

In this sermon, Bishop Pennese speaks in a complex register, invoking the actual experiences of worshippers and contrasting the rejection they may have received at the hands of their families with the experience they deserved to have, and that they can be part of a family that God intended for them. The images of family as non-judgmental, as solidary and reliable, contrast with the real world, but like the enunciation of radical inclusivity, they are aspirational and are effective to the extent that they reinforce ideas about how families are *supposed* to behave. To the extent that blood families have failed to provide the kinds of supports she invokes, TFAM stands as the implicit substitute. The slogan "we are family" thus refers to the community engendered in TFAM rather than being a true-to-life description of anyone's actual experience. It also inserts ideas of justice into reminiscences of family, both making those memories concrete through the use of vernacular examples and also measuring how fully they correspond to cultural expectations (see also Weston 1991, for how this construction works more generally in the ways that lesbians and gay men imagine kinship). The invocation of "family" has been a common theme in LGBT-rights activities over the years, having served as the theme not only of TFAM conferences, but of gay pride parades, with the 1979 song, "We Are Family" by Sister Sledge often serving as a soundtrack for such events.[12] Though none of the TFAM events I attended mentioned the song explicitly, it is safe to assume that congregants understood the allusion.

3   Altar at City of Refuge United Church of Christ, Oakland, California (photo by Veronica Jordan).

Symbolic Representations of Radical Inclusivity

As has been clear throughout this volume, symbolic representations of traditions that TFAM wishes to embrace and/or recognize as part of members' spiritual heritage include both visual and linguistic elements. As detailed earlier, the altar at the Oakland "mother church," City of Refuge, incorporates a Yoruba mask, a totem pole, and a menorah, in addition to a small statue of Jesus. The church also embraces traditions, particularly in the use of language, with which most of the African American members are comfortable. This means, for example, that not all prayers are expressed in "inclusive," non-gender-specific language. When visitors, usually European American, have complained about these practices, Pastor Toni Dunbar explains:

That's because using "him" or "he" is a part of our cultural reality. . . . Rather than saying, you people are not theologically astute because some of your leaders use non-gender-inclusive language; there's something wrong with you. You have to find out why it's not offensive to us, rather than being offended by it. Why is it okay for me to say God, my father? . . . So we've had some of that. And that is European-American hegemony. That's what that is. Man-hating lesbians and woman-hating men, they're not comfortable with us. . . . People who are hiding in the closet and angry about it, they can't do it either, because we say that personal integrity is the most important thing. And if you're not feeling it, you're shortchanging your life.... You know that phenomenon, down low? Down-low folks don't come to our church. The people they have been having sex with are at our church, and they're hiding so hard to keep those folks from knowing, that they have same-sex contacts that if they were to come, there would be an implication.

Pastor Dunbar also explains core religious experiences in ways that make them accessible even to those who don't have a background in the black church. When I ask her about the experience of being filled with the spirit, she astutely assesses my background and explains that it's all about embodiment, which can occur in many ways and with many different kinds of stimuli. In particular, she refers to ecstatic experiences that she suspects (correctly) I might have had with great art, saying that this kind of embodiment is "very similar to music, performance, dance."

Embodiment means to me that [if] you have really embodied worship ... it doesn't just reside in the intellect. When a person is fully actualized and that whole mind-body connection is working, as with an athlete or with a musician, when a person is fully actualized, and they're in the moment, that's when they say, when the whole symphony is focused and acting as one, because they have embodied their education, their knowledge, their feelings, their thoughts, it's all one. That can happen in worship. And it doesn't require that it be any particular faith, because almost any faith has some aspect of that. And so the Pentecostal experience is a moment of complete embodiment to me, where a person has made contact with what they understand to be God with all of their being, mind, soul, emotions. The physicality is there. And they abandon themselves to the experience, as opposed to trying to moderate the experience through understanding. It happens a lot. But there's a moment in everyone's life where they're not doing that. They are simply being and living in the moment. And they're expressing, physically, this complete union and then it goes away, unfortunately, and we go back to trying to piece it together. So for me, it's embodiment.

Much ink has been spilled over the matter of "invented traditions" (Anderson 1991) and how anthropologists should represent their deployment among people we study. Discussion raises questions of which invocations of tradition and history are authentic and what authenticity means to those who use particular symbols (Briggs 1996; Conklin 1997; Graham 2005; Jackson 1995). If the symbols that are elaborated in ceremonies do not factually adhere to historical record, does that make them any less compelling to participants in the event? The use of symbols intended to convey congregants' African roots and those linked to American Indian traditions are important because they introduce (or reinforce) the idea of the complex cultural origins of black worship practices, not because they are necessarily historically accurate depictions of those traditions. Similarly, the elaboration of representations that are identified as "southern" are more important symbolically than they are verifiable portrayals of congregants' backgrounds; the South stands as a way to invoke cultural authenticity, even for those who may never have been there and whose (recent) roots are not grounded there.

We saw in chapter 4 that TFAM preachers regularly draw on histories of the South that congregants share or believe constitute their heritage, and draw worshippers into sermons using gospel music, along with references to African American hair and cuisine. The use of symbolic representations to celebrate radical inclusivity is somewhat different, however, as the symbols do not necessarily have the automatic resonance for worshippers that hair, music, and food do. Some of the symbols displayed on the altar are, indeed, unfamiliar, so the task of the preacher is to link them into the experience of the congregation.

In some ways the symbols on the altar and elsewhere in the sanctuary are simply token representations of the imagined, desired shape of radical inclusivity. No one is required to examine them, and they are not actively invoked in the course of worship. For some members of the congregation, they give voice to identities and explorations that are vital parts of their spiritual life. For others, I suspect, they are just there, not necessarily being noticed explicitly or becoming a part of worship practices. Insofar as the central meaning of "radical inclusivity" remains aspirational, these symbols speak to what TFAM wants to be, regardless of how achieving such aspirations will be achieved.

Benediction: Continuities and Departures

This examination of the Fellowship of Affirming Ministries (TFAM) has revealed an ongoing dialogue between tradition and innovation, between reverence for the past—however it is constructed and imagined—and an embrace of new values and ways of living. Indeed, one might observe that these seemingly contradictory qualities actually buttress one another and make one another more possible. It may seem like a drastic departure from the Metho-Bapti-Costal heritage most TFAM members share to open the doors of its churches, both physically and metaphorically, to whoever chooses to enter, no matter how outrageous or transgressive their religious views, their personal presentation, or their identity. It may seem like a contradiction for a religious organization to be animated by the charismatic persona of its leader, but also to insist that others can do what she does in the future, thus, in a sense undermining the power of her personal charisma. It may be surprising for TFAM members to espouse ideas about coming out that focus less on political goals than on spiritual fulfillment, even as TFAM encourages its members to actively engage with struggles for justice in the public sphere and dignity for all people. TFAM is both entranced by the charisma of Bishop Flunder and skeptical of its universality; and both inspired by invocations of history and tradition, but also able to rethink the relation of each person to the fictions of nostalgia. It makes new meanings out of apparent contradictions, and indeed expands these contradictions as its leaders move its mission into the future.

TFAM is a religious organization that does a number of things at once. It allows worshippers who are (mostly) black and LGBT to reclaim their religious heritage, to insist on the right to have a spiritual experience that fills them with the Spirit in the manner that they understand to be their birthright, and which (re)constitutes a link to the communities in which they were raised. This part of the TFAM mission involves the recuperation of the foundation of moral value from which many LGBT or otherwise stigmatized worshippers have found themselves excluded. Some of this recuperation is tangled with nostalgia, with memories that are real or imagined, but which are saturated with deep emotion regardless. Gaining readmission to one's church family is metaphorically of a piece with reentering one's blood family, both of which may have deep connections with ideas about personal legitimacy and value.

This recuperative mission also reflects the impact of forces outside black communities and black churches that have elevated LGBT people to a new position of civic validity in the United States, revealed in various insignia of respect and citizenship that they may claim (as of this writing): increasingly positive representations in media, access to the public restrooms they feel most comfortable using (by law if not in practice), the right to marry and form a family with their chosen partner, or the right to serve in the military, to mention some prominent recent developments. Being able to worship God in a way that resonates as authentic to them is another such mark of legitimacy, and for those who were raised in the expressive religious traditions of the black church, essential to that undertaking is the yearning to be filled with the Holy Spirit and in this way to access divine aspects of the self. Though the spiritual rewards sought and achieved may be similar, this recuperative undertaking is fundamentally different from the quest for spiritual renewal that animates many other religious movements in the United States, particularly those with a Pentecostal inflection, when they are embraced by people for whom such worship does not derive from heritage (see, for example, Luhrmann 2012). Those new and vigorously expanding religious movements may be rewarding and inspiring, but they do not generally constitute a reclamation of one's birthright.[1]

At the same time that TFAM gives congregants access to their ancestral worship practices, however, it also questions and reconfigures those very traditions. As I have shown, TFAM worship follows forms that have deep histories in black churches, but it also demands space for people whose gender and sexual identities and presentations stray far from what they remember seeing in the churches they attended in years past. TFAM spiritual practices do much more than tolerate such deviations from the norm—they honor and embrace those who display such identities. They remind worshippers that they are made in the image of God and that God's intention for them is revealed in the lives that they lead, while also never forgetting the belief that God is the source of all truth and meaning. This sense of value and esteem ordains a path to community activism, as congregants are urged not to wait for God to care for them, but to step into the world on their own and dedicate themselves to remedying its flaws, be they social, religious, environmental, or political. In other words, even as TFAM invokes the past, it also reconfigures it and discards those elements of religious history that don't support the mission of radical inclusivity and ministering to a population that has long been distanced from black churches. Like the former slave, who swore that she would never read the pages of the Bible that sanctioned slavery (see p. 194, n. 14), the members of TFAM also discard those elements of their heritage that are demeaning and that belittle them.

One way that TFAM is able to achieve this effect is by directing worshippers' attention to the multiple religious roots that may underlie their devotional practices, legitimating all of what worshippers feel is part of their spirituality and also introducing practices that may be new or more attractive. This embrace of eclectic religious and cultural roots effectively cloaks the extent to which TFAM fosters innovation, particularly in terms of its embrace of persons who would otherwise not be valued in a church context. As we have seen, radical inclusivity means many things, but among them is the ability to draw on elements of various worship traditions to create a more welcoming and affirming experience. So while the affective shape of TFAM services uses the expressive vocabulary of Pentecostal worship, doctrine draws on other sources as well: the Methodist emphasis on social action, the congregational autonomy sometimes characteristic of the Baptists (but actually most typical of the UCC), and the unconditional notion of salvation as dependent on accepting Jesus as one's savior, also drawn from the Baptists. As I have shown, radical inclusivity also embraces some non-Christian symbols, both as a way to honor Native American and African ancestors, an expression of openness to all sorts of spiritual truths, and a gesture of welcome to those whose roots lie very far from these sources. While drawing on symbols derived from African and Native American traditions reminds worshippers that their origins are diverse, it also demands that all religious doctrines be given respect and be examined for their efficacy in TFAM worship.

The Fellowship and the Present

How does the story of the Fellowship figure in our understanding of religion in the United States in the current moment? The United States has long been known for the religiosity of its population, particularly in contrast to the levels of church attendance that are typical in Europe (McLeod 2007). Still, the growth of a type of worship that sociologist of religion Nancy Ammerman (1987) calls "Bible believing" has generated widespread concern across the cultural and political spectrum. Ammerman uses this term to refer to an eclectic range of religious adherents variously labeled Fundamentalists, Evangelicals, and Pentecostals, though each of these terms signals a distinct theological position, and often more than one for any single designation. While mainly distinguished by a conservative theology that variously recalls early (apostolic) Christianity, the Puritan heritage of the United States, and a concomitant resistance to modernity, Bible-believing Christians differ considerably in positions they take on matters of doctrine and in their views of social issues and the appropriate level of involvement for them to have in the secular world. Many in the general public assume that they are all politically conservative and hostile to progressive social agendas. A voluminous literature exists on fundamentalism, Bible-believing Christianity, evangelical religion, and Pentecostalism that examines the history and sociology of these movements, as well as their proliferation in the United States and throughout the developing world. So I was challenged to situate my work within the larger study of religion in general and African American religion in the United States.

A particular focus of this literature has been to account for the immense appeal of seemingly conservative religious formations in the twenty-first century, including efforts to explain the explosive public influence many of them have effected in American political life, not to mention their international impact, such as the virulent forms of homophobia that have been stoked by American fundamentalist preachers in such countries as Uganda (Baptiste and Foreign Policy in Focus 2014; Williams 2014).[2] Some scholars, Ammerman (1987) among them, have pointed to an anti-modern thrust that positions affiliation with such churches as a form of resistance to the commodification of everyday life, though it may also promote conservative stances on a range of social and cultural issues that spill over into critiques of governmental action in these arenas, including family planning, marriage policy, the environment, and health care (Coontz 1992; Klassen 2001). Certainly resistance to commodification is a stance adopted by many on the political left as well; a number of commentators have observed that the anarchist streak represented in the Tea Party is mirrored by some of the positions that characterized the Occupy Movement of 2011–12 (Gitlin 2012; Reyes-Chow 2011). But more commonly, the sentiments associated with Bible-believing Christianity have been associated with deeply conservative positions on a range of cultural and political issues.

It is the extreme conservatism of the most visible elements of Bible-believing Christianity that has captured the attention of many scholars concerned with the current political climate, particularly in terms of the heightened enmity between liberals and conservatives in the United States (Putnam and Campbell 2010). This has been nowhere more prominent than in discussions of the massive influence of Pastor Jerry Falwell and his allies on the direction of American political discourse, an influence seen as having unleashed or intensified the "culture wars" that have characterized the tone of much public discussion (Harding 2001; Hartman 2015; Hunter 1991). The acrimony that these debates have fueled provide much of the substance of current discussions of marriage and family (including same-sex marriage), abortion and reproductive rights, the teaching of evolution and scientific approaches to climate change, and other issues.[3] The intense antagonism surrounding such discussion is difficult to resolve under conditions where proponents of particular stances feel themselves to have been called by God to advocate for their positions. Also complicating the current situation are new alliances between formerly antagonistic denominations—namely, conservative and fundamentalist Protestants and Roman Catholics—dramatically in evidence during Republican presidential campaigns since Ronald Reagan, with candidates seemingly competing to enunciate the most extreme and punitive positions on social issues including access to birth control, abortion rights, and marriage equality.

As noted earlier, while the denominations that make up the black church in America have typically taken conservative theological stances and have often stood with other Bible-believing churches in espousing socially conservative positions on the family, many black churches also have a long and deep history of political involvement and engagement with social justice movements. Throughout much of African American history, churches were the primary sites of political mobilization, and black churches certainly parted company with many white churches on matters having to do with civil rights, beginning with struggles against slavery, regardless of areas of agreement on theological issues (Lincoln and

Mamiya 1990; McDaniel 2008). The Fellowship's practices and positions assume their broadest significance as the heirs of these debates.

Despite the personal links of its members to conservative black Christianity, the Fellowship promotes a public vision that differs dramatically from the stance of many Bible-believing denominations in the United States, as well as from those churches that distance themselves from political engagement. I will discuss this further later, but here I merely wish to stress the way that the Fellowship's very existence disrupts often taken-for-granted assumptions about links between conservative Christianity and right-wing politics. Fellowship sermons not only emphasize respect for gender and sexual identities that differ from the norm, but often take positions that would be unlikely to arise in conservative or fundamentalist churches, such as environmental protection, abortion rights, same-sex marriage equality, and transgender rights. However, its involvement in a host of social justice ministries—such as programming for gay youth, HIV/AIDS services, and the orphanage TFAM supports in Zimbabwe—while sometimes focused on populations and issues avoided by black churches, resonates with the long history of black churches as loci for liberationist struggles.

It is in its theological engagement with Scripture that TFAM most actively departs from its conservative Christian roots. Fellowship clergy actively promote the notion that the Scriptures are historical and cultural documents that must be examined in the specific context of their creation to be properly interpreted. TFAM leaders urge congregants to think of the Bible as a source of wisdom, but not as the literal word of God, and certainly not immune from scholarly and critical examination. Toward this end, active members are groomed for future leadership by encouraging them to attend seminary or to gain a critical religious education in some other sort of institution. Some members have attended relatively traditional Bible colleges, but others are the products of innovative programs at liberal theological schools. There are members who have completed degrees at ecumenical or interfaith schools of divinity, including two New York congregants who completed a doctoral program in Interfaith Clinical Education offered at the Hebrew Union College–Jewish Institute of Religion. In other words, TFAM imagines religious education broadly, encouraging members to pursue further training in many different settings. That their educational encounters might also offer them the opportunity to spread ideas about radical inclusivity means that some divinity schools may help these ideas to be disseminated beyond the boundaries of Fellowship congregations.

Even with their challenges to politically conservative positions, and with a membership that differs dramatically in terms of sexual orientation and gender presentation from the typical congregation in a black church, Fellowship members anchor their practices in the worship style most recall from their earlier lives. TFAM worshippers do not seem tempted to dream up trendy new ways of presenting their commitment to Jesus; rather, they are firmly grounded in the "Metho-Bapti-Costal" traditions that Bishop Flunder playfully invokes to indicate a pastiche of practices that are characteristic of the varied observances found in the denominations that constitute the black church in America. According to this logic, Fellowship members can employ selected traditions no matter what personal attributes may have impeded their access to them. What is being enacted here is authenticity and entitlement; they believe that only the use of "traditional" forms can send this message.

Of course, there is more variation in members' spiritual backgrounds than can be conveyed by "Metho-Bapti-Costal" practices; these strategies are understandable as invocations of "invented" traditions and communities (Anderson 1991; Connerton 1989; Halbwachs 1992; Shils 1981). As we saw in chapter 4, historical reconstruction requires more than recapitulating ritual forms and singing familiar hymns. The notion that congregants share a collective history originating in the South (and before that, in Africa) emerges in the use of cultural allusions that often focus on southern food and weather, morsels of grandmotherly wisdom, and reminders of how slavery inflected the not-so-distant past. That this "past" may be grounded more in sentiment than in the specific experiences of worshippers does not impede these images from being powerful evocations of cultural authenticity.

Studies of black religious practices—and especially those that explore the performance of sermons, testimony, gospel music, and prayer—have identified their common features: call-and-response, the improvisational style of sermons, the interaction between preacher and congregation in the creation of sacred space, and the experience of trance and possession. Some have concentrated on drawing out the roots of these observances in African religion and the worship practices of slaves, such as the ring shout (Hinson 2000; Raboteau 1978); others have directed our attention to the connections between the social circumstances that constrained and inspired worshippers under slavery and after Emancipation (Alexander 2011; Baer and Singer 1992; Cone 1997 [1975]; Cox 2001; Davis 1985; Hinson 2000; Hurston 1981; Jackson 2004; Lincoln and Mamiya 1990; Mitchell 1990; Raboteau 1978, 1999). What I wish to stress here is that these forms coexist in the presence of decidedly non-traditional congregants; they are in essence translated to meet the needs of mostly LGBT worshippers. Such translation may occur without any palpable changes in their form or language; it is the worshippers who transform the texts, giving new vigor to histories they believe themselves to share.

The black church's role as the defender of conservative social thinking starkly contrasts with its historic struggle against Jim Crow and lynching, serving as the cradle of the civil rights movement and as a living model of liberation theology. In fact, it has often been the comparison between the black civil rights movement and more recent efforts by LGBT people to secure basic civil entitlements that has made the contrast between the liberationist black church and the black church as a force of social conservatism particularly perplexing. As a logical extension of its obligations to disadvantaged congregants, some in the black church have long focused on a progressive political agenda, including issues like education, prison reform, health care access, voting rights, and affirmative action, allying them with the post–civil rights Democratic Party (Banerjee 2005), but some black church leaders also have taken up the causes espoused by conservative white churches, such as rigid personal morality and opposition to abortion and same-sex marriage, thus pulling them closer to contemporary Republican positions, even as such positions are unlikely to make them vote for Republican candidates. Still other black churches have been decidedly apolitical, even advising their members to refrain from voting. At the same time that many black clergy have been uncompromising opponents of LGBT rights, however, others have taken positions like the Reverend Kelvin Calloway, pastor of the Second AME Church in Los Angeles, who was reported to have said, "Oppression is oppression is oppression. Just because we're not the ones who are being oppressed now, do we not stand with those oppressed now? That is the biblical mandate. That's what Jesus is all about" (Banerjee 2005).[4]

Documenting the shape of these positions as I have written this book has been uniquely challenging. First, the tide seemed to turn after President Barack Obama's May 2012 announcement that his position on same-sex marriage had "evolved" to supporting equal access for gays and lesbians (Calmes and Baker 2012). The president's statement, which followed years during which he avoided taking a definitive position on the issue, gave rise to a veritable flood of responses from across black communities, with the NAACP announcing its agreement with the president less than two weeks later (Barbaro 2012). Some black clergy and other prominent black public figures hastily disassociated themselves from these positions, but others, including former secretary of state Colin Powell, were just as swift in affirming their agreement with the president's position (Bruni 2012). In Maryland, where a referendum on same-sex marriage was then under debate, news of the president's announcement seemed to spark an almost instantaneous shift among the state's African Americans on the issue, results that echoed national polls taken in May 2012 (Cohen 2012; Richen 2013).

The June 2015 decision of the Supreme Court in *Obergefell et al. v. Hodges* made same-sex marriage legal at the federal level and followed the earlier 2013 ruling in the *United States v. Windsor*, which invalidated the Defense of Marriage Act (DOMA). Although this legal ruling would seem to end the matter of opposition to marriage equality, resistance has persisted, especially among some fundamentalist Christians, most notably in the case of the Kentucky county clerk Kim Davis, who refused to issue marriage licenses to anyone (gay or straight) in order to avoid letting same-sex couples receive them, a decision that led to her being jailed for a short time (Fuller 2015). As of this writing, same-sex civil marriage is legal throughout the United States, though individual churches are not mandated to perform such weddings and some local governments have erected obstacles to implementing the law. These changes have moved TFAM's long support for same-sex marriage closer to the center of the political spectrum.

As I write these words, controversy over sexuality has continued among churches on their position vis-à-vis marriage equality for same-sex couples. For many years, the position of black clergy on LGBT rights—especially in relation to such (often) religiously mediated rights as marriage—has ranged from quietly unfavorable to virulently hostile. In the debates over Proposition 8 in California in 2008, African American pastors played a visible role in support of the amendment, which invalidated same-sex marriage in the state. Their participation on this side of the debate, indeed, was so visible that they were widely, though probably inaccurately, credited with responsibility for Proposition 8's success (Abrajano 2010; Egan and Sherrill 2009).

Many conservative religious figures, as well, have used an appeal to "religious freedom" to inveigh against ordinances that would make it possible for transgender persons to use restrooms based on their current gender identity instead of limiting them to facilities that match the sex designation on their birth certificates. These figures have argued that allowing transgender women into women's restrooms would open the way for rapists to disguise themselves as women in order to gain access to these accommodations. The connection between these clashes and religious freedom is hard to discern, though it would seem that conservative religious doctrine is suspicious of efforts by transgender men and women to gain recognition for their chosen gender identities (Moore 2016).[5]

TFAM in the Future

The Fellowship exists in a space between the public and the sacred domains in which meanings are in constant flux and aspirations need frequent readjustment. On the one hand, its very existence owes a great deal to shifting views of sexual and gender non-conformity, while at the same time it has been shaped by the extent to which these views have only partially changed. While discrimination against LGBT people has become less respectable in recent years, and overt expressions of racism are frowned upon (in polite company), we live in a world in which these forms of bigotry and oppression are still vigorous and threatening, albeit rarely explicitly stated.[6] As I finished this book, explanations for the 2016 murders of forty-nine LGBT patrons of an Orlando, Florida, nightclub continue to oscillate between discourses of hate crimes and Islamic terrorism (as though these are definitively separable), inflected with proclamations about gun violence (Ross 2016). In other words, anti-gay violence is revealed to have multiple origins and to ramify in unpredictable directions.

Similarly, the national conversation about the Second Amendment and access to military-style weapons that are extraordinarily destructive sometimes focuses on their impact on minority racial populations—the Charleston church shootings of 2015, gun violence in poor black neighborhoods in cities such as Chicago—and at other times is folded into wider debates about citizenship, due process, and mental health. Radical inclusivity, however, contributes to these discussions by pointing out the shared humanity of all involved in these critical matters and their interdependency. There could hardly exist a better illustration of the complicated meanings that can be drawn from the doctrine of radical inclusivity.

In this book, I have tried to attend to the ways in which shifting and even contradictory meanings and symbols play out in the Fellowship of Affirming Ministries. Through its embrace of radical inclusivity in its most expansive sense, TFAM offers a set of ideas and practices that can be tailored to the needs of particular constituencies, some of which have not yet been defined. It does this even as it makes itself a home for mostly LGBT African Americans who have their roots in traditional black churches. Perhaps paradoxically, both departure from tradition and its celebration are contained in radical inclusivity and in the ways in which TFAM's congregations and worshippers make themselves both guardians of history and pioneers of the future.

Notes

INVOCATION

1. Most names used in this book are the real names of the narrators, who preferred to be fully identified. In some cases, I have used pseudonyms, and those are indicated by the use of quotation marks around the name when it is first used.
2. *Glossolalia* refers to the practice of speaking seemingly unintelligible syllables in the course of ecstatic prayer. It is most commonly observed among Pentecostals and other charismatic Christian sects, though it has also been found among non-Christians. It takes its religious justification from the text of Acts 2, which describes the baptism of fire experienced by the apostles on the Day of Pentecost during which people spoke in other (unknown) languages.
3. Though the Azusa Street Revival is commonly credited with having started Pentecostalism, many scholars trace its origins to earlier Holiness movements (see, for example, Anderson 1979; Synan 1971).
4. This is particularly the case when one is constrained by the cost of air travel, lodging, and car rentals, as well as by the routine obstacles presented by an academic job, with its regular teaching schedule. Research and travel funding is scarce and hard to get, so I was faced with a host of logistical and financial challenges to attending Fellowship events around the country. I tried to do as much research as I could during the summer and breaks in the academic year, and in many cases, I traveled to research sites on weekends or piggybacked research on other travel opportunities that came my way. Still, I was very fortunate during this time to receive funding from the Arts and Humanities Initiative at the University of Iowa (2010–11), a Martin Duberman Fellowship from the Center for

Lesbian and Gay Studies (CLAGS) at the City University of New York (2010-11), and research fellowships from the Louisville Institute and the National Endowment for the Humanities (2015-16). I also benefited enormously from the opportunity to work at the Obermann Center for Advanced Studies at the University of Iowa during my sabbatical semester in spring of 2012.

5. Examples of such dedicated behavior are too numerous to detail here, but a few well-known recent figures whose work fits this pattern are Dorothy Day (Forest 2011), Mother Teresa (Scott 2005), and Dr. Thomas Dooley (Dooley 1962).

6. For a discussion of how this happens in same-sex weddings, see Lewin 1998.

CHAPTER ONE

1. The First and Second Great Awakenings refer to periods of intense religious revival in US history led by evangelical Protestant clergy, many of whom were itinerant preachers who staged revivals in many different geographical locations (Ahlstrom 1972; Kidd 2007; Lambert 1999). These events led to an intensification in religious observance, the formation of new religious movements, and challenges to the authority of established Christian denominations. The Second Great Awakening had considerable influence on the formation and shape of the suffrage, abolition, and temperance movements (Ryan 1983).

2. Lincoln and Mamiya define the black church as consisting of seven major denominations: the African Methodist Episcopal (AME) Church; the African Methodist Episcopal Zion (AMEZ) Church; the Christian Methodist Episcopal (CME) Church; the National Baptist Convention, USA, Incorporated (NBC); the National Baptist Convention of America, Unincorporated (NBCA); the Progressive National Baptist Convention (PNBC); and the Church of God in Christ (COGIC). These seven major historically black denominations account for 80 percent of black Christian church membership (Lincoln and Mamiya 1990: 1). In addition, there are predominantly black local churches in majority white denominations such as the United Methodist Church, the Episcopal Church, and the Roman Catholic Church.

3. See Stack 1996 on return migration to the South as a reclamation of tradition.

4. No matter how severe the rejection that white LGBT people may experience, including being exiled from their religious communities, their families, and having other sources of value in their lives—chosen families, homes, careers—threatened or devalued, they do not have to face the possibility that they are no longer white or that they no longer can claim membership in the particular ethnic group with which they identify. Of course, being white is the unmarked category, the racial default, and as such, not an identity that most white people explicitly embrace unless a special circumstance makes it visible or salient (Bonilla-Silva 2008; Frye 1998; Lipsitz 1998; Painter 2011).

5. The potency of debates about what constitutes "authentic blackness" emerged in a particularly charged fashion as Barack Obama rose to political prominence (Staples 2007). Is a biracial man who was raised in a white family in Hawaii authentically black? What about one who attended and excelled in Ivy League institutions? The debate over authenticity may characterize the experience of black people who achieve academically and have professional ambitions, who find themselves accused of "acting white" (Fordham 1996).
6. Popular coverage of the mass shooting that took place in the Orlando, Florida, gay nightclub Pulse in June 2016 emphasizes the importance of the club as a cultural venue that patrons expected to be "safe." See, for example, Cullen 2016.
7. A rather large body of work in psychology and social work addresses some of these issues. See, for example, Sauvé 1998.
8. Work by other scholars has made clear that not only racial alliances but other structural factors also affect the ability of African Americans to embrace LGBT identities. Natasha Wilson, for example, provides a compelling portrait of impoverished black women in New Orleans whose lives as lesbians are often challenged by their connections to black men, the fathers of their children, who cycle in and out of prison (Wilson 2009). Although these women rarely use the word "lesbian" to describe themselves, they enthusiastically join in the performance of a song they call the "lesbian anthem" when female-dressed drag performers include it in their acts at their local bar. The song's lyrics actually don't refer to lesbianism at all, but to infidelity, a key element of how masculine lesbians (studs) enact their sexuality—or believe that they should. Wilson shows that the song allows bar patrons to articulate their identities even as it makes clear how fragile and contingent these may be.
9. The Centers for Disease Control (CDC) reports that African Americans have the most severe burden of HIV of all racial/ethnic groups in the United States. In data reported for 2014, they account for a higher proportion of new HIV diagnoses, those living with HIV, and those ever diagnosed with AIDS than other racial or ethnic populations. Though there has been some reduction in the impact of HIV/AIDS on black women, their numbers are still high compared to other racial/ethnic groups. And the CDC reports that gay and bisexual men account for more than half of estimated new HIV diagnoses among African Americans (http://www.cdc.gov/hiv/group/racialethnic/africanamericans/, accessed June 15, 2016).
10. This situation is, of course, not limited to black churches. The case of Rev. Ted Haggard in Colorado is one of the most well-known of recent scandals. Instances where pastors have come out have elicited huge controversy as well. When Pastor Jim Swilley of the Atlanta megachurch Church in the Now came out as gay in 2010, he was subjected to public outrage, death threats, and other hostility.
11. Other measures followed, including the acceptance of openly gay and les-

bian pastors (1979), a resolution in support of UUA clergy performing Services of Union between same-gender couples (1984), and establishing policies in support of congregations being designated as "welcoming," a designation that characterized 25 percent of all UUA congregations by 2000. Over the years, the UUA has taken numerous stands in support of LGBT causes (http://archive.uua.org/obgltc/resource/history.html, accessed April 12, 2012).

12. In 1985 the Fifteenth General Synod of the UCC, its national delegate body, passed a resolution entitled "Calling on United Church of Christ Congregations to Declare Themselves Open and Affirming." It followed the implementation of similar policies in individual congregations in preceding years. Since individual congregations in the UCC are self-governing, the resolution does not extend to requiring such non-discrimination of all churches in the denomination, though the UCC website reported in 2012 that about 1,000 of the approximately 5,000 US congregations are open and affirming. In 2003 a new resolution extended the policy to cover transgender persons. The policy has long meant that many UCC churches perform wedding ceremonies for LGBT couples; as of 2005, the denomination actively supported the cause of legal marriage equality (http://www.ucc.org/lgbt/ona.html, accessed April 12, 2012).

13. In Judaism, similar transitions have occurred. Reconstructionist Judaism began to accept gay men and lesbians into the rabbinate in 1985 and issued policies in support of same-sex marriage in 1993. Reform Judaism has also taken gay-supportive positions, changing its earlier policies on the rabbinate in 1990, which had long sought to exclude LGBT applicants (see, for example, the World Congress of Gay, Lesbian, Bisexual, and Transgender Jews: Keshet Ga'avah (http://www.glbtjews.org/, accessed April 17, 2012; Kahn 1989; Salkowitz, Kahn, and Kravitz 1989; Schnoor 2006), and since 1998 allowing individual congregations to decide on whether or not to perform same-sex weddings. They were later joined by Conservative Jews, who since 2006 have allowed the ordination of lesbian and gay rabbis, permitting individual congregations to decide on performing same-sex unions, and since 2012 have disseminated guidelines for performing same-sex weddings (Zeveloff 2012). Not surprisingly, all wings of Orthodox Judaism have maintained their steadfast opposition to homosexuality, in addition to (usually) separating women from worship with men and excluding them from Torah study, and, of course, the rabbinate.

14. The MCC includes some 222 member congregations in 37 countries (as of this writing), with a specific outreach to lesbian, gay, bisexual, and transgender families and communities. Its founder, the Reverend Troy Perry, who is white, started his first church in Los Angeles in 1968. He served as the leader (moderator) of the denomination until 2005, when Reverend Nancy Wilson became the moderator, making the MCC one of the only denominations in the United States to have a female leader.

15. His wife stayed with him after the first time he was "outed," and they moved to California, where he became the pastor of a Church of God in Prophecy (a breakaway from the Church of God) in Los Angeles. All was well until his wife found a copy of the book *The Homosexual in America*, by Donald Webster Cory, hidden under his mattress. She revealed the information to his bishop, who forced him to resign his pulpit after directing him to pray to overcome his homosexual feelings. After the end of his marriage and his connection with his church, Perry worked in various jobs, including serving a stint in the US Army.
16. Although Perry's background was Pentecostal, each congregation in MCC is self-governing, and the style of worship varies dramatically depending upon the background of the pastor and the preferences of congregants. MCC members come from varied (mostly) Christian backgrounds; most are white, though some members of national leadership are African American.
17. Affirming Pentecostal Church International (APCI) is one such organization. Formed in Indianapolis, Indiana, in 2010, APCI has established congregations in numerous countries across Europe, Asia, Africa, and Latin America and also maintains a large number of churches in the United States. Other Pentecostal groups preaching messages of inclusion are the Fellowship of Reconciling Pentecostals International (FRPI), the National Gay Pentecostal Alliance (NGPA), the Apostolic Restoration Mission (ARM), the Covenant Network, and the Global Alliance of Affirming Apostolic Pentecostals (GAAAP).
18. Most Pentecostals adhere to a Trinitarian doctrine that sees God as manifested in the distinct forms of the Father, the Son, and the Holy Spirit. Adherents of oneness theology argue, instead, that God is one and indivisible, manifested in Jesus Christ. They make blessings in the name of Jesus Christ, avoiding the three-part Trinitarian formula (Alexander 2011; Synan 1971). This seemingly technical disagreement has accounted for enormous numbers of church schisms.
19. Unity Fellowship Church Movement (http://www.unityfellowshipchurch.org/mainsite/; accessed April 16, 2012).
20. In other local areas, predominantly black open and affirming churches have also arisen, each with a unique history. For example, in the Atlanta area, Bishop O. C. Allen's Vision Church has been in operation since 2005 (http://www.thevisionchurch.org/). Other such congregations have formed in various localities, some with connections to TFAM and others strictly independent, usually formed around a particularly powerful founding pastor.
21. www.radicallyinclusive.net/content.cfm?id=2006 (accessed July 14, 2009).
22. Glossolalia and other forms of trance and possession have a long history both in the West and in various cultures around the world, a topic to which anthropologists have devoted considerable attention. In the case of Pentecostal manifestations of these altered states of consciousness, the usual interpretation is that they evidence inhabitation by the Holy Spirit (Anderson

NOTES TO PAGE 51

1979). Important works on possession and trance include Lewis 1989, Goodman 1972, and Samarin 1972.

23. At the leadership conference held in Palm Springs in July 2016, I distributed a brief demographic survey to those attending. Eighty-six of 230 attendees completed the surveys (a response rate of 37 percent), and while the results do not reflect the general membership of the entire Fellowship, they do offer some basic information about those involved in TFAM, especially those who are very active. The average age was about 52, with ages ranging between 26 and 89. Three out of the 86 identified themselves in an open-ended question as white or Caucasian, while nearly all others indicated that they were either African American or black (with two specifying Caribbean heritage). Five described themselves as biracial, mixed race, or black-white, and one said he was Latino. Of those 83 who answered an open-ended question about gender, 26 described themselves as male, 52 as female, and 5 used another term such as "non-conforming" (two responses), transgender, gay, or transmale. As for sexual orientation, one person used the term "straight" and 8 some variant on bisexual. The rest used either lesbian or gay to describe themselves, though 20 preferred the term SGL (same-gender-loving) and one chose WLW (woman-loving woman). Since the attendees were those interested in the future leadership of TFAM, the educational level was higher than is probably the case among all members of congregations. Twenty-one had some college, 26 were college graduates, and 41 had graduate-level degrees, the majority of which were a Master of Divinity (M.Div.). Only two attendees described their highest level of education as high school.

Participants' regional origins were quite varied. Of those responding, 28 attendees identified the area where they had been raised as somewhere in the South; 22 as the East; 18 as the West (predominantly California); and 17, the Midwest. Current residences were also varied. Considering that the conference was held in Palm Springs, the largest group of respondents (39) described their current home as being in the West, especially California. Twenty claimed homes in the East; 18 in the South; 8 in the Midwest; and 1 in Hawaii.

When asked about the churches they had attended when they were growing up (if any), some respondents listed more than one. The largest category (34) was Baptist, including such sects as Missionary Baptist, Primitive Baptist, and Original Free Will Baptist. The next largest group was some variety of Pentecostal (26), with 13 saying that they had grown up in the Church of God in Christ (COGIC), and another 13 describing their childhood churches as Pentecostal, Holiness, Apostolic, or non-denominational. Four of those responding named the African Methodist Episcopal (AME) as the church in which they were raised. Thirteen listed other churches, such as Catholic, Presbyterian, Methodist, Lutheran, United Church of Christ (UCC), Jehovah's Witness, and Mormon, while 11 said they did not attend church when they were growing up.

Members of the group who completed the survey showed how much TFAM has influenced members to pursue seminary training. A total of thirty-eight respondents either had completed a program since participating in TFAM, were currently enrolled in one, or were actively planning to attend seminary, in some cases through Project Access, a TFAM program that helps prepare individuals for future religious education. Besides these, four others answered the question with a phrase like "want to" or "not yet," indicating that they are considering such further education. Of course, given that the surveys were completed by those attending a leadership conference, there were probably a disproportionate number of respondents who were involved in higher education in seminaries or schools of theology.

24. This movement was founded in 1927 by Ernest Holmes, who called its teachings Science of Mind. The movement is now under the aegis of the Centers for Spiritual Living, and includes Christian principles and ideas drawn from Buddhism.

CHAPTER TWO

1. It was at Love Center that Bishop Flunder became friends with Sylvester, the drag performer who became a legend in the disco scene of the 1970s and 1980s in San Francisco. Like many other congregants who found their way to Love Center, Sylvester had grown up in COGIC and had found himself rejected from church because of his unorthodox gender presentation. But he yearned for involvement in church, and especially for an extravagant worship style that complemented his theatrical preferences, desires that were realized in the ornate funeral held at Love Center after his death from AIDS in 1988, with friends from all areas of the gay world mourning his passing (Gamson 2005).
2. Bishop Pearson has led a number of congregations in Chicago and Tulsa. He is the author of several books advocating "new thought," including Pearson 2006. Bishop Swilley, the leader of the Atlanta megachurch Church of the Now, got national attention in 2010 when he came out as gay. The book he wrote about this experience was published in 2012.
3. See also Braude (2008) and Brasher (1998) for other accounts of how women managed to achieve leadership positions in American churches. Casselberry (2017) and Frederick (2003) have focused similar inquiries on black churches.
4. In these usages, the term can convey something menacing, as when analysts speak of figures like Hitler possessing charismatic powers.
5. Although Bishop Flunder and other TFAM clergy would hold that God is neither male nor female, most typically use masculine pronouns in referring to God. They argue that God can be in whatever manner worshippers find familiar and comforting, and given their backgrounds, most tend to use masculine pronouns. Bishop Flunder explains that "God can move through any

culture," and she uses this idea to support worshippers' use of language that is meaningful to them and draws on their experience. She emphasizes that worshippers can retain "the atmosphere, style, sound and feel of the Metho-Bapti-Costal church without the oppression perpetuated by some in those traditions" (Flunder 2005: 11).
6. Not all TFAM congregations, however, have a Pentecostal style of worship; Charla Kouadio and Theresa Coley-Kouadio—who co-pastor a TFAM UCC congregation in Springfield, Massachusetts—both come from Baptist upbringings and told me that the freedom to run their church along those lines was an important part of their embrace of TFAM.

CHAPTER THREE

1. The much-acclaimed 2016 film *Moonlight* deals with a young black man as he comes to terms with being gay, beginning in childhood, moving through adolescence, and ending when he is in his twenties. Directed by Barry Jenkins, the film is based on the play *In Moonlight Black Boys Look Blue* by Tarell Alvin McCraney (A24, Plan B Entertainment, and Pastel Productions).
2. "Mother" is an honorific title given to older women in a congregation, described by religious studies scholar Anthea Butler as those who serve as the backbone of the black church. She explains: "Such 'spiritual mothers,' or 'church mothers,' as they are called in the African American church traditions, are women within the congregation who act as advisors to the pastors, as disciplinarians and leaders of wayward church members, and as spiritual avatars to the congregation" (Butler 2007: 12).
3. This is also the church that was the original home of Reverend Troy Perry, the founder of MCC.

CHAPTER FOUR

1. There is also an enormous corpus of work on lesbian and gay life in various communities: e.g., Armstrong 2002; Boyd 2003; Chauncey 1994; Faderman and Timmon 2006; Kennedy and Davis 1993; Newton 1993; Stein 2004. John D'Emilio (1983) offers a sophisticated analysis of the rise of gay communities in the United States after World War II.
2. As E. Patrick Johnson explains in *Sweet Tea* (2008: 17), the term "tea" is a word with multiple meanings in gay black vernacular, particularly indicating gossip or truth-telling. "T Time" thus is a double entendre that draws on other usages of "tea" or "T" including those that refer to "tea dances," "tearooms" (or locations where anonymous public sex may be obtained), and "tea bagging," which refers to particular sexual practices by which a man dips his testicles in another man's mouth. The term "tearoom trade," made famous in Laud Humphreys' book of the same name (1970), draws on the same complex of vernacular.

3. A *chavurah* or "fellowship" is a term used to refer to a group of Jewish friends or acquaintances who assemble to celebrate the Sabbath or a holiday. Such gatherings may provide an alternative to institutional Jewish worship.
4. The blessing, which comes from the Talmud, is recited when experiencing something pleasurable but infrequent, at the start of a holiday, when greeting people one hasn't seen in a long time, or otherwise celebrating something new, unusual, and gratifying. Its translation is "Blessed are you Lord our God, King of the Universe, who has granted us life, sustained us, and enabled us to reach this occasion."
5. The 2013 documentary film *Twenty Feet from Stardom* focused on singers who performed with well-known R & B and rock stars. Virtually all got their start singing in church, as did many who eventually achieved stardom, like Aretha Franklin (Neville 2013).
6. Similar patterns appeared in my research on same-sex weddings in the early 1990s. Many participants felt that these were uniquely authentic since there was no social or family pressure for same-sex couples to declare their unions in a public fashion (Lewin 1998).
7. Singing well (or having rhythm) is popularly construed in the United States as an attribute of blackness, with disparaging comments occasionally appearing about white people and their lack of musical aptitude. Both white people and blacks seem to share this belief. There seems to be no scientific evidence for this stereotype, which may have the same roots as beliefs about exceptional athletic prowess among African Americans.
8. See also Cone 1991 (1972), Douglas 2012, and Moss 2015.
9. Another issue that also emerges when one discusses African American women's hair is the involvement of black women as entrepreneurs in the beauty and cosmetics industry, with many achieving economic success through this work. Madame C. J. Walker offers the most famous example of the potential of hair care products to catapult an individual to great wealth (Rooks 1996), but also significant is the role of hair care as an arena for more modest business success and the importance of the beauty parlor as a site of black women's social engagement and political activism (Gill 2010; Wingfield 2008). The 2009 film by comedian Chris Rock, *Good Hair*, offers an account of the extreme measures some black people are willing to take to tame their hair, including the use of methods that can cause permanent damage.
10. Bishop keeps her natural curl and has her hair cut very short.
11. The conk (derived from congolene, a hair straightener gel made from lye) refers to a process often carried out at home that straightened kinky hair, usually for men. Because of the alkaline composition of the lye, the person applying it had to carefully wash the hair to avoid having the chemicals burn the scalp of the person receiving the treatment (see Byrd and Tharps 2014: 43).
12. See Byrd and Tharps (2014: 86–90) on the Jheri curl.

13. Congregation Sha'ar Zahav (CSZ), a predominantly LGBT synagogue in San Francisco, faced similar challenges in reproducing the memories of worship that congregants with varying backgrounds treasured and demanded. Ritual forms at CSZ were accordingly characterized as "Reconservadox."
14. The process of choosing which parts of the Bible one should embrace and which one might want to discard recalls the story that Howard Thurman told about his grandmother, a former slave. She refused to let him include the letters of Paul when he read her the Bible because these were the parts of Scripture slave owners favored to send the message that slaves should be obedient to their masters. "'I vowed to myself,' she said, 'that if freedom ever came and I learned to read, I would never read that part of the Bible!'" (Thurman, quoted in Darden 2004: 34).

CHAPTER FIVE

1. The Fellowship, "What Is Radical Inclusivity?," 2011 (http://radically inclusive.com/what-is-radical-inclusivity; accessed February 7, 2017).
2. This work parallels responses to criticisms of African American family structure, such as that which appeared in the infamous Moynihan Report (1965). See, for example, Stack 1974; Valentine 1968; Williams 1992, and work that sought to repudiate Oscar Lewis's theories of the "culture of poverty" (Leacock 1971).
3. Some of these individuals would probably see themselves as transgender today, but that identity label had not yet come into general usage at the time of this research (Valentine 2007).
4. I am grateful to Tim Wolfe for clarifying the meaning of Pentecost as a charter for radical inclusivity.
5. Wicca, also known as pagan witchcraft, refers to a new religious movement that first gained prominence in England in the mid-twentieth century. It became popular among some second-wave feminists whose interest in goddess worship led them to practices they felt could be the basis for a new feminist spirituality (Spretnak 1981).
6. E. Patrick Johnson (2003) calls our attention to one of the more perplexing instances of cultural appropriation in his account of an all-white, mostly atheist, Australian gospel choir. Despite their geographical, racial, and cultural distance from gospel performance, the Café of the Gate of Salvation produces music that has amazing "authenticity," even as the choir does not aspire to imitating the black gospel sound. In other words, their performance surpasses the identity of the singers, revealing ways that a performance genre like gospel can expand its meanings for different performers—and presumably different audiences. The multi-vocal nature of the Australian choir's performance was particularly striking when it performed in the Baptist House of Prayer in Harlem, transporting worshippers and overcoming the appar-

7. A *kippah*, also called a *yamulka*, is a skullcap or small head covering worn by men, but sometimes also by women. A *tallit katan* is a ritual garment worn by observant Jewish men under their other clothing, which has *tsitsis*, or tassels, that hang down and are visible; it is also often just called a *tsitsis*. The tassels, attached to the four corners of the garment, are intended to remind the wearer of his religious obligations or *mitzvot*.
8. I also felt that, given my belief system, participating in the Eucharist would be disrespectful.
9. I am indebted to Dawne Moon for calling my attention to this important literature.
10. Here Bishop gestures toward her own large body.
11. *Aché* (also sometimes transcribed as *àshe* or *axé*) is a Yoruba word that is often used to indicate the connection that pastors and congregants have, or wish to have, with their West African origins. It is associated with "spiritual command, the power-to-make-things-happen, God's own enabling light made accessible to men and women" (Thompson 1983: 5) and with "the power and authority embodied in human agents, animals, and inanimate objects. . . . [T]he 'life force' that is inherent in all things and creatures" (Matory 2005: 123). Anthropologist J. Lorand Matory reports, as well, that throughout the West African diaspora, it can be understood to mean "amen" or "let it be," or in Brazil "cool!" or "right on!" and is a common feature of conversation.
12. The song has a wide range of popular culture references, including as the theme of the Pittsburgh Pirates in the 1979 World Series and the Democratic National Convention in 2004 (https://en.wikipedia.org/wiki/We_Are_Family_(song)#References).

BENEDICTION

1. One might make the same observation about the proliferation of Pentecostal worship in parts of the world where it has little historical foundation, such as Africa and Latin America.
2. Bishop Christopher Senyonjo stands out as the only Ugandan clergyperson who spoke up for the rights of LGBT people. He was excommunicated from the Anglican Church and stripped of his pension, but has subsequently worked with several progressive religious organizations in Uganda and the United States, including TFAM.
3. A national uproar followed the 2016 passage of a North Carolina law configured as a religious freedom measure that restricts transgender persons to using public restrooms according to the sex on their birth certificate. In like fashion, religious conservatives opposed to providing birth control to their

employees have claimed that the requirement to do so that appears in the Affordable Care Act (aka Obamacare) violates their religious freedom. Prominent recent cases that have taken this position and been heard by the US Supreme Court are those brought by Hobby Lobby and the Little Sisters of the Poor, a Roman Catholic order of nuns.

4. Attorney General Loretta Lynch explained the support for the rights of transgender people to use whichever restrooms matched their gender identity, comparing restrictions on restroom use to the Jim Crow policies of racial separation in such public facilities as restrooms and drinking fountains. (http://www.nytimes.com/reuters/2016/05/09/us/09reuters-north-carolina-lgbt.html, accessed May 10, 2017).

5. A similar strategy has surfaced among religious organizations that have resisted implementing mandates in the Affordable Care Act (aka Obamacare) for the provision of contraceptive services with no out-of-pocket cost to patients: see the group of cases recently considered by the Supreme Court, *Zubik v. Burwell* (http://www.scotusblog.com/case-files/cases/zubik-v-burwell/; accessed July 6, 2016). With attempts to dismantle ("repeal and replace") the ACA early in the Trump administration, the outcome of these controversies remains unclear as of this writing.

6. The early weeks of the Trump administration seem to have made racial and ethnic diatribes more acceptable, but as I write these words, the final form that alt-right figures in the White House will take has yet to be revealed. The impact of all of these unfolding ideological struggles remains difficult to discern, as of this writing, though controversies over matters that once seemed settled, contraception, for example, have emerged and continue to rage.

References Cited

Abrajano, Marisa. 2010. "Are Blacks and Latinos Responsible for the Passage of Proposition 8? Analyzing Voter Attitudes on California's Proposal to Ban Same-Sex Marriage in 2008." *Political Research Quarterly* 63(4): 922–32.

Abrams, Andrea C. 2014. *God and Blackness: Race, Gender, and Identity in a Middle Class Afrocentric Church*. New York: New York University Press.

Abu-Lughod, Lila. 1991. "Writing Against Culture." In *Recapturing Anthropology: Working in the Present*, ed. R. G. Fox, pp. 137–62. Santa Fe: School of American Research Press.

Achtemeier, Mark. 2014. *The Bible's Yes to Same-Sex Marriage: An Evangelical's Change of Heart*. Louisville, KY: Westminster John Knox Press.

Adam, Barry D. 2009. "How Might We Create Collectivity That We Would Want to Belong To?" In *Gay Shame*, ed. David M. Halperin and Valerie Traub, pp. 301–11. Chicago: University of Chicago Press.

African American Heritage Hymnal. 2001. Chicago: GIA Publications.

Ahlstrom, Sydney E. 1972. *A Religious History of the American People*. New Haven, CT: Yale University Press.

Alba, Richard D. 1990. *Ethnic Identity: The Transformation of White America*. New Haven, CT: Yale University Press.

Alexander, Estrelda Y. 2011. *Black Fire: One Hundred Years of African American Pentecostalism*. Downers Grove, IL: IVP Academic.

Alexander, Paul. 2009. *Signs and Wonders: Why Pentecostalism Is the World's Fastest Growing Faith*. San Francisco: Jossey-Bass.

Ammerman, Nancy T. 1987. *Bible Believers: Fundamentalists in the Modern World*. New Brunswick, NJ: Rutgers University Press.

Anderson, Allan. 2004. *An Introduction to Pentecostalism*. Cambridge: Cambridge University Press.

Anderson, Allan, Michael Bergunder, Andre F. Droogers, and Cornelius Van den Laan. 2010. *Studying Global Pentecostalism: Theories and Methods*. Berkeley: University of California Press.

Anderson, Benedict. 1991. *Imagined Communities: Reflections on the Origin and Spread of Nationalism*. London: Verso.

Anderson, Robert Mapes. 1979. *Vision of the Disinherited: The Making of American Pentecostalism*. Oxford: Oxford University Press.

Anderson, Victor. 1998. "Deadly Silence: Reflections on Homosexuality and Human Rights." In *Sexual Orientation and Human Rights in American Religious Discourse*, ed. Saul M. Olyan and Martha Nussbaum, pp. 185–200. New York: Oxford University Press.

Armstrong, Elizabeth A. 2002. *Forging Gay Identities: Organizing Sexuality in San Francisco, 1950–1994*. Chicago: University of Chicago Press.

Arnold, Lee. 2002. "Troy Perry." In *Before Stonewall: Activists for Gay and Lesbian Rights in Historical Context*, ed. V. L. Bullough, pp. 393–98. New York: Harrington Park Press.

Austin-Broos, Diane J. 1997. *Jamaica Genesis: Religion and the Politics of Moral Orders*. Chicago: University of Chicago Press.

Baer, Hans A., and Merrill Singer. 1992. *African-American Religion in the Twentieth Century: Varieties of Protest and Accommodation*. Knoxville: University of Tennessee Press.

Bailey, Marlon M. 2013. *Butch Queens Up in Pumps: Gender, Performance, and Ballroom Culture in Detroit*. Ann Arbor, MI: University of Michigan Press.

Baker, Lee D. 1998. *From Savage to Negro: Anthropology and the Construction of Race, 1896–1954*. Berkeley: University of California Press.

Banerjee, Neela. 2005. "Black Churches Struggle Over Their Role in Politics." *New York Times*, March 6.

Banks, Ingrid. 2000. *Hair Matters: Beauty, Power, and Black Women's Consciousness*. New York: New York University Press.

Baptiste, Nathalie, and Foreign Policy in Focus. 2014. "It's Not Just Uganda: Behind the Christian Right's Onslaught in Africa." https://www.thenation.com/article/its-not-just-uganda-behind-christian-rights-onslaught-africa/ (accessed July 6, 2016).

Barbaro, Michael. 2012. "N.A.A.C.P. Endorses Same-Sex Marriage." *New York Times*, May 19.

Barth, Frederik, ed. 1969. *Ethnic Groups and Boundaries*. Boston: Little Brown.

Barton, Bernadette. 2012. *Pray the Gay Away: The Extraordinary Lives of Bible Belt Gays*. New York: New York University Press.

Bates, Aryana. 2005. "Liberation in Truth: African American Lesbians Reflect on Religion and Their Church." In *Gay Religion*, ed. S. Thumma and E. R. Gray, pp. 221–37. Lanham, MD: Altamira Press.

Battle, Michael. 2006. *The Black Church in America: African American Christian Spirituality*. Malden, MA: Wiley-Blackwell.

Bauman, Richard. 1977. *Verbal Art as Performance*. Long Grove, IL: Waveland Press.

REFERENCES CITED

———. 1986. *Story, Performance, and Event: Contextual Studies of Oral Narrative.* Cambridge: Cambridge University Press.

———. 2004. *A World of Others' Words: Cross-Cultural Perspectives on Intertextuality.* Malden, MA: Wiley Blackwell.

Bauman, Richard, and Charles L. Briggs. 2003. *Voices of Modernity: Language Ideologies and the Politics of Inequality.* Cambridge: Cambridge University Press.

Beam, Joseph. 1986. *In the Life: A Black Gay Anthology.* Boston: Alyson.

Bean, Carl. 2010. *I Was Born This Way: A Gay Preacher's Journey through Gospel Music, Disco Stardom, and a Ministry in Christ.* New York: Simon and Schuster.

Beemyn, Brett, ed. 1997. *Creating a Place for Ourselves: Lesbian, Gay, and Bisexual Community Histories.* New York: Routledge.

Best, Wallace D. 2005. *Passionately Human, No Less Divine.* Princeton, NJ: Princeton University Press.

Bevans, Stephan B. 1992. *Models of Contextual Theology.* Maryknoll, NY: Orbis Books.

Bielo, James S. 2009. *Words upon the Word: An Ethnography of Evangelical Group Bible Study.* New York: New York University Press.

———. 2011. *Emerging Evangelicals: Faith, Modernity, and the Desire for Authenticity.* New York: New York University Press.

Blount, Brian K. 1995. *Cultural Interpretation: Reorienting New Testament Criticism.* Eugene, OR: Wipf and Stock Publishers.

Blumhofer, Edith Waldvogel. 1993. *Restoring the Faith: the Assemblies of God, Pentecostalism, and American Culture.* Urbana: University of Illinois Press.

Boellstorff, Tom. 2005. "Between Religion and Desire: Being Muslim and Gay in Indonesia." *American Anthropologist* 107(4): 575–85.

———. 2007. "Queer Studies in the House of Anthropology." *Annual Review of Anthropology* 36:17–35.

Bonilla-Silva, Eduardo. 2008. *Racism without Racists: Color-Blind Racism and the Persistence of Racial Inequality in the United States.* Lanham, MD: Rowman & Littlefield.

Borker, Ruth A. 1984. "'Moved by the Spirit': Constructing Meaning in a Brethren Breaking of Bread Service." *Text* 6(3): 317–37.

Bourdieu, Pierre. 1977. *Outline of a Theory of Practice.* Cambridge: Cambridge University Press.

Bourguignon, Erika, ed. 1973. *Religion, Altered States of Consciousness, and Social Change.* Columbus: Ohio State University Press.

Boyd, Nan Alamilla. 2003. *Wide Open Town: A History of Queer San Francisco, to 1965.* Berkeley: University of California Press.

Boykin, Keith. 1996. *One More River to Cross: Black and Gay in America.* New York: Anchor Books.

———. 2005. *Beyond the Down Low: Sex, Lies, and Denial in Black America.* New York: Carroll and Graf.

Boym, Svetlana. 2001. *The Future of Nostalgia.* New York: Basic Books.

Brasher, Brenda E. 1998. *Godly Women: Fundamentalism and Female Power*. New Brunswick, NJ: Rutgers University Press.

Braude, Ann. 2008. *Sisters and Saints: Women and American Religion*. Oxford: Oxford University Press.

Brekus, Catherine A. 1998. *Strangers and Pilgrims: Female Preaching in America, 1740–1845*. Chapel Hill: University of North Carolina Press.

Brennan, Emily. 2011. "The Unbelievers." *New York Times*, November 25. http://www.nytimes.com/2011/11/27/fashion/african-american-atheists.html?emc=eta1.

Briggs, Charles L. 1996. "The Politics of Discursive Authority in Research on the 'Invention of Tradition.'" *Cultural Anthropology* 11(4): 435–69.

Brown, Diane R., and Lawrence E. Gary. 1991. "Religious Socialization and Educational Attainment among African Americans: An Empirical Assessment." *Journal of Negro Education* 60(3): 411–26.

Brownson, James. 2013. *Bible, Gender, Sexuality: Reframing the Church's Debate on Same-Sex Relationships*. Cambridge: Eerdmans.

Bruni, Frank. 2012. "Blacks and Marriage Equality: An Update." *New York Times*, May 25.

Brusco, Elizabeth E. 1995. *The Reformation of Machismo: Evangelical Conversion and Gender in Colombia*. Austin: University of Texas Press.

Butler, Anthea D. 2007. *Women in the Church of God in Christ: Making a Sanctified World*. Chapel Hill: University of North Carolina Press.

Byrd, Ayana, and Lori Tharps. 2014. *Hair Story: Untangling the Roots of Black Hair in America*. New York: St. Martin's.

Callahan, Allen Dwight. 2006. *The Talking Book: African Americans and the Bible*. New Haven: Yale University Press.

Calmes, Jackie, and Peter Baker. 2012. "Obama Endorses Same-Sex Marriage, Taking Stand on Charged Social Issue." *New York Times*, May 10: A1.

Caplan, Pat. 1997. "Approaches to the Study of Food, Health and Identity." In *Food, Health and Identity*, ed. Pat Caplan, pp. 1–31. London: Routledge.

Caplow, Theodore. 1985. "Contrasting Trends in European and American Religion." *Sociological Analysis* 46(2): 101–8.

Carbado, Devon W., Dwight A. McBride, and Donald Weise, eds. 2011. *Black Like Us: A Century of Lesbian, Gay, and Bisexual African American Fiction*. San Francisco: Cleis Press.

Cass, Vivienne C. 1979. "Homosexuality Identity Formation." *Journal of Homosexuality* 4(3): 219–35.

Casselberry, Judith. 2017. *The Labor of Faith: Gender and Power in Black Apostolic Pentecostalism*. Durham: Duke University Press.

Chauncey, George. 1994. *Gay New York: Gender, Urban Culture, and the Making of the Gay Male World, 1890–1940*. New York: Basic Books.

Chaves, Mark. 1997. *Ordaining Women: Culture and Conflict in Religious Organizations*. Cambridge, MA: Harvard University Press.

Cheng, Patrick S. 2012. *From Sin to Amazing Grace: Discovering the Queer Christ.* New York: Seabury Books.

Cohen, Cathy J. 1996. "Contested Membership: Black Gay Identities and the Politics of AIDS." In *Queer Theory/Sociology*, ed. S. Seidman, pp. 362–94. Cambridge, MA: Blackwell Publishers.

———. 1999. *The Boundaries of Blackness: AIDS and the Breakdown of Black Politics.* Chicago: University of Chicago Press.

Cohen, Micah. 2012. "Signs of Shift among African-Americans on Same-Sex Marriage." In *FiveThirtyEight* (May). New York: New York Times.

Collins, Patrica Hill. 1991. *Black Feminist Thought: Knowledge, Consciousness, and the Politics of Empowerment.* New York: Routledge.

———. 2004. *Black Sexual Politics: African Americans, Gender, and the New Racism.* New York: Routledge.

Cone, James H. 1991 (1972). *The Spirituals and the Blues: An Interpretation.* Maryknoll, NY: Orbis Books.

———. 1997 (1975). *God of the Oppressed.* Maryknoll, NY: Orbis Books.

———. 2011. *The Cross and the Lynching Tree.* Maryknoll, NY: Orbis Books.

Conerly, Gregory. 2001. "Are You Black First or Are You Queer?" In *The Greatest Taboo: Homosexuality in Black Communities*, ed. D. Constantine-Simms, pp. 7–23. Los Angeles: Alyson Books.

Conklin, Beth A. 1997. "Body Paint, Feathers, and VCRs: Aesthetics and Authenticity in Amazonian Activism." *American Ethnologist* 24(4): 711–37.

Connerton, Paul. 1989. *How Societies Remember.* Cambridge: Cambridge University Press.

Constantine-Simms, D., ed. 2000. *The Greatest Taboo: Homosexuality in Black Communities.* Los Angeles: Alyson Publications.

Coontz, Stephanie. 1992. *The Way We Never Were: American Families and the Nostalgia Trap.* New York: Basic Books.

Cox, Harvey. 2001. *Fire from Heaven: The Rise of Pentecostal Spirituality and the Reshaping of Religion in the Twenty-First Century.* Cambridge, MA: Da Capo Press.

Creed, Gerald W. 2006. "Community as Modern Pastoral." In *The Seductions of Community: Emancipations, Oppressions, Quandaries*, ed. G. W. Creed, pp. 23–48. Santa Fe, NM: School of American Research Press.

Csordas, Thomas J. 1997. *Language, Charisma, and Creativity: The Ritual Life of a Religious Movement.* Berkeley: University of California Press.

———. 2002. *Body/Meaning/Healing.* New York: Palgrave Macmillan.

Cullen, Dave. 2016. "Mass Murder at the Gay Bar: When a Refuge Becomes the Target," *Vanity Fair*, June 13. http://www.vanityfair.com/news/2016/06/dave-cullen-on-orlando-shooting (accessed June 24, 2016).

Dank, Barry. 1971. "Coming Out in the Gay World." *Psychiatry* 34(2): 180–97.

Darden, Robert. 2004. *People Get Ready: A New History of Black Gospel Music.* New York: Bloomsbury.

REFERENCES CITED

Davis, Gerald L. 1985. *I Got the World in Me and I Can Sing It, You Know: A Study of the Performed African-American Sermon*. Philadelphia: University of Pennsylvania Press.

Decena, Carlos Ulises. 2011. *Tacit Subjects: Belonging and Same-Sex Desire among Dominican Immigrant Men*. Durham: Duke University Press.

D'Emilio, John. 1983. *Sexual Politics, Sexual Communities: The Making of a Homosexual Minority in the United States, 1940–1979*. Chicago: University of Chicago Press.

———. 2004. *Lost Prophet: The Life and Times of Bayard Rustin*. Chicago: University of Chicago Press.

Dickel, Simon. 2012. *Black/Gay: The Harlem Renaissances, the Protest Era, and the Constructions of Black Gay Identity in the 1980s and '90s*. East Lansing: Michigan State University Press.

Dieter, Melvin Easterday. 1996. *The Holiness Revival of the Nineteenth Century*. Lanham, MD: Scarecrow Press.

Dodson, Jualynne E. 2002. *Engendering Church: Women, Power, and the AME Church*. Lanham, MD: Rowman and Littlefield.

Dodson, Jualynne E., and Cheryl Townsend Gilkes. 1995. "There's Nothing Like Church Food: Re-Membering Community and Feeding the Embodied S/spirit(s)." *Journal of the American Academy of Religion* 63(3): 519–38.

Dooley, Agnes W. 1962. *Promises to Keep: The Life of Dr. Thomas A. Dooley*. New York: Farrar, Straus, and Cudahy.

Douglas, Kelly Brown. 1999. *Sexuality and the Black Church: A Womanist Perspective*. Maryknoll, NY: Orbis Books.

———. 2012. *Black Bodies and the Black Church: A Blues Slant*. New York: Palgrave Macmillan.

Douglas, Mary. 1971. "Deciphering a Meal." In *Myth, Symbol, and Culture*, ed. C. Geertz, pp. 61–81. New York: W. W. Norton and Company.

———. 1984. "Standard Social Uses of Food: Introduction." In *Food in the Social Order: Studies of Food and Festivities in Three American Communities*, ed. Mary Douglas, pp. 1–39. New York: Russell Age Foundation.

Dubey, Madhu. 2003. *Signs and Cities: Black Literary Postmodernism*. Chicago: University of Chicago Press.

Du Bois, W. E. B. 1994 (1903). *The Souls of Black Folk*. New York: Dover.

Duggan, Lisa. 2003. *The Twilight of Equality? Neoliberalism, Cultural Politics, and the Attack on Democracy*. Boston: Beacon Press.

Egan, Patrick J., and Kenneth Sherrill. 2009. "California's Proposition 8: What Happened, and What Does the Future Hold?" National Gay and Lesbian Task Force Policy Institute.

Elisha, Omri. 2011. *Moral Ambition: Mobilization and Social Outreach in Evangelical Megachurches*. Berkeley University of California Press.

Erzen, Tanya. 2006. *Straight to Jesus: Sexual and Christian Conversions in the Ex-Gay Movement*. Berkeley: University of California Press.

Espinosa, Gastón. 2014. *Latino Pentecostals in America: Faith and Politics in Action*. Cambridge, MA: Harvard University Press.
Faderman, Lillian, and Stuart Timmon. 2006. *Gay LA: A History of Sexual Outlaws, Power Politics, and Lipstick Lesbians*. New York: Basic Books.
Fiorenza, Elisabeth Schüssler. 1993. *Discipleship of Equals: A Critical* Ekklēsia-*logy of Liberation*. New York: Crossroad.
Flunder, Yvette A. 2005. *Where the Edge Gathers: Building a Community of Radical Inclusivity*. Cleveland: Pilgrim Press.
Fordham, Signithia. 1996. *Blacked Out: Dilemmas of Race, Identity, and Success at Capital High*. Chicago: University of Chicago Press.
Forest, Jim. 2011. *All Is Grace: A Biography of Dorothy Day*. Maryknoll, NY: Orbis Books.
Foucault, Michel. 1990. *An Introduction*. Vol. 1 of *History of Sexuality*. New York: Vintage.
Frazier, E. Franklin. 1957. *Black Bourgeoisie: The Rise of a New Middle Class in the United States*. Glencoe, IL: The Free Press and Falcon's Wing.
———. 1974 (1964). *The Negro Church in America*. New York: Schocken.
Frederick, Marla F. 2003. *Between Sundays: Black Women and Everyday Struggles of Faith*. Berkeley: University of California Press.
———. 2015. *Colored Television: American Religion Gone Global*. Stanford: Stanford University Press.
Fuller, Jaime. 2015. "Kentucky County Clerk Who Refused to Issue Marriage Licenses Sent to Jail." *New York*, September 3. http://nymag.com/daily/intelligencer/2015/09/kim-davis-sent-to-jail-in-kentucky.html (accessed October 30, 2015).
Gamson, Joshua. 2005. *The Fabulous Sylvester*. New York: Picador.
Geertz, Clifford. 1973. *The Interpretation of Cultures*. New York: Basic Books.
Genovese, Eugene D. 1972. *Roll, Jordan, Roll: The World the Slaves Made*. New York: Random House.
Gerber, Lynne. 2011. *Seeking the Straight and Narrow: Weight Loss and Sexual Reorientation in Evangelical America*. Chicago: University of Chicago Press.
Ghavami, Negin, and Kerri L. Johnson. 2011. "Comparing Sexual and Ethnic Minority Perspectives on Same-Sex Marriage." *Journal of Social Issues* 67(2): 394–412.
Gilkes, Cheryl Townsend. 2001. *If It Wasn't for the Women . . . : Black Women's Experience and Womanist Culture in Church and Community*. Maryknoll, NY: Orbis Books.
Gill, Tiffany M. 2010. *Beauty Shop Politics: African American Women's Activism in the Beauty Industry*. Urbana: University of Illinois Press.
Ginsburg, Faye D. 1989. *Contested Lives: The Abortion Debate in an American Community*. Berkeley: University of California Press.
Gitlin, Todd. 2012. *Occupy Nation: The Roots, the Spirit, and the Promise of Occupy Wall Street*. New York: HarperCollins.

REFERENCES CITED

Glaude, Eddie S., Jr. 2003. "Of the Black Church and the Making of a Black Public." In *African American Religious Thought: An Anthology*, ed. C. West and E. S. Glaude Jr., pp. 338–65. Louisville, KY: Westminster John Knox Press.

Goffman, Erving. 1963. *Stigma: Notes on the Management of Spoiled Identity*. Englewood Cliffs, NJ: Prentice-Hall.

Gomes, Peter J. 1996. "The Bible and Homosexuality: The Last Prejudice." In *The Good Book: Reading the Bible with Mind and Heart*, 144–72. San Francisco: Harper.

Gomez, Jewelle L. 1983. "A Cultural Legacy Denied and Discovered: Black Lesbians in Fiction by Women." In *Home Girls: A Black Feminist Anthology*, ed. B. Smith, pp. 110–23. New York: Kitchen Table: Women of Color Press.

Goodman, Felicitas D. 1972. *Speaking in Tongues: A Cross-Cultural Study of Glossolalia*. Chicago: University of Chicago Press.

Goodman, Felicitas D., Jeannette Henney, and Esther Pressel. 1974. *Trance, Healing, and Hallucination: Three Field Studies of Religious Experience*. New York: Wiley-Interscience.

Goodstein, Laurie. 2012. "Unions That Divide: Churches Split Over Question of Gay Marriage." *New York Times*, May 14.

———. 2017. "Methodist High Court Rejects First Openly Gay Bishop's Consecration." *New York Times*, April 28.

Gorman, E. Michael. 1980. "A New Light on Zion: A Study of Three Homosexual Religious Congregations in Urban America." PhD diss., University of Chicago.

Graham, Laura R. 2005. "Image and Instrumentality in a Xavante Politics of Existence Recognition: The Public Outreach Work of Eténhiritipa Pimentel Barbosa." *American Ethnologist* 32(4): 6232–641.

Gray, Mary L. 2009. *Out in the Country: Youth, Media, and Queer Visibility in Rural America*. New York: New York University Press.

Griffin, Horace L. 2006. *Their Own Receive Them Not: African American Lesbians and Gays in Black Churches*. Cleveland: Pilgrim Press.

Gross, Larry. 1993. *Contested Closets: The Politics and Ethics of Outing*. Minneapolis: University of Minnesota Press.

———. 1999. "Contested Closets: The Politics and Ethics of Outing." In *The Columbia Reader on Lesbians and Gay Men in Media, Society, and Politics*, ed. L. Gross and J. D. Woods, pp. 421–28. New York: Columbia University Press.

———. 2001. *Up from Invisibility: Lesbians, Gay Men, and the Media in America*. New York: Columbia University Press.

Gushee, David P. 2015. *Changing Our Mind*. Canton, MI: Read the Spirit Books.

Halbwachs, Maurice. 1992. *On Collective Memory*, trans. L. A. Coser. Chicago: University of Chicago Press.

Halperin, David M. 1995. *Saint Foucault: Toward a Gay Hagiography*. New York: New York University Press.

Halperin, David M., and Valerie Traub, eds. 2009. *Gay Shame*. Chicago: University of Chicago Press.

Harding, Susan F. 2001. *The Book of Jerry Falwell: Fundamentalist Language and Politics*. Princeton, NJ: Princeton University Press.

Harris, Craig G. 1986. "Cut Off from among Their People." In *In the Life: A Black Gay Anthology*, ed. J. Beam, pp. 63-67. Boston: Alyson Publications.

Harris, Fredrick C. 1999. *Something Within: Religion in African American Political Action*. New York: Oxford University Press.

Harris, Michael W. 1992. *The Rise of the Gospel Blues: The Music of Thomas Andrew Dorsey in the Urban Church*. New York: Oxford University Press.

Harrison, Faye V. 1995. "'Give Me That Old-Time Religion': The Genealogy and Cultural Politics of an Afro-Christian Celebration in Halifax County, North Carolina." In *Religion in the Contemporary South: Diversity, Community, and Identity*, ed. O. K. White Jr. and D. White, pp. 34-45. Athens: University of Georgia Press.

Hartman, Andrew. 2015. *A War for the Soul of America: A History of the Culture Wars*. Chicago: University of Chicago Press.

Hawkeswood, William G. 1996. *One of the Children: Gay Black Men in Harlem*. Berkeley: University of California Press.

Heineman, Kenneth J. 1998. *God Is a Conservative: Religion, Politics, and Morality in Contemporary America*. New York: New York University Press.

Helminiak, Daniel A. 2000 (1994). *What the Bible Really Says about Homosexuality*. Tajique, NM: Alamo Square Press.

Herdt, Gilbert. 1992. "'Coming Out' as a Rite of Passage: A Chicago Study." In *Gay Culture in America: Essays from the Field*, ed. G. Herdt, pp. 29-67. Boston: Beacon Press.

Herdt, Gilbert, and Andrew Boxer. 1993. *Children of Horizons: How Gay and Lesbian Teens Are Leading a New Way Out of the Closet*. Boston: Beacon Press.

Herskovits, Melville. 1990 (1941). *The Myth of the Negro Past*. Boston: Beacon Press.

Higginbotham, Evelyn Brooks. 1993. *Righteous Discontent: The Women's Movement in the Black Baptist Church, 1880-1920*. Cambridge, MA: Harvard University Press.

Hine, Darlene Clark. 1989. "Rape and the Inner Lives of Black Women in the Middle West: Preliminary Thoughts on the Culture of Dissemblance." *Signs* 14(4): 912-20.

Hinson, Glenn. 2000. *Fire in My Bones: Transcendence and the Holy Spirit in African American Gospel*. Philadelphia: University of Pennsylvania Press.

Holtzman, Jon D. 2006. "Food and Memory." *Annual Review of Anthropology* 35: 361-78.

hooks, bell. 1989. *Talking Back: Thinking Feminist, Thinking Black*. Boston: South End Press.

———. 2001. *Salvation: Black People and Love*. New York: HarperCollins

Humphreys, Laud. 1970. *Tearoom Trade: Impersonal Sex in Public Places*. Chicago: Aldine.

REFERENCES CITED

Hunter, James D. 1991. *Culture Wars: The Struggle to Define America*. New York: Basic Books.

Hurston, Zora Neale. 1981. *The Sanctified Church: The Folklore Writings of Zora Neale Hurston*. Berkeley: Turtle Island.

Jackson, Jean. 1995. "Culture, Genuine and Spurious: The Politics of Indianness in the Vaupés, Colombia." *American Ethnologist* 22(1): 3–27.

Jackson, Jerma A. 2004. *Singing in My Soul: Black Gospel Music in a Secular Age*. Chapel Hill: University of North Carolina Press.

Jackson, Mahalia, and Evan McLeod Wylie. 1966. *Movin' on Up: The Warmly Personal Story of America's Favorite Gospel Singer*. New York: Hawthorn Books.

Jacobson, Matthew Frye. 1998. *Whiteness of a Different Color: European Immigrants and the Alchemy of Race*. Cambridge, MA: Harvard University Press.

Jefferson, Margo. 2015. *Negroland: A Memoir*. New York: Pantheon.

Johnson, E. Patrick. 2000. "Feeling the Spirit in the Dark: Expanding Notions of the Sacred in the African American Gay Community." In *The Greatest Taboo: Homosexuality in Black Communities*, ed. D. Constantine-Simms, pp. 88–109. Los Angeles: Alyson Publications.

———. 2003. *Appropriating Blackness: Performance and the Politics of Authenticity*. Durham, NC: Duke University Press.

———. 2008. *Sweet Tea: Black Gay Men of the South, an Oral History*. Chapel Hill: University of North Carolina Press.

Johnson, J. M. 1982. "Influence of Assimilation on the Psychosocial Adjustment of Black Homosexual Men." PhD diss., California School of Professional Psychology.

Kahn, Yoel H. 1989. "Judaism and Homosexuality: The Traditionalist/Progressive Debate." *Journal of Homosexuality* 18(3–4): 47–82.

Kalčik, Susan. 1984. "Ethnic Foodways in America: Symbol and the Performance of Identity." In *Ethnic and Regional Foodways in the United States: The Performance of Group Identity*, ed. L. K. Brown and K. Mussell, pp. 37–65. Knoxville: University of Tennessee Press.

Keane, Webb. 2007. *Christian Moderns: Freedom and Fetish in the Mission Encounter*. Berkeley: University of California Press.

Keil, Charles. 1966. *Urban Blues*. Chicago: University of Chicago Press.

Kennedy, Elizabeth Lapovsky. 1996. "'But We Would Never Talk about It': The Structures of Lesbian Discretion in South Dakota, 1928–1933." In *Inventing Lesbian Cultures in America*, ed. Ellen Lewin, pp. 15–39. Boston: Beacon Press.

———. 2002. "'These Natives Can Speak for Themselves': The Development of Lesbian and Gay Community Studies in Anthropology." In *Out in Theory: The Emergence of Lesbian and Gay Anthropology*, ed. E. Lewin and W. L. Leap, pp. 93–109. Champaign-Urbana: University of Illinois Press.

Kennedy, Elizabeth Lapovsky, and Madeline D. Davis. 1993. *Boots of Leather, Slippers of Gold: The History of a Lesbian Community*. New York: Routledge.

Kidd, Thomas S. 2007. *The Great Awakening: The Roots of Evangelical Christianity in Colonial America*. New Haven: Yale University Press.

Klassen, Pamela E. 2001. *Blessed Events: Religion and Home Birth in America*. Princeton, NJ: Princeton University Press.
Klein, Lillian R. 2000. *Deborah to Esther: Sexual Politics in the Hebrew Bible*. Minneapolis: Fortress Press.
Kleinman, Arthur. 1988. *The Illness Narratives: Suffering, Healing, and the Human Condition*. New York: Basic Books.
Krasniewicz, Louise. 1992. *Nuclear Summer: The Clash of Communities at the Seneca Women's Peace Encampment*. Ithaca, NY: Cornell University Press.
Krieger, Susan. 1983. *The Mirror Dance: Identity in a Women's Community*. Philadelphia: Temple University Press.
Kwilecki, Susan. 1987. "Contemporary Pentecostal Clergywomen: Female Christian Leadership, Old Style." *Journal of Feminist Studies in Religion* 3(2): 57–75.
La Barre, Weston. 1980. *Culture in Context: Selected Writings of Weston La Barre*. Durham, NC: Duke University Press.
Lambert, Frank. 1999. *Inventing the "Great Awakening."* Princeton, NJ: Princeton University Press.
Lawless, Elaine J. 1988. *Handmaidens of the Lord: Pentecostal Women Preachers and Traditional Religion*. Philadelphia: University of Pennsylvania Press.
Leacock, Eleanor Burke, ed. 1971. *The Culture of Poverty: A Critique*. New York: Simon and Schuster.
Leap, William L. 1996. *Word's Out: Gay Men's English*. Minneapolis: University of Minnesota Press.
Lee, Justin. 2013. *Torn: Rescuing the Gospel from the Gays-vs.-Christians Debate*. New York: Jericho Books.
Lemann, Nicholas. 1991. *The Promised Land: The Great Black Migration and How It Changed America*. New York: Knopf.
Leong, Pamela. 2006. "Religion, Flesh, and Blood: Re-Creating Religious Culture in the Context of HIV/AIDS." *Sociology of Religion* 67(3): 295–311.
Levine, Lawrence W. 1977. *Black Culture and Black Consciousness: Afro-American Folk Thought from Slavery to Freedom*. Oxford: Oxford University Press.
Lewin, Ellen. 1991. "Writing Lesbian and Gay Culture: What the Natives Have to Say for Themselves." *American Ethnologist* 18(4): 786–92.
———. 1993. *Lesbian Mothers: Accounts of Gender in American Culture*. Ithaca, NY: Cornell University Press.
———. 1998. *Recognizing Ourselves: Lesbian and Gay Ceremonies of Commitment*. New York: Columbia University Press.
———. 2009. *Gay Fatherhood: Narratives of Family and Citizenship in America*. Chicago: University of Chicago Press.
Lewis, I. M. 1989. *Ecstatic Religion: An Anthropological Study of Spirit Possession and Shamanism*. London: Routledge.
Lincoln, C. Eric, and Lawrence H. Mamiya. 1990. *The Black Church in the African American Experience*. Durham, NC: Duke University Press.
Lindholm, Charles. 1990. *Charisma*. Malden, MA: Blackwell.
———. 2008. *Culture and Authenticity*. Malden, MA: Blackwell.

REFERENCES CITED

———, ed. 2013. *The Anthropology of Religious Charisma*. New York: Palgrave Macmillan.
Lipsitz, George. 1998. *The Possessive Investment in Whiteness: How White People Profit from Identity Politics*. Philadelphia: Temple University Press.
Lorde, Audre. 1982. *Zami: A New Spelling of My Name—A Biomythography*. Freedom, CA: Crossing Press.
Lowenthal, David. 1985. *The Past Is a Foreign Country*. Cambridge: Cambridge University Press.
———. 1989. "Nostalgia Tells It Like It Wasn't." In *The Imagined Past: History and Nostalgia*, ed. C. Shaw and M. Chase, pp. 18–32. Manchester: Manchester University Press.
Luhrmann, T. M. 2012. *When God Talks Back: Understanding the American Evangelical Relationship with God*. New York: Knopf.
Marcus, George E. 1998. *Ethnography through Thick and Thin*. Princeton, NJ: Princeton University Press.
Matory, James Lorand. 2005. *Black Atlantic Religion: Tradition, Transnationalism, and Matriachy in the Afro-Brazilian Candomblé*. Princeton, NJ: Princeton University Press.
McCune, Jeffrey Q., Jr. 2014. *Sexual Discretion: Black Masculinity and the Politics of Passing*. Chicago: University of Chicago Press.
McDaniel, Eric L. 2008. *Politics in the Pews: The Political Mobilization of Black Churches*. Ann Arbor: University of Michigan Church.
McLeod, Hugh. 2007. *The Religious Crisis of the 1960s*. New York: Oxford University Press.
McNeill, John. 1976. *The Church and the Homosexual*. Boston: Beacon Press.
McQueeney, Krista. 2009. "'We Are God's Children, Y'All': Race, Gender, and Sexuality in Lesbian- and Gay-Affirming Congregations." *Social Problems* 56(1): 151–73.
Metzger, Bruce M. 2001. *The Bible in Translation: Ancient and English Versions*. Grand Rapids, MI: Baker Academic.
Miller, Adrian. 2013. *Soul Food: The Surprising Story of an American Cuisine, One Plate at a Time*. Chapel Hill: University of North Carolina Press.
Miller, Donald E., and Tetsunao Yamamori. 2007. *Global Pentecostalism: The New Face of Christian Social Engagement*. Berkeley: University of California Press.
Miller, Nicole, and Beth Burkhart, dirs. 2006. *The Believers*. San Francisco: Frameline.
Mintz, Sidney W., and Richard Price. 1992 (1976). *The Birth of African-American Culture: An Anthropological Perspective*. Boston: Beacon Press.
Mitchell, Henry H. 1990. *Black Preaching: The Recovery of a Powerful Art*. Nashville: Abingdon Press.
Moon, Dawne. 2004. *God, Sex, and Politics: Homosexuality and Everyday Theologies*. Chicago: University of Chicago Press.
———. 2014. "Beyond the Dichotomy: Six Religious Views of Homosexuality." *Journal of Homosexuality* 61(9): 1215–41.

Moore, Mignon R. 2010. "Black and Gay in L.A.: The Relationships Black Lesbians and Gay Men Have with Their Racial and Religious Communities." In *Black Los Angeles: American Dreams and Racial Realities*, ed. D. Hunt and A. Ramon, pp. 188–212. New York: New York University Press.

———. 2011. *Invisible Families: Gay Identities, Relationships and Motherhood among Black Women*. Berkeley: University of California Press.

Moore, Russell. 2016. "The Real Meaning of Transgender Bathrooms." Religion News Service. http://religionnews.com/2016/05/13/what-the-transgender-bathroom-debate-means-for-you/ (accessed June 27, 2016).

Morgan, Robert, and John Barton. 1988. *Biblical Interpretation*. Oxford: Oxford University Press.

Morrison, Toni, ed. 1992. *Race-ing Justice, En-Gendering Power: Essays on Anita Hill, Clarence Thomas, and the Construction of Social Reality*. New York: Pantheon.

Moss, Otis, III. 2015. *Blue Note Preaching in a Post-Soul World: Finding Hope in an Age of Despair*. Louisville, KY: Westminster John Knox Press.

Mumford, Kevin. 2016. *Not Straight, Not White: Black Gay Men from the March on Washington to the AIDS Crisis*. Chapel Hill: University of North Carolina Press.

Murray, Stephen O. 1979. "The Institutional Elaboration of a Quasi-Ethnic Community." *International Review of Modern Sociology* 9(2): 155–75.

Myerhoff, Barbara. 1992. "A Death in Due Time: Conviction, Order, and Continuity in Ritual Drama." In *Remembered Lives: The Work of Ritual, Storytelling, and Growing Older*, ed. M. Kaminsky, pp. 159–90. Ann Arbor: University of Michigan Press.

National Council of Churches of Christ in the USA. 1989. Holy Bible, with the Apocryphal/Deuterocanonical Books, New Revised Standard Edition. New York: Oxford University Press.

Neitz, Mary Jo. 1987. *Charisma and Community: A Study of Religious Commitment within the Charismatic Renewal*. New Brunswick, NJ: Transaction Books.

Neville, Morgan, dir. 2013. *Twenty Feet from Stardom*. Radius–The Weinstein Company.

Newman, Richard. 2009. *Freedom's Prophet: Bishop Richard Allen, the AME Church, and the Black Founding Fathers*. New York: New York University Press.

Newton, Esther. 1979 (1972). *Mother Camp: Female Impersonators in America*. Chicago: University of Chicago Press.

———. 1993. *Cherry Grove, Fire Island: Sixty Years in America's First Gay and Lesbian Town*. Boston: Beacon Press.

Nida, Eugene A. 1964. *Toward a Science of Translating: With Special Reference to Principles and Procedures Involved in Bible Translating*. Leiden: E. J. Brill.

Noll, Mark A. 2006. *The Civil War as a Theological Crisis*. Chapel Hill: University of North Carolina Press.

Oakes, Len. 1997. *Prophetic Charisma: The Psychology of Revolutionary Religious Personalities*. Syracuse, NY: Syracuse University Press.

O'Brien, Jodi. 2004. "Wrestling the Angel of Contradiction: Queer Christian Identities." *Culture and Religion* 5(2): 179–202.

REFERENCES CITED

Olson, Lynne. 2002. *Freedom's Daughters: The Unsung Heroines of the Civil Rights Movement from 1830 to 1970*. New York: Scribner.

Painter, Nell Irvin. 2011. *The History of White People*. New York: W. W. Norton.

Pearson, Bishop Carlton. 2006. *The Gospel of Inclusion: Reaching Beyond Religious Fundamentalism to the True Love of God*. San Francisco: Azusa Press International.

Perry, Troy D. 1972. *The Lord Is My Shepherd and He Knows I'm Gay: The Autobiography of the Reverend Troy D. Perry*. Los Angeles: Universal Fellowship Press.

Personal Narratives Group, ed. 1989. *Interpreting Women's Lives: Feminist Theory and Personal Narratives*. Bloomington: Indiana University Press.

Pew Forum on Religion and Public Life. 2009. *A Religious Portrait of African-Americans and Religion*. Washington, DC: Pew Research Center.

Piazza, Michael. 1994. *Holy Homosexuals: The Truth about Being Gay or Lesbian and Christian*. Dallas: Sources of Hope Publishing House.

Pinn, Anthony B. 2014. *Writing God's Obituary: How a Good Methodist Became a Better Atheist*. Amherst, NY: Prometheus Books.

Pitt, Richard N. 2009. "'Still Looking for My Jonathan': Gay Black Men's Management of Religious and Sexual Identity Conflicts." *Journal of Homosexuality* 57(1): 39–53.

———. 2010. "'Killing the Messenger': Religious Black Gay Men's Neutralization of Anti-Gay Religious Messages." *Journal for the Scientific Study of Religion* 49(1): 56–72.

Pitts, Walter F., Jr. 1993. *Old Ship of Zion: The Afro-Baptist Ritual in the African Diaspora*. Oxford: Oxford University Press.

Polikoff, Nancy. 2009. *Beyond (Straight and Gay) Marriage: Valuing All Families under the Law*. Boston: Beacon Press.

Porter, Stanley E., and Richard Hess. 2005. *Translating the Bible*. London: A & C Black.

Potts, John. 2009. *A History of Charisma*. London: Palgrave Macmillan.

Povinelli, Elizabeth A. 2001. "Radical Worlds: The Anthropology of Incommensurability and Inconceivability." *Annual Review of Anthropology* 30: 319–34.

Powell, Brian, Catherine Bolzendahl, Claudia Geist, and Lala Carr Steelman. 2010. *Counted Out: Same-Sex Relations and Americans' Definitions of Family*. New York: Russell Sage Foundation.

Putnam, Robert D., and David E. Campbell. 2010. *American Grace: How Religion Divides and Unites Us*. New York: Simon and Schuster.

Raboteau, Albert J. 1978. *Slave Religion: The Invisible Institution in the Antebellum South*. New York: Oxford University Press.

———. 1999. *Canaan Land: A Religious History of African Americans*. New York: Oxford University Press.

Ramberg, Lucinda. 2014. *Given to the Goddess: South Indian Devadasis and the Sexuality of Religion*. Durham, NC: Duke University Press.

Ransby, Barbara. 2005. *Ella Baker and the Black Freedom Movement: A Radical Democratic Vision*. Chapel Hill: University of North Carolina Press.

Raspa, Richard. 1985. "Exotic Foods among Italian-Americans in Mormon Utah: Food as Nostalgic Enactment of Identity." In *Ethnic and Regional Foodways in the United States: The Performance of Group Identity*, ed. L. K. Brown and K. Mussell, pp. 185–94. Knoxville: University of Tennessee Press.

Ray, Krishnendu. 2004. *The Migrant's Table: Meals and Memories in Bengali-American Households*. Philadelphia: Temple University Press.

Read, Kenneth. 1981. *Other Voices: The Style of a Male Homosexual Tavern*. Novato, CA: Chandler and Sharp.

Reyes-Chow, Bruce. 2011. "The Tea Party and Occupy Wall Street Movements: Similarities and Differences." *Huffington Post*, November 1. http://www.huffingtonpost.com/bruce-reyeschow/tea-party-occupy-movement_b_1062824.html (accessed March 31, 2017).

Richen, Yoruba, dir. 2013. *The New Black*. San Francisco: California Newsreel.

Robbins, Joel. 2004. *Becoming Sinners: Christianity and Moral Torment in a Papua New Guinea Society*. Berkeley: University of California Press.

Roberts, John W. 1989. *From Trickster to Badman: The Black Folk Hero in Slavery and Freedom*. Philadelphia: University of Pennsylvania Press.

Rogers, Jack. 2009. *Jesus, the Bible, and Homosexuality: Explode the Myths, Heal the Church*. Louisville, KY: Westminster John Knox Press.

Rooks, Noliwe M. 1996. *Hair Raising: Beauty, Culture, and African American Women*. New Brunswick, NJ: Rutgers University Press.

Rosaldo, Renato. 1989. *Culture and Truth: The Remaking of Social Analysis*. Boston: Beacon Press.

Ross, Janell. 2016. "Hate Crime? Terrorism? Mass Shooting? How the Increasingly Blurred Lines Lead to a Blurry Response." *Washington Post*, June 14. https://www.washingtonpost.com/news/the-fix/wp/2016/06/14/hate-crime-terrorism-mass-shooting-how-the-increasingly-blurred-lines-lead-to-a-blurry-response/ (accessed July 6, 2016).

Ross, Marlon B. 2005. "Beyond the Closet as Raceless Paradigm." In *Black Queer Studies: A Critical Anthology*, ed. E. Patrick Johnson and Mae G. Henderson, pp. 161–89. Durham, NC: Duke University Press.

Roth, Benita. 2003. *Separate Roads to Feminism: Black, Chicana, and White Feminist Movements in America's Second Wave*. Cambridge: Cambridge University Press.

Rouget, Gilbert. 1985. *Music and Trance: A Theory of the Relations between Music and Possession*. Chicago: University of Chicago Press.

Russell, Letty M., ed. 1985. *Feminist Interpretations of the Bible*. Louisville, KY: Westminster Press.

Ryan, Mary P. 1983. *Cradle of the Middle Class: The Family in Oneida County, New York, 1790–1865*. Cambridge: Cambridge University Press.

Salkowitz, Selig, Yoel H. Kahn, and Leonard S. Kravitz, eds. 1989. *Homosexuality and the Rabbinate: Papers Delivered at the 100th Convention of the Central Conference of American Rabbis*. New York: Central Conference of American Rabbis.

Samarin, William J. 1972. *Tongues of Men and Angels: The Religious Language of Pentecostalism*. New York: Macmillan.

Sanders, Cheryl J. 1996. *Saints in Exile: The Holiness-Pentecostal Experience in African American Religion and Culture*. New York: Oxford University Press.
Sarris, Greg. 1993. *Keeping Slug Woman Alive: A Holistic Approach to American Indian Texts*. Berkeley: University of California Press.
Sauvé, John R. 1998. "Issues Facing Gay Black Males in College." *Journal of College Student Psychotherapy* 13(2): 21–39.
Savin-Williams, Ritch C. 2005. *The New Gay Teenager*. Cambridge, MA: Harvard University Press.
Schmidt, Leigh Eric. 2000. *Hearing Things: Religion, Illusion, and the American Enlightenment*. Cambridge, MA: Harvard University Press.
Schnoor, Randal F. 2006. "Being Gay and Jewish: Negotiating Intersecting Identities." *Sociology of Religion* 67(1): 43–60.
Schwarz, A. B. Christa. 2003. *Gay Voices of the Harlem Renaissance*. Bloomington: Indiana University Press.
Scott, David. 2005. *A Revolution of Love: The Meaning of Mother Teresa*. Chicago: Loyola Press.
Sedgwick, Eve K. 1990. *The Epistemology of the Closet*. Berkeley: University of California Press.
Sedmak, Clemens. 2002. *Doing Local Theology: A Guide for Artisans of a New Humanity*. Maryknoll, NY: Orbis Books.
Sernett, Milton C. 1997. *Bound for the Promised Land: African American Religion and the Great Migration*. Durham, NC: Duke University Press.
Severson, Kim, and Robbie Brown. 2011. "Charismatic Church Leader, Dogged by Scandal, to Stop Preaching for Now." *New York Times*, December 4.
Shallenberger, David. 1998. *Reclaiming the Spirit: Gay Men and Lesbians Come to Terms with Religion*. New Brunswick, NJ: Rutgers University Press.
Shils, Edward. 1965. "Charisma, Order, and Status." *American Sociological Review* 30(2): 199–213.
———. 1981. *Tradition*. Chicago: University of Chicago Press.
Shokeid, Moshe. 1995. *A Gay Synagogue in New York*. New York: Columbia University Press.
Signorile, Michelangelo. 1999. "How I Brought Out Malcolm Forbes—and the Media Flinched." In *The Columbia Reader on Lesbians and Gay Men in Media, Society, and Politics*, ed. Larry Gross and James D. Woods, pp. 429–31. New York: Columbia University Press.
Smith, Barbara, ed. 1983. *Home Girls: A Black Feminist Anthology*. New York: Kitchen Table: Women of Color Press.
Snorton, C. Riley. 2014. *Nobody Is Supposed to Know: Black Sexuality on the Down Low*. Minneapolis: University of Minnesota Press.
Southern, Eileen. 1983. *The Music of Black Americans: A History*. New York: W. W. Norton.
Spencer, Jon Michael. 1987. *Sacred Symphony: The Chanted Sermon of the Black Preacher*. New York: Greenwood Press.

Spong, John Shelby. 1988. *Living in Sin? A Bishop Rethinks Human Sexuality*. San Francisco: Harper and Row.

Spretnak, Charlene, ed. 1981. *The Politics of Women's Spirituality: Essays by Founding Mothers of the Movement*. New York: Anchor.

Stack, Carol. 1974. *All Our Kin: Strategies of Survival in a Black Community*. New York: Harper and Row.

———. 1996. *Call to Home: African Americans Reclaim the Rural South*. New York: Basic Books.

Staples, Brent. 2007. "Decoding the Debates over the Blackness of Barack Obama." *New York Times*, February 11.

Steedman, Carolyn Kay. 1987. *Landscape for a Good Woman: A Story of Two Lives*. New Brunswick, NJ: Rutgers University Press.

Stein, Arlene. 2001. *The Stranger Next Door: The Story of a Small Community's Battle over Sex, Faith, and Civil Rights*. Boston: Beacon

Stein, Marc. 2004. *City of Sisterly and Brotherly Loves: Lesbian and Gay Philadelphia, 1945–1972*. Chicago: University of Chicago Press.

Stockley, Grif. 2005. *Daisy Bates: Civil Rights Crusader from Arkansas*. Oxford: University of Mississippi Press.

Sutton, David E. 2001. *Remembrance of Repasts: An Anthropology of Food and Memory*. Oxford: Berg.

Swilley, Bishop Jim. 2012. *First, the Good News: The Positive Truth about God, the Gospel, and What It Really Means to Be Gay*. Atlanta: Church in the Now Publishing.

Synan, Vinson. 1971. *The Holiness-Pentecostal Tradition: Charismatic Movements in the Twentieth Century*. Grand Rapids, MI: William B. Eerdmans.

Taylor, Robert Joseph, Linda M. Chatters, and Jeff Levin. 2004. *Religion in the Lives of African Americans: Social, Psychological, and Health Perspectives*. Thousand Oaks, CA: Sage.

Thomas, Kendall. 1997. "'Ain't Nothin' Like the Real Thing': Black Masculinity, Gay Sexuality, and the Jargon of Authenticity." In *The House That Race Built*, ed. W. Lubiano, pp. 116–35. New York: Random House.

Thompson, Robert Farris. 1983. *Flash of the Spirit: African and Afro-American Art and Philosophy*. New York: Random House.

Thumma, Scott. 2005. "Negotiating a Religious Identity: The Case of the Gay Evangelical." In *Gay Religion*, ed. S. Thumma and E. R. Gray, pp. 67–82. Lanham, MD: Altamira Press.

———. 2006. "'Open and Affirming' of Growth: The Challenge of Liberal Lesbian, Gay and Bisexual-Supportive Congregational Growth." In *Why Liberal Churches Are Growing*, ed. M. Percy and I. Markham, pp. 100–118. London: I & T Clark International.

Tinney, James S. 1986. "Why a Gay Black Church?" In *In the Life: A Black Gay Anthology*, ed. J. Beam, pp. 70–86. Boston: Alyson Publications.

Tobin, Kay, and Randy Wicker. 1972. *The Gay Crusaders*. New York: Paperback Library.

REFERENCES CITED

Turner, Victor. 1967. *The Forest of Symbols: Aspects of Ndembu Ritual*. Ithaca, NY: Cornell University Press.

———. 1969. *The Ritual Process: Structure and Anti-Structure*. Ithaca, NY: Cornell University Press.

———. 1987. *The Anthropology of Performance*. New York: PAJ Publications.

Valentine, Charles A. 1968. *Culture and Poverty: Critique and Counterproposals*. Chicago: University of Chicago Press.

Valentine, David. 2007. *Imagining Transgender: An Ethnography of a Category*. Durham, NC: Duke University Press.

Vines, Matthew. 2014. *God and the Gay Christian: The Biblical Case in Support of Same-Sex Relationships*. New York: Convergent Books.

Walker, Alice. 1983. *In Search of Our Mothers' Gardens*. New York: Harcourt Brace.

Walton, Jonathan L. 2009. *Watch This!: The Ethics and Aesthetics of Black Televangelism*. New York: New York University Press.

Warner, R. Stephen. 1995. "The Metropolitan Community Churches and the Gay Agenda: The Power of Pentecostalism and Essentialism." In *Religion and the Social Order: Sex, Lies, and Sanctity: Religion and Deviance in Contemporary North America*, ed. Mary Jo Neitz and Marion S. Goldman, pp. 81–108, Greenwich, CT: JAI Press.

Weber, Max. 1968a. *Economy and Society I*. New York: Bedminister Press.

———. 1968b. *On Charisma and Institution Building*, ed. S. N. Eisenstadt. Chicago: University of Chicago Press.

Weeks, Jeffrey. 1979. *Coming Out: Homosexual Politics in Britain from the Nineteenth Century to the Present*. London: Quartet Books.

Weston, Kath. 1991. *Families We Choose: Lesbians, Gays, Kinship*. New York: Columbia University Press.

———. 1993. "Lesbian/Gay Studies in the House of Anthropology." *Annual Review of Anthropology* 22: 339–67.

———. 1995. "Get Thee to a Big City: Sexual Imaginary and the Great Gay Migration." *GLQ: A Journal of Lesbian and Gay Studies* 2(3): 253–77.

Wharry, Cheryl. 2003. "Amen and Hallelujah Preaching: Discourse Functions in African American Sermons." *Language in Society* 32: 203–25.

White, James F. 1989. *Protestant Worship: Traditions in Transition*. Louisville, KY: Westminster John Knox Press.

Wiegman, Robyn. 1995. *American Anatomies: Theorizing Race and Gender*. Durham, NC: Duke University Press.

Wiggins, Daphne C. 2005. *Righteous Content: Black Women's Perspectives of Church and Faith*. New York: New York University Press.

Wilcox, Clyde, and Carin Robinson. 2011. *Onward Christian Soldiers?: The Religious Right in American Politics*. Boulder, CO: Westview Press.

Wilcox, Melissa M. 2003. *Coming Out in Christianity*. Bloomington: Indiana University Press.

Wilk, Richard R. 1999. "'Real Belizean Food': Building Local Identity in the Transnational Caribbean." *American Anthropologist* 101(2): 244–55.

Wilkerson, Isabel. 2010. *The Warmth of Other Suns: The Epic Story of America's Great Migration*. New York: Random House.
Williams, Brett. 1992. "Poverty among African Americans in the Urban United States." *Human Organization* 51(2): 164–74.
Williams, Raymond. 1973. *The Country and the City*. New York: Oxford University Press.
Williams, Robert. 1992. *Just as I Am: A Practical Guide to Being Out, Proud, and Christian*. New York: Crown.
Williams, Roger Ross, dir. 2014. *God Loves Uganda*. New York: First Run Features.
Williams-Forson, Psyche A. 2006. *Building Houses Out of Chicken Legs: Black Women, Food, and Power*. Chapel Hill: University of North Carolina Press.
Willner, Ann, Ruth. 1984. *The Spellbinders: Charismatic Political Leadership*. New Haven: Yale University Press.
Wilson, James F. 2011. *Bulldaggers, Pansies, and Chocolate Babies: Performance, Race, and Sexuality in the Harlem Renaissance*. Ann Arbor: University of Michigan Press.
Wilson, Natasha Sandraya. 2009. "A Queer Situation: Poverty, Prisons, and Performance of Infidelity and Instability in the New Orleans Lesbian Anthem." In *Out in Public: Reinventing Lesbian/Gay Anthropology in a Globalizing World*, ed. E. Lewin and W. L. Leap, pp. 104–22. Malden, MA: Wiley-Blackwell.
Wingfield, Adia Harvey. 2008. *Doing Business with Beauty: Black Women, Hair Salons, and Racial Enclave Economy*. Lanham, MD: Rowman and Littlefield.
Wolf, Margery. 1992. *A Thrice-Told Tale: Feminism, Postmodernism, and Ethnographic Responsibility*. Stanford, CA: Stanford University Press.
Wolkomir, Michelle. 2006. *Be Not Deceived: The Sacred and Sexual Struggles of Gay and Ex-Gay Christian Men*. New Brunswick, NJ: Rutgers University Press.
Wright, Kai. 2008. *Drifting toward Love: Black, Brown, Gay, and Coming of Age on the Streets of New York*. Boston: Beacon Press.
Young, Jason R. 2007. *Rituals of Resistance: African Atlantic Religion in Kongo and the Low Country South in the Era of Slavery*. Baton Rouge: Louisiana State University Press.
Zeveloff, Naomi. 2012. "Conservatives Give Gay Wedding Guidance." *Jewish Daily Forward*, June 8.
Zimmerman, Bonnie. 1984. "The Politics of Transliteration: Lesbian First-Person Narratives," *Signs* 9(4): 663–82.

Index

Abrajano, Marisa, 40, 182
Abrams, Andrea C., 118
Abu-Lughod, Lila, 17
Achtemeier, Mark, 162
Adam, Barry D., 95
African Methodist Episcopal Church (AME), 33, 48, 60, 64, 116, 147, 150, 181
Ahlstrom, Sydney E., 186n1
Alba, Richard D., 131
Alexander, Estrelda Y., 6–8, 49, 126, 180, 189n18
Alexander, Paul, 7
Ammerman, Nancy T., 161, 177–78
Anderson, Allan, 8, 20–21
Anderson, Benedict, 146, 172, 180
Anderson, Robert Mapes, 7, 21, 49–50, 185n3, 189n22
Anderson, Victor, 28
anti-Semitism, 2, 50
Armstrong, Elizabeth A., 192n1
Arnold, Lee, 46
Austin-Broos, Diane J., 7
Azusa Street Revival, 6–8, 49–50, 62–64, 130, 141–44, 185n3

Baer, Hans A., 32, 180
Bailey, Marlon M., 147
Baker, Lee D., 96
Baker, Peter, 181
Banerjee, Neela, 181
Banks, Ingrid, 136
Baptiste, Nathalie, 177
Barbaro, Michael, 181–82
Barth, Frederik, 131–32

Barton, Bernadette, 15, 90–91, 93, 161–62
Barton, John, 160–61
Bates, Aryana, 28, 47
Battle, Michael, 28–29, 32
Bauman, Richard, 20, 156
Beam, Joseph, 38, 97
Bean, Carl (pastor), 47, 61, 162
Beemyn, Brett, 9–10, 147
Best, Wallace D., 7, 32, 63–64, 130–31
Bevans, Stephan B., 160
Bible study, 161–62
Bielo, James S., 7, 14, 21
black churches: Chicago, 63–64; denominations, 186n2; and Emerging Churches/megachurches, 21; formation, 47–48; and LGBT individuals, 35–37, 39–43, 50–51, 90–92, 97; political activism, 8, 14–15, 25, 31–33; Praise Center, 3–5, 9; public dimensions, 31; responses to HIV/AIDS, 43–45; social work, 64; TFAM and traditional, 6; women in, 33–35; worship styles, 47. *See also* gospel music; "Metho-Bapti-Costal"; nostalgia
Blount, Brian K., 160
Blumhofer, Edith Waldvogel, 49
Boellstorff, Tom, 15, 147
Bonilla-Silva, Eduardo, 186n4
Borker, Ruth A., 156
Bourdieu, Pierre, 139
Bourguignon, Erika, 20–21

INDEX

Boxer, Andrew, 94-95
Boyd, Nan Alamilla, 192n1
Boykin, Keith, 97
Boym, Svetlana, 124
Brasher, Brenda E., 191n3
Braude, Ann, 191n3
Brekus, Catherine A., 62-63
Brennan, Emily, 33
Briggs, Charles L., 156, 172
Brown, Robbie, 43-44
Brownson, James, 162
Bruni, Frank, 182
Burkhart, Beth, 123
Butler, Anthea D., 34-35, 62, 192n2
Byrd, Ayana, 136-38, 193n11

Callahan, Allen Dwight, 152, 158-59
Calmes, Jackie, 181
Campbell, David E., 178
Caplan, Pat, 131
Caplow, Theodore, 33
Carbado, Devon W., 37
Cass, Vivienne C., 94
Casselberry, Judith, 191n3
charisma: Bishop Flunder, 23-24, 53-55, 66, 68-86, 87-88; calling, 65-66; charismatic gifts, 126, 141; COGIC, 34-35; Pentecostal, 7-8, 106, 185n2; research, 14, 21, 66-68; TFAM, 9, 66, 174
Chatters, Linda M., 33
Chauncey, George, 192n1
Chaves, Mark, 34
Cheng, Patrick S., 162
Chicago, IL: Anthony Sullivan (pastor), 72; black churches, 63-64; Carl Madgett, 110; Carlton Pearson (bishop), 191n2; Chicago Theological Seminary (CTS), 2-6; churches and southern churches, 104-7; gospel music, 129-31; gun violence, 183; LGBT community, 27, 94-95; Phyllis Pennese (bishop), 19-20; Pillar of Love, 12, 18, 119, 127, 145, 149; soul food, 133; TFAM, 112; United Church of Christ, 151
Church of God in Christ. *See* COGIC
City of Refuge: altar, 152, 171; Bishop Flunder's charisma, 75-79, 87; departure from COGIC, 55-56; formation, 59-61; Jewish congregants, 157; Lewin research, 5-6, 12; move to Oakland, 79-85; music, 123; services, 153-55

COGIC: Azusa Street Revival, 50; black church denominations, 150, 186n2; demonization of homosexuality, 101; departure from, 54-56, 58-59, 73-74, 86, 141-42, 190n23, 191n1; doctrine, 72; female limitations, 34-35, 61-62, 64, 128; gospel music, 128-29; hypocrisy, 113; nostalgia, 118-19; order of service, 9; Pentecostal segregation, 6-7; political activism, 25; Tinney excommunication, 48
Cohen, Cathy J., 36, 39, 43, 146
Cohen, Micah, 182
Collins, Patricia Hill, 31, 35, 96
coming out: Bishop Flunder, 100-102, 125; "disfellowshipping," 107-10; "Don't ask, don't tell," 90; *Families We Choose* (Weston), 16; National Coming Out Day, 2; political activism, 94-96, 110, 113-14; racial complications, 96-99; spiritual needs, 90-91; stories, 24, 38, 89-90, 90-91, 92-94, 97; TFAM, 24, 99-102, 110-14, 125, 174
Cone, James H., 130, 158-59, 180
Conerly, Gregory, 37-38, 41
Conklin, Beth A., 172
Connerton, Paul, 180
Constantine-Simms, D., 43
Coontz, Stephanie, 177-78
Cox, Harvey, 7, 8, 180
Creed, Gerald W., 147
Csordas, Thomas J., 9, 20-21
Cullen, Dave, 187n6

Dallas, TX, 6
Dank, Barry, 94
Darden, Robert, 118-19, 126, 130, 194n14
Davis, Angela, 136
Davis, Gerald L., 17, 68-69, 115, 125, 163-64, 167, 180
Davis, Madeline D., 9-10, 37, 192n1
Decena, Carlos Ulises, 97-98
D'Emilio, John, 37, 192n1
Dickel, Simon, 37
Dieter, Melvin Easterday, 49
"disfellowshipping," 107-10
divinity, 1
Dodson, Jualynne E., 62, 135
"Don't ask, don't tell," 22, 41-43, 56, 90
Dooley, Agnes W., 186n5
Douglas, Kelly Brown, 28, 41

Douglas, Mary, 131–34
Dubey, Madhu, 119
Du Bois, W. E. B., 31, 35, 38
Duggan, Lisa, 95, 158
Dunbar, Toni (pastor), 153–55, 160, 171–72

Egan, Patrick J., 182
Elaw, Zilpha, 63
Elisha, Omri, 7, 21
Erzen, Tanya, 15, 95, 147
Espinosa, Gastón, 7

Faderman, Lillian, 192n1
Families We Choose (Weston), 16
Fiorenza, Elisabeth Schüssler, 65
Flunder, Yvette (bishop): Azusa Street Revival, 49–50; biblical scholarship, 162–63; blessings, 53–54; calling, 58–60; charisma, 23–24, 53–55, 66, 68–86, 87–88; City of Refuge, 12; COGIC, 54–56; coming out, 100–102, 125; female preaching in America, 61–66; gospel music, 128; hair care, 136–39, 193n10; Lewin research, 5–6, 12–13, 18–19; Love Center, 48, 58–59, 191n1; memories of food, 134–35; "Metho-Bapti-Costal," 54, 140, 148–49, 168, 174, 180, 191n5; Mother Langston, 103–4, 142–43; "oppression sickness," 141–43; sermons, 68–70, 78–86, 135, 152; teaching positions, 13; TFAM, 44, 48–49, 50–51, 60–61, 86–87, 140–41
Fordham, Signithia, 187n5
Forest, Jim, 186n5
Foucault, Michel, 96
Frazier, E. Franklin, 28, 30–31
Frederick, Marla F., 62, 65
Fuller, Jaime, 182

Gamson, Joshua, 191n1
gay rights, 4, 24, 38, 47, 92, 95, 97, 162
Geertz, Clifford, 20–21
Genovese, Eugene D., 28
Gerber, Lynne, 15, 95
Ghavami, Negin, 40
Gilkes, Cheryl Townsend, 62, 135
Gill, Tiffany M., 193n9
Ginsburg, Faye D., 17
Gitlin, Todd, 178
Glaude, Eddie S., Jr., 31
God's Trombones (Johnson), 159

Goffman, Erving, 40, 91
Gomes, Peter J., 87
Gomez, Jewelle L., 38
Goodman, Felicitas D., 20–21, 126
Goodstein, Laurie, 45
Gorman, E. Michael, 44, 90
gospel music: Bishop Flunder, 128; choirs, 18, 58–59, 123, 157, 194n6; gay musicians, 106; nostalgia, 118–19; research, 180–81; TFAM, 128–31, 144, 173
Graham, Laura R., 156, 172
Gray, Mary L., 92–93, 95, 96
Griffin, Horace L., 28, 30, 41, 92, 142, 147
Gross, Larry, 95
Gushee, David P., 162

hair care, 135–39, 193nn9–10
Halbwachs, Maurice, 180
Halperin, David M., 95–97
Harding, Susan F., 20–21, 178
Harris, Craig G., 43
Harris, Fredrick C., 32
Harris, Michael W., 118–19
Harrison, Faye V., 32, 117
Hartman, Andrew, 21, 178
Hawkeswood, William G., 11, 38–39
Heineman, Kenneth J., 20–21
Helminiak, Daniel A., 87, 94, 160–61, 162–63
Herdt, Gilbert, 94–95
Herskovits, Melville, 7, 28, 141
Hess, Richard, 161
Higginbotham, Evelyn Brooks, 31–32, 33–34, 62
Hine, Darlene Clark, 97
Hinson, Glenn, 17, 125, 128–29, 167, 180–81
Holtzman, Jon D., 118
hooks, bell, 36–37, 136
Humphreys, Laud, 192n2
Hunter, James D., 20–21, 178
Hurston, Zora Neale, 126, 180–81

Jackson, Jean, 172
Jackson, Jerma A., 118–19, 128–29, 180–81
Jackson, Mahalia, 130
Jefferson, Margo, 7, 136
Johnson, E. Patrick., 11, 28, 40–42, 97, 131, 146, 192n2, 194n6
Johnson, J. M., 37–38
Johnson, James Weldon, 159
Johnson, Kerri L., 40

INDEX

Judaism, 1-2, 50, 122, 150-52, 156-58, 188n13

Kahn, Yoel H., 188n13
Kalcik, Susan, 118, 131-32
Keane, Webb, 20-21
Keil, Charles, 129-30
Kennedy, Elizabeth Lapovsky, 9-10, 37, 98, 119, 147, 192n1
Kidd, Thomas S., 186n1
Klassen, Pamela E., 177-78
Klein, Lillian R., 65
Kleinman, Arthur, 16
Krasniewicz, Louise, 17
Kravitz, Leonard S., 188n13
Krieger, Susan, 147
Kwilecki, Susan, 65-66

La Barre, Weston, 68
Lambert, Frank, 186n1
Las Vegas, NV, 5, 18, 71, 79, 142, 156
Lawless, Elaine J., 64-65
Leacock, Eleanor Burke, 194n2
Leap, William L., 16
Lee, Ann, 62-63
Lee, Jarena, 63
Lee, Justin, 162
Lemann, Nicholas, 32
Leong, Pamela, 47
Levin, Jeff, 33
Levine, Lawrence W., 130
Lewin, Ellen, 2, 10-11, 16, 22, 93, 148, 186n6, 193n6
Lewis, Oscar, 194n2
Lincoln, C. Eric, 28, 147, 178-79, 180-81, 186n2
Lindholm, Charles, 21, 67, 125
Lipsitz, George, 186n4
Lorde, Audre, 38
Love Center, 48, 58-59, 191n1
Lowenthal, David, 117, 124
Luhrmann, T. M., 7, 9, 20-21, 175

Madgett, Carl, 110-12
Mamiya, Lawrence H., 28, 147, 178-79, 180-81, 186n2
Marcus, George E., 13
Matory, James Lorand, 141, 195n11
McCune, Jeffrey Q., Jr., 96-97
McDaniel, Eric L., 178-79

McLeod, Hugh, 33, 177
McNeill, John, 162
McQueeney, Krista, 43, 91
"Metho-Bapti-Costal," 54, 140, 148-49, 168, 174, 180, 191n5
Metropolitan Community Church (MCC): Bible study, 161-62; black congregates, 46-47, 91-92; conferences, 5, 135; denominational status, 150; formation, 45-46, 188n14, 192n3; Lewin research, 12; safe spaces, 10; TFAM, 51, 58-61; worship style, 109, 145, 189n16
Metzger, Bruce M., 87, 162
Miller, Adrian, 132-34
Miller, Donald E., 20-21
Miller, Nicole, 123
Mintz, Sidney W., 7, 28-29
Mitchell, Henry H., 68, 115, 125-26, 180-81
Moon, Dawne, 15, 45, 93, 195n9
Moore, Mignon R., 11, 39-41
Moore, Russell, 182-83
Morgan, Robert, 160-61
Morrison, Toni, 30-31, 119
Mumford, Kevin, 11, 37
Murray, Stephen O., 9-10, 119, 147
Myerhoff, Barbara, 20

National Coming Out Day, 2
Neitz, Mary Jo, 9
Neville, Morgan, 193n5
Newman, Richard, 147
Newton, Esther, 9-10, 37, 147, 192n1
New York City, 6, 38-39, 74
Nida, Eugene A., 162
Noll, Mark A., 45
nostalgia: black identity, 113; "community," 119; food, 134-35; "gustatory nostalgia," 118; hair care, 135-39, 193n9; "old-time," 32, 115-18, 127-28, 140-43; TFAM, 23-24, 174-75; worship, 118-19, 123-25

Oakes, Len, 67-68, 71-72
Oakland, CA, 5-6, 12, 48, 58-59, 68-69, 79-85, 123, 152, 171
O'Brien, Jodi, 94
"old-time," 32, 115-18, 127-28, 140-43. *See also* nostalgia
Olson, Lynne, 35
Open Door, Church of the, 4-5
"oppression sickness," 141-43

INDEX

Painter, Nell Irvin, 186n4
Palm Springs, CA, 5, 190n23
Pearson, Carlton (bishop), 61, 151, 191n2
Pennese, Phyllis (bishop), 4–5, 13–14, 19–20, 86–87, 133, 149–50, 163–70
Perry, Troy D. (reverend), 45–46, 93–94, 162, 188n14, 189nn15–16, 192n3
Piazza, Michael, 162
Pillar of Love, 12, 18, 119, 127, 145, 149
Pinn, Anthony B., 33
Pitt, Richard N., 42–43, 91
Pitts, Walter F., Jr., 7
Polikoff, Nancy, 10–11
political activism: beauty parlors, 193n9; black churches, 8, 14–15, 25, 31–33; "black experience, *the*," 36–38, 187n5; charisma, 67; church scholarship, 21; COGIC, 25; coming out, 94–96, 110, 113–14; fundamentalism, 177–79; gay rights, 4, 24, 38, 47, 92, 95, 97, 162; TFAM, 22, 50, 140–41, 174, 176, 178–82
Porter, Stanley E., 161
Potts, John, 66–67
Povinelli, Elizabeth A., 15
Powell, Brian, 40
Powell, Colin, 181–82
Praise Center, 3–5, 9
Price, Richard, 7, 28–29
Putnam, Robert D., 178

Raboteau, Albert J., 7, 28–30, 126, 152, 160, 180–81
radical inclusivity: Azusa Street Revival, 6–8, 64, 141–44; Bible study, 160–63, 179; Bishop Pennese sermon, 163–70; black traditions, 156, 183–84; cause of distress, 155–56; community, 146–48; Lewin research, 12–13, 19; order of services, 119–25; "safe space," 158; seminary training, 158–63, 179; slaves' oral tradition, 158–60; social commentary, 183; symbolic representations, 171–73, 176; TFAM doctrine, 6, 8–9, 15–16, 22–26, 48–52, 148–50, 152–55, 176; TFAM's nondenominational status, 150–52
Ramberg, Lucinda, 21
Ransby, Barbara, 35
Raspa, Richard, 132
Ray, Krishnendu, 118
Read, Kenneth, 37

Reyes-Chow, Bruce, 178
Richen, Yoruba, 182
Robbins, Joel, 7, 20–21
Roberts, John W., 29
Robinson, Carin, 20–21
Rogers, Jack, 162
Rooks, Noliwe M., 136, 193n9
Rosaldo, Renato, 16
Rosh Hashanah, 1
Ross, Janell, 183
Ross, Marlon B., 96
Roth, Benita, 35
Rouget, Gilbert, 20–21
Russell, Letty M., 65
Ryan, Mary P., 186n1

Salkowitz, Selig, 188n13
Samarin, William J., 20–21, 126
Sanders, Cheryl J., 33
Sanders, Troy (pastor), 89–90, 102–4, 142–43, 152
San Francisco, CA: COGIC, 54, 191n1; Heald College, 56; LGBT community, 147; Sylvester (drag performer), 191n1; synagogues, 1, 10, 157; TFAM, 48, 101. *See also* City of Refuge
Sarris, Greg, 16
Sauvé, John R., 187n7
Savin-Williams, Ritch C., 94
Schmidt, Leigh Eric, 20
Schnoor, Randal F., 188n13
Schwarz, A. B. Christa, 37
Scott, David, 186n5
Sedgwick, Eve K., 96
Sedmak, Clemens, 160
sermons: Bishop Flunder, 68–70, 78–86, 135, 152; Bishop Pennese, 4, 163–70; black preaching, 68–69; fundamental hypocrisy, 113; God's intention, 93–94; gospel music, 128; homophobic, 41, 57, 103, 105; improvisations, 126–27, 180; Lewin research, 6, 17; Pastor Williams, 115–16; Pillar of Love, 120; "sermonphones," 126; social callings, 140–41, 179. *See also* charisma; nostalgia
Sernett, Milton C., 64
Severson, Kim, 43–44
Sha'ar Zahav, 1, 157, 194n13
Shallenberger, David, 10, 44, 90–91
Sherrill, Kenneth, 182

Shils, Edward, 66–67, 180
Shokeid, Moshe, 10, 44, 90–91
Signorile, Michelangelo, 95
Singer, Merrill, 32, 180
Smith, Barbara, 38
Smith, Lucy (elder), 63–64
Snorton, C. Riley, 96–97
soul food, 131–35
Southern, Eileen, 130
Spencer, Jon Michael, 126
Spong, John Shelby, 93–94
Spretnak, Charlene, 194n5
Springfield, MA, 6, 192n6
Stack, Carol, 117–19, 186n3, 194n2
Staples, Brent, 187n5
Steedman, Carolyn Kay, 17
Stein, Arlene, 45
Stein, Gertrude, 37
Stein, Marc, 192n1
Stockley, Grif, 35
Sullivan, Anthony (pastor), 72–73, 79
Sutton, David E., 118
Swilley, Jim (bishop), 61, 151, 187n10, 191n2
Sylvester (drag performer), 191n1
Synan, Vinson, 6–7, 62, 185n3, 189n18

Taylor, Robert Joseph, 33
TFAM (the Fellowship of Affirming Ministries): Bishop Flunder, 44, 48–49, 50–51, 60–61, 86–87, 140–41; Chicago, 112; coming out, 24, 99–102, 110–14, 125, 174; doctrine, 6, 8–9, 15–16, 22–26, 48–52, 148–50, 152–55, 176; formation, 60–61; gospel music, 128–31, 144, 173; Metropolitan Community Church (MCC), 51, 58–61; nostalgia, 23–24, 174–75; political activism, 22, 50, 140–41, 174, 176, 178–82; San Francisco, 48, 101; and traditional black churches, 6
Thomas, Kendall, 37
Thompson, Robert Farris, 195n11
Thumma, Scott, 10, 44–45
Timmon, Stuart, 192n1
Tindell, Kevin (pastor), 2–4, 9
Tinney, James S., 47–48, 147
Tobin, Kay, 46
"traditional." *See* "old-time"
traditional black churches and TFAM, 6
Turner, Victor, 20–21, 127

United Church of Christ (UCC), 10, 19–20, 72, 91–92, 120–21, 151, 171, 188n12

Valentine, Charles A., 194n2
Valentine, David, 194n3
Vines, Matthew, 162

Walker, Alice, 35
Walker, Madame C. J., 193n9
Walton, Jonathan L., 65–66
Warner, R. Stephen, 46
Washington, DC, 2, 6, 10, 37, 48, 82, 145
"We are family," 141, 148–49, 163–70
Weber, Max, 66–68, 71–72, 87
Weeks, Jeffrey, 95
Weston, Kath, 16, 92–93, 119, 147–48, 170
Wharry, Cheryl, 125–26
White, James F., 62
Wicker, Randy, 46
Wiegman, Robyn, 96
Wiggins, Daphne C., 34, 62
Wilcox, Clyde, 20–21
Wilcox, Melissa M., 10, 44, 147
Wilk, Richard R., 118
Wilkerson, Isabel, 32, 117
Williams, Brett, 194n2
Williams, Raymond, 119
Williams, Robert, 162
Williams-Forson, Psyche A., 135
Willner, Ann Ruth, 21, 67
Wilson, James F., 37
Wilson, Nancy (reverend), 188n14
Wilson, Natasha Sandraya, 187n8
Wingfield, Adia Harvey, 193n9
Wolf, Margery, 17
Wolfe, Tim, 194n4
Wolkomir, Michelle, 95, 146, 161–62
worship, 1
Wright, Kai, 97
Wright, Rev. Dr. Jeremiah, 105–6
Wylie, Evan McLeod, 130

Yamamori, Tetsunao, 20–21
Yom Kippur, 1–2, 122
Young, Jason R., 29

Zeveloff, Naomi, 188n13
Zimmerman, Bonnie, 16, 92

www.ingramcontent.com/pod-product-compliance
Lightning Source LLC
Chambersburg PA
CBHW021944290426
44108CB00012B/957